Page deliberately left blank

Stay up to date with the latest research

VOLUME 668

NOVEMBER 2016

THE ANNALS

of The American Academy of Political
and Social Science

*The Middle East and Regional
Transition, Terrorism, and Countering
Violent Extremism: What the Next
President Will Face*

Special Editors:
RAND BEERS
Dartmouth College
RICHARD A. CLARKE
Middle East Institute
EMILIAN PAPADOPOULOS
Good Harbor Security Risk Management
PAUL SALEM
Middle East Institute

⑤SAGE

Los Angeles I London I New Delhi
Singapore I Washington DC I Melbourne

Origin and Purpose. The Academy was organized December 14, 1889, to promote the progress of political and social science, especially through publications and meetings. The Academy does not take sides in controverted questions, but seeks to gather and present reliable information to assist the public in forming an intelligent and accurate judgment.

Meetings. The Academy occasionally holds a meeting in the spring extending over two days.

Publications. THE ANNALS of The American Academy of Political and Social Science is the bimonthly publication of the Academy. Each issue contains articles on some prominent social or political problem, written at the invitation of the editors. These volumes constitute important reference works on the topics with which they deal, and they are extensively cited by authorities throughout the United States and abroad.

Subscriptions. THE ANNALS of The American Academy of Political and Social Science (ISSN 0002-7162) (J295) is published bimonthly—in January, March, May, July, September, and November—by SAGE Publications, 2455 Teller Road, Thousand Oaks, CA 91320. Periodicals postage paid at Thousand Oaks, California, and at additional mailing offices. POSTMASTER: Send address changes to The Annals of The American Academy of Political and Social Science, c/o SAGE Publications, 2455 Teller Road, Thousand Oaks, CA 91320. Institutions may subscribe to THE ANNALS at the annual rate: $1070 (clothbound, $1209). Individuals may subscribe to the ANNALS at the annual rate: $122 (clothbound, $180). Single issues of THE ANNALS may be obtained by individuals for $38 each (clothbound, $52). Single issues of THE ANNALS have proven to be excellent supplementary texts for classroom use. Direct inquiries regarding adoptions to THE ANNALS c/o SAGE Publications (address below).

All correspondence concerning membership in the Academy, dues renewals, inquiries about membership status, and/or purchase of single issues of THE ANNALS should be sent to THE ANNALS c/o SAGE Publications, 2455 Teller Road, Thousand Oaks, CA 91320. Telephone: (800) 818-SAGE (7243) and (805) 499-0721; Fax/Order line: (805) 375-1700; e-mail: journals@sagepub.com. *Please note that orders under $30 must be prepaid.* For all customers outside the Americas, please visit http://www.sagepub.co.uk/customerCare.nav for information.

Printed on acid-free paper

THE ANNALS

© 2016 by The American Academy of Political and Social Science

Editorial Office: 202 S. 36th Street, Philadelphia, PA 19104-3806
For information about individual and institutional subscriptions address:
SAGE Publications
2455 Teller Road
Thousand Oaks, CA 91320

For SAGE Publications: Peter Geraghty (Production) and Mimi Nguyen (Marketing)

From India and South Asia,
write to:
SAGE PUBLICATIONS INDIA Pvt Ltd
B-42 Panchsheel Enclave, P.O. Box 4109
New Delhi 110 017
INDIA

From Europe, the Middle East,
and Africa, write to:
SAGE PUBLICATIONS LTD
1 Oliver's Yard, 55 City Road
London EC1Y 1SP
UNITED KINGDOM

International Standard Serial Number ISSN 0002-7162
ISBN 978-1-5063- 7893-0 (Vol. 668, 2016) paper
ISBN 978-1-5063-7892-3 (Vol. 668, 2016) cloth
Manufactured in the United States of America. First printing, November 2016

Please visit http://ann.sagepub.com and under the "More about this journal" menu on the right-hand side, click on the Abstracting/Indexing link to view a full list of databases in which this journal is indexed.

Information about membership rates, institutional subscriptions, and back issue prices may be found on the facing page.

Advertising. Current rates and specifications may be obtained by writing to The Annals Advertising and Promotion Manager at the Thousand Oaks office (address above). Acceptance of advertising in this journal in no way implies endorsement of the advertised product or service by SAGE or the journal's affiliated society(ies) or the journal editor(s). No endorsement is intended or implied. SAGE reserves the right to reject any advertising it deems as inappropriate for this journal.

Claims. Claims for undelivered copies must be made no later than six months following month of publication. The publisher will supply replacement issues when losses have been sustained in transit and when the reserve stock will permit.

Change of Address. Six weeks' advance notice must be given when notifying of change of address. Please send the old address label along with the new address to the SAGE office address above to ensure proper identification. Please specify the name of the journal.

THE ANNALS

OF THE AMERICAN ACADEMY OF POLITICAL AND SOCIAL SCIENCE

Volume 668   November 2016

IN THIS ISSUE:

The Middle East and Regional Transition, Terrorism, and Countering Violent Extremism: What the Next President Will Face

Special Editors: RAND BEERS, RICHARD A. CLARKE, EMILIAN PAPADOPOULOS, and PAUL SALEM

Introduction

Section I

Section II

Conclusion

FORTHCOMING

New Developments in Data Collection: Linking Data across Levels
Special Editors: SANDRA HOFFERTH and EMILIO MORAN

Regulatory Intermediaries in the Age of Governance
Special Editors: KENNETH W. ABBOTT, DAVID LEVI-FAUR,
and DUNCAN SNIDAL

Introduction

Terrorism in Perspective: A Review for the Next American President

The next American president will encounter a landscape with regard to terrorism, and specifically violent Islamist extremism, that is challenging and also much changed from eight years ago, when President Obama took office. The changes relate to failed and failing states in the Middle East and surrounding region, the terrorist organizations themselves, how the United States has dealt with the problem of terrorism, and how the problem has manifested in Europe. Even if the United States and its allies continue to retake territory from Daesh (or ISIS) and are able to disrupt other terrorist organizations, the problems of violent Islamist extremism and the societal and demographic conditions that enable it will persist. This volume seeks to define the problem and set it in context, and to offer some paths and priorities for the next president and her or his administration, including in the emerging and promising field of countering violent extremism (CVE).

Keywords: terrorism; countering violent extremism; Middle East; Daesh; ISIS; president; security

By
RICHARD A. CLARKE
and
EMILIAN PAPADOPOULOS

Eight years ago, as Senators Barack Obama and John McCain prepared for their campaigns against each other and for the American presidency, *The ANNALS* commissioned us to prepare the volume, "Terrorism: What the Next

Richard A. Clarke is chairman of the Middle East Institute and an internationally renowned expert on cybersecurity, homeland security, and national security. Clarke served as a senior White House advisor to three presidents through an unprecedented 11 consecutive years of White House service, including as Special Advisor to the President for Cyber Security, National Coordinator for Security and Counter-terrorism, and Special Assistant to the President for Global Affairs. He also served as Assistant Secretary of State and held other positions in the State Department and the Pentagon. He is author of the New York Times *bestseller* Against All Enemies *(Free Press 2004), among other books. He taught at Harvard Kennedy School, is an on-air consultant for ABC News on terrorism and cyber-security, and is chairman of Good Harbor Security Risk Management.*

Correspondence: contact@goodharbor.net

DOI: 10.1177/0002716216672896

President Will Face." That 2008 volume of *The ANNALS* brought together lead-ing academic experts and practitioners to examine the multifaceted problem of terrorism. Many of the recommendations in the volume were implemented in whole or in significant part, in some cases by the authors themselves, many of whom were appointed by President Obama to positions in his administration. Some of the recommendations stand today and will be repeated in this volume because, in our opinion, they have not been implemented to the necessary degree. The analysis eight years ago also failed to anticipate many of the signifi-cant shifts that would occur—changes that have altered in fundamental ways the nature of the problem.

We are honored to be asked again by *The ANNALS* to oversee a special vol-ume of analyses and recommendations, which may help the new American presi-dent and his or her administration to place the seemingly familiar problem of terrorism into perspective and suggest some paths and priorities at the outset of the new presidency. We are especially grateful that two distinguished experts agreed to assist us in recruiting expert authors, working with them, and editing the two halves of this volume. We think of the volume in two halves because we conceive the terrorism problem as two closely related sets of concerns. First, ter-rorism is one of the forces riling the nation-states of the Middle East. Second, terrorism is an issue of domestic security for the United States and its Western allies, particularly in Europe.

Paul Salem directs the analysis of terrorism in the Middle East in section one of the volume. Salem is the vice president for policy and research at the oldest think tank in the United States dedicated to the study of the Arab world, the 70-year-old Middle East Institute (MEI). Prior to joining MEI, Salem was the founding director of the Carnegie Middle East Center in Beirut, Lebanon.

Leading our analysis of terrorism as a domestic security concern was Rand Beers, who has 40 years of experience in U.S. national security and, uniquely, served on the White House's National Security Council staff, where he focused on terrorism for Ronald Reagan and Barack Obama and every president in between. In addition, he served in senior confirmation positions in the Department of State and the Department of Homeland Security.

Again, as eight years ago, we have gathered leading scholars and practitioners to explore different aspects of terrorism. We are very grateful for their participa-tion. Before we begin our review of their work, there are two important framing questions to consider. First, what is the definition of terrorism as we conceive of it in this volume? Second, how is the issue of terrorism different from that in *The ANNALS* volume prepared for the new American president eight years ago?

Emilian Papadopoulos is president of Good Harbor Security Risk Management, a boutique consulting firm that advises boards, CEOs, and executives on cyber security risk. He frequently publishes and speaks at industry conferences on emerging cyber security issues. Previously, he advised clients in the Middle East on national security, counterterrorism, and urban security. Before joining Good Harbor, he was a political and economic officer with Foreign Affairs Canada and worked at the Canadian Embassy in Washington, D.C., where he helped to launch the Embassy's Connect2Canada diaspora initiative.

Defining Terror

Eight years ago, we began our volume of *The ANNALS* by noting that terrorism (organized violence designed to change a government, its policies, or societal values) had been used for centuries but that "the problem for the new President is that terrorism is now widely being used, among other tactics, by extremist groups claiming affiliation with one of the world's main religions, Islam" (Clarke and Papadopoulos 2008, 7). That remains the problem.

In 2008 we noted, "rather than call them terrorists, it is best to think about them as violent Islamist extremists" (Clarke and Papadopoulos 2008, 7). We used the word *Islamist*, not *Islamic*, to denote a deviant current that claims to adhere to the Muslim religion, while actually violating many of its key tenets and attempting to create or gain control of the instruments of state governance.

Of course, there are many non-Islamist terrorist groups throughout the world. Indeed, most terrorist acts in the world are carried out by groups having nothing to do with Islam (RAND Corporation 2009). The same is true within the United States, where terrorists motivated by a cause having nothing to do with religion commit the majority of violent acts of terror (Kurzman and Schanzer 2015). They, however, are not within the scope of this volume, though notably many of the solutions emerging to counter violent Islamist extremism may apply as well to countering violent extremism writ large, and vice versa.

We focus only on violent Islamist extremism because it has posed and will likely continue for some time to pose the greatest threat of disruption to the greatest number of nation-states. It is a problem in a region of the Arab world from Morocco to Iraq and the Arabian Peninsula, into the non-Arab nations of Iran, Afghanistan, Pakistan, and India. *The region*, as we use the term in this volume, describes those nations and the Muslim nations in Africa from Somalia on the Indian Ocean, across the Sahel and Central Africa, to Nigeria on the Atlantic. (We do not focus here on Southeast Asia—an area that we considered in *The ANNALS* volume eight years ago—because the problem has been relatively contained there, and terrorism from this region has not affected Europe or the United States to the same degree as terrorism from "the region," as discussed in this volume.) Violent Islamist extremists have also brought their conflict outside the region to the streets of Western Europe, the United States, Australia, Canada, and elsewhere.

In the region of the Middle East and Africa, these violent extremists are essentially fighting a civil war within Islam, attempting to stage a coup d'état with only a small minority of the population supporting them. They are seeking to replace existing states and governments, putting themselves in power, under the guise of creating theocracies, or one large "Caliphate." They see Western nations as a roadblock to their plans, "propping up" what they label "apostate regimes" in majority Muslim nations. Attacking those Western countries and their values; and portraying the Western governments as oppressing Muslims at home and abroad, and as being "at war with Islam" are essential elements in the ideological appeal of the violent Islamist extremists. Violence against Western countries is part of the campaign of the terrorists, designed chiefly to convince Western governments to withdraw from what they see as "their region." Thus, the problem of terrorism by these violent extremists is primarily a struggle to determine who governs majority Muslim nations in this region, and how they do so. It is, however, a problem that has violent spillover effects outside that region, as well.

Eight Years of Change

We cannot simply refer the new American administration to the recommendations we made eight years ago because much about this problem has changed in that time. The changes have come in four categories: in states in the region, in the terrorist organizations themselves, in the way in which the United States has dealt with the problem, and in the manner in which the problem has manifested itself in Europe. These four factors have also interacted and shaped each other in important ways. It is valuable, before launching into an analysis of where we are today, to recall how we got here.

States in the region

Eight years ago there was one fully failed state in the region, Somalia. Afghanistan and Iraq had gone through the ravage of invasion and regime change, and were both being ripped by civil wars. Another, Lebanon, had failed in the mid-1970s but then achieved a precarious kind of stasis of factional control. What appeared to be strong, autocratic governments ruled elsewhere across these majority-Muslim nations. Then, beginning in 2011, a wave of revolts hit six existing regimes, rippling from the Maghreb in the Mediterranean to the Arab Gulf and Indian Ocean. This wave resulted in the greatest series of leadership changes since the rise of the "strong man" Arab nationalist regimes in the 1960s that swept out the last vestiges of colonialism and its leftover royals. That tectonic movement that began in 2011 was, in a bit of a misnomer, called the "Arab Spring."

Uprisings occurred in Tunisia, Libya, Egypt, Syria, Bahrain, and Yemen. It is important to understand that they were not, however, Islamist revolts, at least not initially. Instead, most were explosions of frustration at the ineffectiveness of the authoritarian regimes, which had been unsuccessful in dealing with the socioeconomic challenges of population growth or the rising political and social justice demands of an increasingly informed and empowered youth generation. The rebellions were about serious unemployment and a lack of government services, corruption, and gross economic inequalities, rather than interpretations of the Koran or the desire for a Caliphate (Anderson 2011).

Violent Islamist extremist groups, notably the new group Daesh, did, however, take advantage of the opening created by the revolts, notably in Syria, but subsequently in Libya, Egypt, and Yemen, as well. Except in Egypt, where an authoritarian regime was reestablished and a form of order re-created, the revolts in those nations ravaged the infrastructure and created failed states without an effective central government, with factions ruling regions and continuing in armed conflict. (The conflict in Syria then interacted with the then-low-level civil war in Iraq in important ways that we examine further.) These failed states and their civil wars have acted as an accelerant to the growth of violent extremist groups, attracting fighters; providing a strong propaganda narrative; and delivering territory, funding, and materiel resources on a level never before attained by a terrorist group in the region.

Iran, a largely non-Arab Islamic nation, also played a role after the outbreak of the Arab Spring. Already heavily engaged in the low-level civil war in Iraq through support of the Shia-dominated regime in Baghdad, Iran became even more deeply involved in the revolt in Syria. Its role caused the revolt to take on aspects of a Sunni-Shia conflict. Iran stimulated the Shia revolt against the government in Bahrain, prompting Saudi Arabia and the United Arab Emirates (UAE) to intervene militarily. Iran supported the Houthi movement, which led the Zaidi Shiite community to revolt in Yemen, again provoking Saudi Arabia and the UAE to intervene militarily.

Saudi Arabia and the UAE, which have become increasingly involved militarily throughout the region, are among the states of the region where the governmental systems have not changed and revolt has not occurred. The monarchical regimes in Morocco, Jordan, Qatar, Oman, and Kuwait have also remained stable.

Thus, as the new American president takes office, as contrasted with 2008, there are new governments in Tunisia, where a form of democracy seems to be working; and in Egypt, where another authoritarian regime faces challenges in achieving security, stability, legitimacy, and growth. In Libya, Syria, Iraq, Yemen, Somalia, and Afghanistan, civil wars or significant rebellions continue. In all of those conflicts violent Islamist extremists—terrorist groups—are among the major combatants against the central government or what passes for one. This swath of active civil war, combat, and destruction is unprecedented in the modern history of the region. It has turned cities into rubble, created millions of refugees, and made much of the region a breeding ground and training field for terrorism.

The terrorist groups in the region

In 2008, we wrote extensively about al-Qaeda and about what we called its "franchise groups." *The ANNALS* volume then described the need for attacking al-Qaeda's leadership along the Afghan-Pakistan border. The Obama administration did just that, greatly expanding the use of armed drones and targeted killing of the leadership of "al-Qaeda Central" and to a lesser extent against the leaders of its franchise groups al-Qaeda in the Arabian Peninsula (AQAP) in Yemen, al-Shabaab in Somalia, and al-Qaeda in Iraq. As a result, al-Qaeda Central appeared to decline significantly. The group the United States continued to fight in Afghanistan was the Taliban, not al-Qaeda. Al-Qaeda in Iraq was reduced after 2008 to a small group in hiding, at least until 2012.

Then, when the revolt against President Assad began in Syria at the tail end of the Arab Spring, al-Qaeda in Iraq moved many of its remaining assets to Syria to join the fight there. The success of their operations in Syria gave the group a new, larger life. They soon broke off from al-Qaeda Central, and under the name ISIS (or Daesh, as many of their Arab opponents and we derisively call them) returned to Iraq in a spectacular manner. Taking advantage of the Shia government in Baghdad's ill treatment of majority Sunni cities, Daesh, reinforced by foreign fighters from dozens of nations, swept into Iraq and seized major cities, ejecting the feckless Iraqi Army and seizing its American-supplied equipment.

Suddenly Daesh controlled large amounts of territory in both Syria and Iraq, including major cities. The Syrian-Iraqi border in effect disappeared. Daesh contended, not without some merit, that a new state—"the Islamic State"—was born. They declared the revival of the Caliphate a century after its abolition by Mustafa Kemal Ataturk in 1924. Unlike al-Qaeda, which vaguely promised a new caliphate some day, Daesh had created it in a year. Inspired by this phenomenal success, about thirty thousand disaffected Muslim youth from Europe, North America, and mainly from Muslim-majority nations around the world flocked to the Caliphate. Never before had a terrorist group in the region controlled a territory as immense or with as large a population.

Daesh ran large cities, including Mosul, the second largest city in Iraq. It collected taxes and provided services. Daesh had a treasury of tens of millions of dollars, taken from banks and "earned" from the sale of hostages and oil from wells and refineries within its territory. Its military inventory included tanks and other armored vehicles. On the Internet, its propaganda machine achieved heights of sophistication never before seen from a terrorist group. Groups in Africa and Afghanistan announced that they were part of Daesh. A team from Syria-Iraq went to Libya and grabbed control of a city of ~100,000 people, Sirte, creating another "province" of the Caliphate.

Self-activated, radicalized individuals in the United States, Europe, Canada, Australia, and elsewhere committed terrorist acts in the name of Daesh. In addition to these "lone wolves," organized terrorist cells staged major attacks in Europe and attempted other attacks elsewhere. The terrorists creating and attempting these attacks included both violent Islamist extremists who had grown up in Europe and refugees from the Middle East.

Daesh eclipsed other Islamist terrorist groups, even though AQAP grabbed territory in Yemen, al-Shabaab hung on in Somalia, the Taliban advanced in Afghanistan, and a mélange of terrorist groups plagued Pakistan. (In response, the residual leadership of al-Qaeda Central created al-Qaeda on the Indian subcontinent and began recruiting in the densely packed and lawless neighborhoods of Karachi.)

At one point Daesh, assisted by other factions, seemed to be on the verge of overthrowing the Baghdad and Damascus regimes, as well as the Kurdish autonomous government in Erbil. The United States, which had withdrawn militarily from Iraq, sent forces back to provide air support and active "advisors" to Kurdish militia and the Iraqi Army. Russia, in its largest military intervention in the region in recent history, sent forces to Syria. Iran stepped up its military presence in both Iraq and Syria, including dispatching forces of its Lebanese ally, Hezbollah, to support the Damascus regime. European and Arab nations also employed their air forces in coordinated strikes by "the Coalition" against Daesh. Gradually, these interventions allowed the indigenous forces fighting Daesh to halt the group's advances and then to regain some territory. Daesh's oil revenues were reduced by Coalition bombing. High casualties among Daesh forces reduced the group's appeal to foreign fighters, reducing the number of new recruits.

Daesh appeared to be contained and had lost control of cities in Syria, Iraq, and Libya. Those cities, however, are now in ruins, and many among their populations are still refugees. Those conditions may generate a new wave of violent extremism. The dramatic rise and the beginning of the fall of the group may have led many observers to think that Daesh was *the problem*. It was, however, only an extreme manifestation of the underlying resentment of the status quo and the yearning for an Islamic success story, one that promised to improve the condition of those with little hope in the slums of major cities in the region and in Europe. The leadership of Daesh was remarkably effective and accomplished much quickly, but even without the group, that resentment and those longings would still have existed, and a small minority of those affected would have found means of expression, sometimes extreme and possibly even violent. If and when Daesh is successfully suppressed, the environmental, social, and demographic conditions that allowed it to thrive and grow will continue. A bulging age cohort of Muslims under 30, in the region and in Europe, will continue to seek employment, improved living conditions, increased respect, greater equality, and meaning in their lives. Few of the existing governments can address those desires. Of the tens of millions who will be frustrated, most will continue to reject violent extremist groups like Daesh, as has been the case until now; but some will be sympathetic to such groups, and a slim minority may support them actively, creating once again the supporting conditions for another organized, capable terrorist movement.

Europe and violent Islamist extremism

France had dealt with Algerian-related terrorism for decades, since the 1950s. Other European nations had been a stage for Palestinian terrorist groups, particularly in the 1970s. England and Spain had both seen major al-Qaeda terrorist attacks early in the century. Daesh, however, managed to inspire some Muslims born or raised in Western Europe to go to the Middle East to fight for the new Caliphate. It inspired others to stage "lone-wolf" attacks in Europe and elsewhere. Daesh also infiltrated a handful of terrorists into Europe. Major Daesh-related terrorist incidents rocked Paris in 2015 and Brussels in 2016. Others in Europe were prevented, including in England and Germany (Troianovski and Turner 2016).

The civil wars in the region triggered an unprecedented mass migration of refugees into Europe, creating political crises throughout the European Union and challenging its "borderless" system of internal national boundaries. The

combination of the refugee deluge and the Daesh terrorist attacks in Europe
prompted anti-immigrant and anti-Islamic political reactions, which heightened
the sense among many Muslims that they were being discriminated against, that
they were hated by many Europeans. For European Muslims who lived in predominantly Islamic neighborhoods with high unemployment and lower living
standards than the rest of their nations, this backlash added to a sense of resentment and discontent. What had been true for decades became more obvious to
the media and political figures: many Western European nations had done a poor
job of integrating Muslim immigrants into the mainstream of their societies.
Violent Islamist extremist groups could find some supporters in the ranks of the
discontented in the isolated Muslim communities. Political groups on the Right
sought to take advantage of fears of terrorism and Muslims for electoral gain,
creating a feedback effect and exacerbating relations among religious groups and
communities in Europe.

The United States and terrorism

The fevered American reaction to the terrorist attacks of 9/11 had begun to
dissipate at the outset of the Obama presidency. Although he increased attacks
against al-Qaeda, President Obama sought to withdraw the U.S. military from the
wars in Iraq and Afghanistan. In Iraq, all U.S. forces were eventually withdrawn.
The predominantly Shia government in Baghdad subsequently ceased support
for the U.S.-created Sunni militias and engaged in a campaign to marginalize
Sunni leaders. That anti-Sunni effort led directly to the success of Daesh in Iraq,
which, in turn, caused the return of U.S. forces (the U.S. Air Force in close air
support missions and U.S. Army Special Forces and other combat "advisors").
After a surge of thirty thousand additional troops early in his administration,
President Obama later withdrew the bulk of U.S. forces in Afghanistan and
turned the combat mission over to the Afghan National Army. However, the
United States was unable to pull out all its forces as planned because of the growing pressure of the Taliban.

Despite the continuing presence of some U.S. forces in Iraq and Afghanistan,
American casualties dwindled and U.S. combat-related fatalities became a rare
event (Defense Manpower Data Center 2011). Although U.S. drone strikes also
declined significantly, they continued to occur occasionally against several terrorist targets in Somalia, Libya, Yemen, Pakistan, Afghanistan, Iraq, and Syria. U.S.
fighter aircraft closely supported air strikes against Daesh, which continued on a
regular basis in both Iraq and Syria. Among the American people, nonetheless,
the sense that their country was actively engaged in war against terrorist groups
diminished. So too did the potential for popular support of any new, large-scale
American military involvement in the region. "War fatigue" and a sense that such
large-scale U.S. military interventions produced few positive outcomes were
much more widespread in 2016 than they had been earlier in the century.

While the terrorist attacks at Fort Hood, the Boston Marathon, San
Bernardino, and Orlando were tragedies and heavily covered in the news, terrorist events in the United States were relatively few and far between and were

self-actuated, largely "lone-wolf" incidents. While any death or injury from terrorism is unacceptable, and governments should engage in vigorous mitigation and prevention efforts, the actual number of Islamist terrorism–related fatalities in the United States over the last eight years has been low. At the time of writing, there have been nine Islamist-related incidents in the United States since Barack Obama took office in 2009, resulting in ninety-one total casualties. The average of about twelve fatalities a year in the United States from terrorist threats contrasts with more than eleven thousand gun homicides a year in the United States and more than thirty-five thousand fatal vehicular accidental deaths in the United States per year (Centers for Disease Control and Prevention 2013). The media and political reaction to the terrorist-related fatalities is, however, far greater than the number of deaths would suggest. These attacks and the images of terrorism in Europe stimulated some anti-Islamic political rhetoric in the United States, particularly in 2016.

Although a few American Muslims attempted to join Daesh or other terrorist groups, such as al-Shabaab in Somalia, the Islamic community in the United States continues overwhelmingly to reject violent extremism and to cooperate with law enforcement against potential terrorists. Federal law enforcement and intelligence agencies brought approximately seventy prosecutions for attempted support to Daesh over the eight years and had more than nine hundred suspects under some degree of surveillance in 2015 (Vidino and Hughes 2015). These numbers are considerably lower than similar data about Europe. The Islamic community in America has been better accepted and integrated into society than it has been in many European nations, but Daesh's effective propaganda still appealed to some disaffected youth in the United States.

The tolerance of the American people for "homeland security" measures and expenditures has generally continued over the last eight years, although, as time has passed since 9/11 and government domestic intelligence activities have become clearer, there has been a growing sense of awareness and concern with government electronic espionage efforts and possible infringements on privacy and civil liberties in the name of counterterrorism. Media reports of NSA activities, as revealed by a former National Security Agency (NSA) contractor, contributed to a sense in some circles that there might be government overreach when it came to counterterrorism surveillance. Congress did amend the post-9/11 "Patriot Act" to curtail some types of electronic surveillance.

The U.S. software industry reacted to the reports of NSA surveillance by increasing the use of encryption for publicly available e-mail and chat programs. That trend touched off a debate between "Silicon Valley" and the Federal Bureau of Investigation (FBI). The FBI alleged the encryption made the FBI's counterterrorism surveillance more difficult and justified its request for government-controlled access to decryption methods. Congress, which was split between those concerned chiefly with civil liberties protection and those more motivated by counterterrorism, seemed unlikely to act favorably on the FBI's request.

Terrorism had not been an issue during the 2000 presidential cycle, despite the fact that al-Qaeda attacked the destroyer USS *Cole* during the final month of the campaign. In 2004, President George W. Bush made counterterrorism the central focus of his successful reelection bid. By 2008 the issue had evolved, but it stayed central to the campaign. A nation weary of Americans fighting and dying in the Middle East elected a candidate in 2008 who promised to be strong on counterterrorism but also pledged to end the wars and certain ethically question-able practices such as torture and open-ended incarceration at Guantanamo. By 2012, after the financial crisis of 2007–2009, terrorism had diminished as a source of concern to voters, compared with economic issues. However, the rise of Daesh propelled terrorism back into the center of the 2016 election (Gallup 2015).

Day One in the West Wing

Thus, the American president elected in 2016 and the national security team that comes to office in 2017 will face a landscape transformed from what we wrote about eight years ago. The high water mark of Daesh's control of cities and lands will have passed, but the wellspring of ideology and discontent into which it taps will still be strong.

Six nations in the region lie in shambles, with millions of their people in refu-gee camps. Rebuilding and repairing the damage from the spasm of civil wars would cost hundreds of billions of dollars, if funds were available. Political settle-ments seem far off. Failed, factionalized states seem likely to continue for the foreseeable future. Other nations in the region face acute stability challenges, due in part to population growth outpacing economic development.

Europe faces twin problems of Islamic refugees from the wars and economic failures, and Islamic citizens who are not well integrated into European society. And in the United States, a large and costly bureaucracy seeks to prevent Islamist terrorism. For a variety of reasons, including the relatively few extremists in the United States; and the country's relatively welcoming approach to assimilation, support from Muslim communities, and effective intelligence and law enforce-ment, there have been few major incidents, but the risk remains and the toler-ance of the American people for any Islamist terrorism in their country remains extremely low.

Thus, the new president should ask, (1) What is the nature of the problem or problems we call "terrorism?" (2) How much is enough in the way of effort and resources to deal with this set of issues? and (3) What are likely to be the most effective programs and policies to address the underlying problems, and to mini-mize the damage that can be done by Islamist terrorism? With those questions in mind, this volume of *The ANNALS* reviews the problem as it manifests itself in "the region" and then examines the spillover effects in Europe and the United States.

References

Anderson, Lisa. 2011. Demystifying the Arab Spring: Parsing the differences between Tunisia, Egypt, and Libya. *Foreign Affairs* 90 (3): 2–7.

Centers for Disease Control and Prevention. 2013. *Deaths: Final data for 2013.* National Vital Statistics Report 41. Washington, DC: U.S. Department of Health and Human Services.

Clarke, Richard A., and Emilian Papadopoulos. 2008. Terrorism: The first portfolio for the next president. In "Terrorism" What the next president will face." *The ANNALS of the American Academy of Political and Social Science* 618.

Defense Manpower Data Center. 2011. *Defense casualty analysis system.* Washingotn, DC: U.S. Department of Defense. Available from https://www.dmdc.osd.mil.

Gallup. 9 December 2015. Terrorism in the United States. Gallup Public Polling. Available from http://www.gallup.com/poll/4909/terrorism-united-states.aspx.

Kurzman, Charles, and David Schanzer. 2015. *Law enforcement assessment of the violent extremism threat.* Durham, NC: Triangle Center on Terrorism and Homeland Security, Duke University.

RAND Corporation. 2009. RAND database of worldwide terrorism incidents. RAND National Security Research Division. Available from http://www.rand.org/nsrd/projects/terrorism-incidents.html.

Troianovski, Anton, and Zeke Turner. 2 June 2016. Germany arrests three in suspected Islamic State plot to attack Düsseldorf. *Wall Street Journal.*

Vidino, Lorenzo, and Seamus Hughes. 2015. *ISIS in America.* Washington, DC: George Washington University.

Section I

This article serves as an introduction to the first section of this volume, a section that focuses on the drivers of instability and radicalization in the Middle East and ways to counter them. This introduction provides a brief sketch of some of the key issues that are dealt with in more detail in this section and a brief précis of what each author addresses in his or her individual article.

Keywords: Middle East; failed states; terrorism; radicalization; regional order; civil wars

Region in Transition

By
PAUL SALEM

The Middle East is going through the most intense period of instability in its modern history. This is partly the result of the dual shocks of the U.S.-led invasion of Iraq in 2003 and the Arab uprisings of 2011: the toppling of the Iraqi state destabilized a precarious regional order and unleashed a regional and sectarian war; the Arab uprisings destabilized a precarious state order and unleashed state collapse and civil war in several countries. But the turmoil is also the result of long-simmering dysfunctions of repressive governments; sluggish and unequal economies; growing populations; tightening land and water resources; and unresolved questions of political identity, the role of religion, and social structure.

Violent sectarian nonstate actors have taken advantage of these conditions to spread their influence. Shiite militias such as Hezbollah spread to neighboring Syria, the popular mobilization units rose to rival the national army in Iraq, and the Houthi militia overran the Yemeni capital. Sunni militias rose to fill the void of

Paul Salem is vice president for policy and research at the Middle East Institute, in Washington D.C. He is the author of numerous books, reports, and articles on issues of political change, transition, and conflict, as well as the regional and international relations of the Middle East.

Correspondence: psalem@mei.edu

DOI: 10.1177/0002716216671908

collapsing states in Syria, Libya, and Yemen, and al-Qaeda took advantage of these conditions to stage a major resurgence. While al-Qaeda prioritized attacks on the West, an even more radical wing of al-Qaeda, which prioritized attacks on Shiites and "unbelievers" in Muslim lands and the establishment of a Caliphate, broke away from al-Qaeda and founded the so-called Islamic State, or ISIS. Al-Qaeda and Islamic State are now locked in competition for primacy in Syria, Libya, Yemen, and other arenas. Both pose a current and future danger to U.S. and Western security.

The fight against these terrorist groups proceeds at various levels. The U.S.-led coalition to defeat ISIS has made slow but steady progress in both Iraq and Syria. These defeats are important not only to deny ISIS territory but also to reverse its own narrative in which it spun its early victories in Syria and Iraq as proof of divine favor and a major reason for Islamist extremists around the world to join it. ISIS is also responding to rollback in Syria and Iraq by building affiliates in Libya, Sinai, Yemen, and elsewhere and by staging attacks in Europe and attempting to do the same in the United States. Al-Qaeda is playing a long game, letting ISIS take the brunt of current attacks and meanwhile embedding in societies in Syria, Libya, and Yemen, building networks that it hopes will provide it with staying power after the ISIS phenomenon loses steam.

The fight against terrorist groups, however, also requires addressing the conditions that enabled this latest resurgence. Prime among these are regional state collapse and regional conflict. There was no significant terrorist presence in Iraq before 2003, or in Syria and Libya before the uprisings there that led to state collapse and civil war. Trying to permanently eradicate terrorist groups in vast stretches of ungoverned space is a game of whack-a-mole if their sway is not replaced with sustainable state power; there is no way around the necessity to end local civil wars and rebuild state sovereignty. Even small and relatively weak states such as Lebanon and Jordan have been able to keep terrorist groups off their territory, while larger and more powerful states—once they collapsed—have provided havens for them. Ending civil wars is not easy and will require concerted application of political power and complex diplomacy; rebuilding the capacity of shattered states to regain control of their territory will also take coordinated international support.

Regional conflict has also been a driver of the terrorist surge and needs to be urgently addressed. The Middle East has seen regional conflict before. The Arab-Israeli conflict raged for years, but it favored the consolidation of militarized police states rather than Islamist extremist groups. Nasserist Egypt and conservative Saudi Arabia were locked in proxy conflict for much of the 1960s, but that generally helped to spread the ideology of socialist Arab nationalism, not sectarian radicalism. The current conflict between Iran and Saudi Arabia, two petro states on opposite sides of the sectarian Sunni-Shii divide, has created the conditions that have weaponized sectarian identities, destabilized states, and enabled Islamist terrorist groups, both Sunni and Shii.

There is nothing necessary or inevitable about Iranian-Saudi or Sunni-Shii conflict. The current conflict is the result of a confluence of factors from the Iranian Revolution in 1979, the Iran-Iraq war of 1980–1988, regime change in

Iraq in 2003, civil war in Syria and Yemen post-2011, and the nuclear deal with Iran in 2015. But the current conflict is a lose-lose proposition for both Iran and Saudi Arabia—let alone for the peoples of the region. The two governments share interests in state security, regional stability, and economic growth; however, they are currently locked in a violence trap that neither seems to know how to get out of.

De-escalating regional distrust and conflict and building a more stable regional order is as challenging as it is necessary. The nuclear deal with Iran showed what strong American leadership, and a smart balance between coercive power and diplomatic creativity, can achieve. That same combination of leadership, power, and diplomacy needs to be brought to bear to get Iran to conform to international norms of behavior in regional affairs and to build a less conflictual and more stable order among the region's main players.

Part One of the current volume brings together a number of experts in the field of terrorism and security to provide analysis and insights into current conditions in the Middle East, the enabling factors for the rise of terrorist groups, the dynamics within those groups, and recommended policies to confront and eventually defeat them.

The first contribution is from Marc Lynch, a professor of political science and director of the Project on Middle East Political Science at The George Washington University and author of *The Arab Uprising: The Unfinished Revolutions of the Middle East* (Public Affairs 2012). He examines the key dynamics in the full or partial collapse of four Arab states—Syria, Yemen, Libya, and Iraq; he explains the links among state collapse, civil war, and the enabling of terrorist organizations. Most importantly, he assesses the likely conditions of those four countries during the first year of the next president's first term and suggests policy approaches to wind down or resolve those conflicts, reconstitute state sovereignty, and deny territory to terrorist groups.

The second article is written by me, Paul Salem, vice president for policy and research at the Middle East Institute and author of *Broken Orders: The Causes and Consequences of the Arab Uprisings* (Dar An-Nahar Press 2013 [in Arabic]). My article is titled "Working toward a Stable Regional Order," and in it I examine the conditions that have led to the collapse of regional order and the escalation of proxy conflict between Iran and the Gulf Arab countries. Further, I describe what leadership role the next U.S. president can play in marshalling international and regional influence to de-escalate dangerous regional conflict and build a more stable regional order—an order that would be far less hospitable to radical sectarian terrorist groups.

Charles Lister's article is an examination of the internal dynamics within both the Islamic State and al-Qaeda and the growing competition between the two. Charles Lister is a senior fellow at the Middle East Institute and the author of *The Syrian Jihad: Al-Qaeda, the Islamic State and the Evolution of an Insurgency* (Oxford University Press 2016). He explains how this competition is both straining and strengthening the two groups. He explores how the United States and its allies in the war on terror can exploit points of weakness in both groups, particularly elements of their rivalry.

The next contribution is from Bernard Haykel, a professor of Near Eastern Studies at Princeton University and a foremost authority on the ideology of the Islamic State and al-Qaeda. His article lays out the ideological worldview of these two principal terrorist groups and examines their narratives as they and their adherents see them. The author uses this template to explore which successes and failures are most critical to their own narrative and how that knowledge can suggest policies that weaken their own internal cohesion and dampen their appeal to Islamist extremists globally.

The final article of this section is from John Allen, a retired Marine Corps four-star general who was commander of the International Security Assistance Force and U.S. Forces Afghanistan (USFOR-A) between September 2014 and October 2015 and U.S. Special Presidential Envoy for the Global Coalition to Counter ISIL. He draws on lessons learned from the U.S.-led alliance's experience fighting terrorism in both Afghanistan and the Middle East, providing policy guidance for the next president in terms of building on America's large anti-ISIS coalition and crafting policies and priorities that would more effectively weaken and defeat these terrorist groups.

These five articles taken together provide a rich and multilayered analysis of the depth of the challenges plaguing today's Middle East, emphasize the links between these challenges and the rise of terrorist groups, and indicate the level of wisdom and nuanced complexity that will have to be part of any sustained and successful strategy to defeat terror groups in the long run and prevent them from coming back. The individual authors, of course, do not see eye to eye on all matters; nor do these articles claim to provide a comprehensive examination of the conditions of today's turbulent Middle East—that will always have to be an ongoing and wider endeavor. But the authors do agree that the war on terror must be understood as not only a battle of killing terrorists where and when they pop up, in an endless game of whack-a-mole, but that it must be conceived of as a wider strategy that addresses the conditions that enable and empower such groups and that has not only a military component but political, diplomatic, and socioeconomic components as well. This view requires a sober assessment of the structural dysfunctions of the region and ways to address them; a keen understanding of the terrorist groups, their organization, and their ideology; and a deep appreciation for what is meant by strategy, and what level of complexity and public commitment has to be built into it.

I do not seek to draw conclusions prematurely in an introduction, but leave the reader to engage with these expert texts on their own terms. Overall conclusions and policy recommendations are drawn together in the final concluding essay of this volume.

Failed States and Ungoverned Spaces

By
MARC LYNCH

State failure and proxy war have consumed key Arab states such as Iraq, Libya, Syria, and Yemen, with massive humanitarian consequences. Local power struggles have been exacerbated by regional and international interventions. The next American administration must act to resolve these wars and assist the reconstruction of shattered states. Rather than new military interventions, the United States should focus on the international enforcement of military de-escalation to accomplish these goals. This article explores the distinctive challenges for U.S. policy in each of these conflicts.

Keywords: Libya; Syria; Yemen; failed states; intervention; civil war

The Obama administration was correct to see the positive potential of the Arab uprisings, which began in late 2010, to offer an unprecedented possibility of transitions to democracy and meaningful change across the Middle East and in North Africa. In some countries, such as Egypt and Tunisia, the downfall of long-ruling presidents opened up the possibility for new political bargains. But those transitions have long since given way to autocratic retrenchment across most of the region; and several key states, most notably Iraq, Libya, Yemen, and Syria, collapsed under the pressure of the uprisings or have lost effective control over significant parts of their territory. The economic, geopolitical, and humanitarian consequences of these state failures and proxy wars have been catastrophic. This article examines why these states failed, their current status, and

Marc Lynch is a professor of political science at The George Washington University. He is the director of the Project on Middle East Political Science, a senior nonresident associate at the Carnegie Endowment for International Peace, and contributing editor to the Washington Post's Monkey Cage *political science page.*

Correspondence: mlynch@gwu.edu

DOI: 10.1177/0002716216666028

how the next president might begin to approach these states in a constructive fashion.

The damage done by failed states almost beggars the imagination. Syria's war is by far the worst of the conflicts, with an estimated 400,000 people killed and some 11 million displaced from their homes (International Crisis Group 2016; Syria Center for Policy Research 2016). Yemen, in addition to the nearly 3,000 dead and millions displaced, has experienced a near collapse of its healthcare, water, and sanitation systems and near famine conditions in much of the country (International Crisis Group 2016). Libya's civil war has claimed at least 4,000 dead, ground the economy and oil production to a halt, and driven refugees out across the region (Wehrey 2016a). The Islamic State of Iraq and the Levant has seized control of a wide swathe of Syria and Iraq and has established footholds in conflict zones such as Libya and the Sinai.

These failed states have had disruptive effects far beyond their own borders. Jihadist groups such as al-Qaeda and the Islamic State have carved out strong-holds in these failed states and ungoverned spaces, using these bases to extend their regional and global reach and to attract new generations of jihadist fighters. Refugee flows threaten to overwhelm already fragile neighbors such as Jordan, Lebanon, and Tunisia and have triggered political crises across Europe. The wars have driven extreme forms of sectarianism and polarization, which have exacerbated social and political conflicts elsewhere.

There is little doubt that this constellation of crisis will demand the attention of the next president, but there is considerable disagreement about the most appropriate policies to confront them. The next president will face strong pressure to escalate U.S. involvement in these wars, especially Syria, in search of a victory, to demonstrate success where Obama failed, and to curry favor with hawkish regional allies keen for American military action. This temptation should be resisted, because such interventions will likely leave the United States even more deeply enmeshed in unwinnable quagmires. While Iraq's U.S.-backed military campaign against ISIS has enjoyed some success, the conditions do not exist in the other war zones to replicate those efforts. The focus should instead be on ending the war in Yemen, supporting the UN's diplomatic efforts to rebuild Libya's state, and forging international agreement on the de-escalation of Syria's war. While none of these initiatives has yet succeeded in ending the civil wars, they should be the foundation for the next president's approach. The costs of the regional proxy wars have been too high to continue. Escalated direct military intervention will only invite higher levels of counterintervention and perpetuate a mutually destructive stalemate.

Instead, the next president should urgently seek ways to de-escalate the wars and begin to rehabilitate these failed states. This will require securing or building on ceasefires, and pressuring regional powers on all sides of the conflict to support military de-escalation and rebuilding efforts. Sustaining such conflict resolution will require a major multilateral investment in rebuilding these countries, facilitating the return of refugees, and protecting fragile transitional regimes. The resources necessary for such reconstruction will not be easily found, given the magnitude of the problems, but the costs would be significantly lower than those associated with military campaigns and far more likely to produce sustainable improvements in regional conditions.

Another temptation will be to double down on authoritarian regimes, seeking to rebuild strong states with the ability to militarily control their territory. This too should be resisted. Military campaigns to establish and sustain central state control often disrupt local orders more than stabilize them. Yemen's military campaigns against the Houthis and al-Qaeda in the Arabian Peninsula in the 2000s arguably did more to destabilize the country's political order than to defeat these local challengers (International Crisis Group 2016). Egypt's repeated military campaigns in the Sinai have made conditions worse rather than better (Ashour 2015; Sabry 2015). The consolidation of authoritarian rule by Nuri al-Maliki in Iraq following the "surge" laid the foundations for the subsequent resurgence of Sunni insurgency (Al-Ali 2014). Support for building strong and professional militaries is an essential step in the reconstruction of these failed states, but as the painful experience of Iraq demonstrates, military aid, advising, and training will fail if not harnessed to meaningful political reforms. Military assistance should be embedded within a political strategy designed to support the consolidation of states rooted in the rule of law and respect for human rights.

Why States Failed

The Arab uprising mobilized millions of citizens across the region to demand political change. While most Arab states found ways to manage the challenge, whether beginning democratic transitions or crushing their challengers, several experienced rapid escalation from peaceful protest to armed conflict. Regime violence in Libya and Syria triggered spirals of escalation as protestors took up arms in self-defense. Crucially, those challengers found ample sources of external support from regional powers and transnational networks that saw opportunities to weaken their rivals. External financial, media, and military support to these insurgencies shifted local balances of power, intensifying and accelerating their challenge to states. External support typically proved sufficient to sustain insurgencies but insufficient to overthrow regimes. As conflicts dragged on and the human costs grew, insurgencies tended to become more extreme ideologically. Their effects were increasingly felt transnationally, as well: Syria's war contributed to reigniting Iraq's Sunni insurgency, while Islamic State affiliates moved opportunistically into Libya and Egypt's Sinai.

The Islamic State emerged out of these externally fueled wars and failing states. The concern that ungoverned spaces and failed states would provide sanctuary for jihadist organizations long predates the Arab uprisings of 2011. Failed states such as Somalia, the Democratic Republic of the Congo, Sudan, Iraq, and Yemen caused enormous human suffering and facilitated the rise of violent extremist groups. Few other Arab states failed to that degree over the course of the 2000s, but the façade of stability was misleading. Indicators of rising fragility grew ever more apparent: growing economic inequality, corruption, political stagnation, abusive security services, and inadequate state services. Popular protests and strikes multiplied. Terrorist attacks and entrenched insurgencies by al-Qaeda affiliates struck across the region.

The progressive hollowing out of autocratic states left states such as Iraq, Libya, Syria, and Yemen without the capacity to survive the combination of popular uprising and regional proxy wars. These countries typically had poorly institutionalized states and strong regional identities at tension with the central national identity. Iraq continued to struggle with the legacies of a decade of civil war and sectarian misgovernance. They also faced regional interventions, which undermined rather than strengthened the control of the central state. Each country has witnessed the collapse of central state authority over significant portions of its territory and the emergence of alternative contenders for political legitimacy. Each has seen extremist jihadist movements take advantage of the chaos to seize and control territory. And each has experienced daunting levels of dispossession, displacement, and death. None will be easy to put back together, even if the fighting were to end. But that nonetheless must be the priority for the next administration. The destabilizing impact of state collapse, transnational insurgencies, and humanitarian catastrophe pose a major threat not only to American interests but to the people of the region.

A closer look at the major cases of failed states can help to identify some of the key themes and issues that will confront the next administration.

Yemen

Yemen's war is rooted in the failure of the Gulf Cooperation Council (GCC)–led transitional process to produce a viable national consensus (International Crisis Group 2015b, 2016). That transition began after months of intense political conflict over the fate of then-President Ali Abdullah Saleh. The GCC-brokered deal transferred power to Saleh's vice president, Abd Rabbuh Mansur Hadi, who was then duly legitimated through a one-candidate election. Saleh himself was granted immunity and the right to remain politically active, a fateful decision that left him free to work against the consolidation of a new regime. An extended United Nations–led national dialogue conference was designed to bring all sectors of the Yemeni political landscape into talks over a new constitution. In practice, key constituencies felt excluded from this national dialogue.

When the new constitution seemed poised to redraw federal districts in ways harmful to the interests of the northern Shi'ite Houthi Movement, they swept into Sanaa. They pursued President Hadi to Aden after he escaped house arrest. On March 26, 2015, Saudi Arabia declared the launch of a military campaign to restore Hadi to power and defeat the Houthis. While the Saudis assembled a sizable coalition, and enticed coalition partners to provide ground troops, they and their local allies proved unable to recapture the country militarily. A protracted stalemate ensued, during which intense Saudi bombing inflicted increasing humanitarian and infrastructural damage. A ceasefire and peace talks began in mid-April 2016, though few were optimistic about their prospects, and by August they appeared to have failed.

Yemen's war has the best prospects for ending before the inauguration of the next U.S. president, simply because it is in almost every way the easiest to end. Unlike either of the other two wars, in Yemen there is a single state actor who can unilaterally decide to end the military campaign. Saudi Arabia elected to launch the military campaign to reverse the seizure of Sanaa and Aden by the Houthi Movement and forces loyal to former President Ali Abdullah Saleh. Riyadh viewed the Houthi takeover through the lens of what it believed to be Iran's rising power in the region. While Saudi Arabia has formed a sizable Arab coalition in support of this war, with strong partnership from the United Arab Emirates and various forms of military support from several other Arab states, ultimately the decision to continue or end the war lies with Riyadh.

Saudi Arabia has been unable to achieve its war objectives through its air campaign or the introduction of an array of limited ground forces. It has made some military progress, including the liberation of parts of Aden, and has dropped enormous volumes of bombs. It does not seem close to achieving its minimal goal of restoring former President Hadi to office, though, to say nothing of its maximal goals of eradicating the Houthi movement.

Saudi Arabia has invested a great deal of its prestige in this war, and it fears the perception of an Iranian victory or its own failure. It will be very difficult for Saudi Arabia to end the war without achieving its stated objectives. At the same time, the humanitarian costs of the war have attracted growing international scrutiny, a small but growing number of Coalition troops have been killed, the financial costs are mounting at a time of low oil prices and serious fiscal crisis, and Saudi Arabia is paying growing (if still small) domestic political costs for an open-ended war. Other external participants in the war coalition will likely follow the Saudi lead. The terms of this deal may include the formal return of Hadi to power, but within a political arrangement that protects the vital interests of the Houthis and other key actors.

Such a deal might include promises of significant Gulf financial assistance for reconstruction, run through the central government, along with commitments to rebuild Yemeni security forces. Peacekeepers are unlikely to be on offer, though Saudi Arabia or its partners may attempt to keep troops on the ground through the implementation phase (strengthening the hand of the new government but making the troops an attractive target for spoilers). Power will likely continue to devolve to the local level, and ongoing local violence will continue to afflict much of the country. Economic development and humanitarian relief will be difficult to deliver without the return of security. The end of the war will likely not end either the political conflict or Yemen's deep problems, but it could at least allow for the urgently needed rebuilding of a shattered economy and society. If the war has not ended before the inauguration of the next president, then pushing for a rapid resolution in Yemen should be a top priority.

Libya

Libya's war is rooted in the failure of the post-Qaddafi state to establish effective authority or to resolve deep differences over the country's political structure

(Wehrey 2016b). Libya's failure to disarm militias following the war, a decision rooted in the unavoidable military realities on the ground, left the central state unable to provide security or to enforce decisions taken by the country's political leadership. The concentration of power at the local level and in militias outside the structure of the state left a vacuum that no actor has been able to fill.

It is easy to forget that post-Qaddafi Libya initially enjoyed considerable positive momentum. It held a series of elections, producing legislative bodies with real, albeit contested, democratic legitimacy. The General National Congress (GNC), elected in November 2011, generated great enthusiasm but soon proved unable to pass legislation or address the country's problems. The Benghazi attack on the U.S. consulate in September 2012 proved devastating, however, as the United States pulled back from a suddenly politically toxic country, and many Libyans recoiled in horror from the inability of the military to prevent militias from such a brazen attack. In 2013, new elections were held for the House of Representatives, but the very low turnout left its credibility in question. The GNC refused to stand down, leaving Libya with two competing parliaments, neither able to exercise effective sovereign control. Military forces backed by external powers attached themselves to each of these dueling political coalitions: Dignity, led by General Khalid Hiftar; and Dawn, an Islamist and militia-backed coalition.

As these political struggles unfolded, Libya has struggled to establish basic state functions (Pack, Mezran, and Eljarh 2014). Security forces were outgunned by powerful militias, which refused to hand over their guns to an uncertain and politicized state. Oil production has been targeted, with devastating effects on the nascent economy. The government was unable to provide even rudimentary services to much of the country, leaving gaps easily exploited by jihadist groups such as Ansar al-Sharia and the Islamic State.

United Nations–led mediation has pushed to overcome these gaps by brokering the formation of a unity government, called the Government of National Accord (GNA; International Crisis Group 2015a). While securing the approval of the dueling governments and competing militias has been difficult, significant progress was made. This new unity government would in principle be the conduit for increased international assistance, including external military assistance against ISIS and help to disarm militias and establish public order. For all the intense suspicion of the GNA and of international actors, most of the actors involved, both inside and outside of Libya, do recognize the importance of ending the war. The economic collapse, and especially the precarious state of the oil industry, harms the interests of all. The establishment of footholds for the Islamic State shows clearly the potentially disastrous effects of continued state failure.

This does not make resolving the civil war a simple task. Libya's problem continues to be the absence of an effectively sovereign state and the high level of fragmentation even within the two large blocs (Wehrey 2016b). Significant pockets of resistance remain to the terms of the GNA. Militias will not likely disarm in the absence of firm guarantees of their future security and power, which will not be possible any time soon. There will therefore be rampant spoilers, including not only the Islamic State but also militias and factions breaking away from the two major blocs. Still, here again the urgent imperative should be establishing a minimal political consensus to allow the consolidation of the state, the restoration of basic services, and the production of oil to restart the economy. The next president should continue to strongly support the GNA and be willing to provide significant assistance, while resisting pressure for more direct military involvement.

Syria

Syria's war grew out of President Bashar al-Assad's savage repression of a civic uprising (Hokayem 2013; Abboud 2016; Lister 2015). Determined to avoid the fates of Mubarak or Qaddafi, Assad deployed graduated military force in an attempt to crush the uprising. His efforts instead fueled the uprising, which rapidly spiraled into a major revolt. Escalating regime violence pushed Syrians to take up arms in self-defense and ultimately led to an insurgency to overthrow the Assad regime. They found eager and willing external sponsors, but the opposition struggled to unify into a coherent political or military force. As the insurgency captured significant territory, Assad's regime received increasingly direct support from Hezbollah, Iran, and Russia. Jihadist trends became increasingly powerful, some fighting alongside the rebels and others battling both rebels and the government to carve out what would become the Islamic State. Syrian Kurds established their own uneasy place between the regime, the rebels, and ISIS. In 2015 Russia intervened directly in support of the government and, despite the agreement on a Cessation of Hostilities, has spearheaded an offensive that has encircled Aleppo. The war has proven utterly catastrophic, with some 400,000 dead and over 10 million displaced (International Crisis Group 2016).

International and local politics interacted in especially toxic ways in Syria. Some GCC states and Turkey provided arms and material support, even as the Syrian rebels gravitated toward Islamist extremism. The United States struggled to find effective local partners on the battlefield. The Free Syrian Army remained divided, unable to exercise authority over the fragmented military field and in constant tension with the political leadership of the opposition. The growing power of jihadist movements, and their intermingling with the Free Syrian Army and other "moderate" rebels, posed an ever more profound challenge. Assad's regime, for its part, became ever more dependent on external backers, including Hezbollah, Iran, Shi'ite militia fighters from Iraq and further afield, and Russia.

All of this has made Syria's war one of the most intractable of all possible types of wars (Lynch 2013, 2016). It has high degrees of competitive external intervention, significant fragmentation among the opposition, a daunting array of spoilers, and remote prospects of external enforcement mechanisms. Syria's strategic stalemate is unlikely to change, despite the advances made by the government with Russian support. Neither side is likely to be able to defeat the other. Local power balances are shaped by the level of external support, and every move by the external supporters of one side has been countered by increased support from external supporters of the other side. Increased American military support to the rebels would more likely invite increased Russian support for Assad than decisively tip the balance.

Even if Assad were to fall or the rebels were to be driven from Aleppo, the war would likely not end. Assad is unlikely to be able to regain legitimacy with a brutalized population or to prevent the continuation of insurgency. The best-case scenario from a Western perspective—a transitional government led by a coalition of moderates from both the regime and opposition—would likely only invite a renewed insurgency from hardliners on both sides. Powerful spoilers such as Jubhat al-Nusra would likely continue to fight. Nor does an international peacekeeping force able to enforce an agreement seem remotely likely. Inserting American forces directly would be a disastrous mistake. Few traditional contributors to peacekeeping missions are likely to be eager to send forces to Syria. The Turkish military, seen by many as the best chance, would face profound problems given its history with Syria and its active role in backing one side of the war, and it would also clash directly with Syrian Kurdish forces that have carved out an area of control along much of the Syrian Turkish border. American-led efforts to build the core of a new Syrian opposition army have had little success.

The Cessation of Hostilities agreed upon in late February of 2016 surprised most observers by holding for almost two months before violence surged again in Aleppo. The difficulty of a sustained ceasefire remains obvious, given that neither the regime nor the opposition has given up hopes of victory, and powerful spoilers such as Jubhat al-Nusra remain active. The regime's advance on Aleppo and continued bombing of rebel areas demonstrated graphically that the logic of war continued to dominate. Still, there are signs of growing exhaustion on both sides and a greater convergence between Russia and the United States on the importance of de-escalation. Negotiations are unlikely to bring about an end to the war in the near term. Neither side believes that the other is sincere about negotiating, and neither side can offer credible commitments to not carry out reprisals following a negotiated agreement. Still, the relative durability of the Cessation of Hostilities suggests that more partial, temporary de-escalation is possible. An international accord that acknowledges the impossibility of victory by either side and instead focuses on humanitarian reconstruction and civilian protection offers the next administration the best chance for stabilizing Syria.

Iraq

The Iraqi state that emerged from the rigors of U.S. occupation and a brutal civil war has struggled to establish effective sovereignty or authority. Former prime minister Nuri al-Maliki presided over a corrupt, sectarian regime that failed to produce either political consensus or effective governance. Maliki did not take advantage of the reduction of violence achieved through the so-called Surge of 2006–2007 to create a durable political accommodation. Instead, as the perceived utility of the awakenings declined, his government pushed these Sunni fighters aside. Following his contested reappointment as prime minister in 2010 and the withdrawal of U.S. troops, his rule became increasingly sectarian and unaccountable (Al-Ali 2014; Haddad 2016).

The Islamic State of Iraq, never fully defeated, continued to wage a lower-level but still quite bloody campaign of terrorist attacks over 2010–2011. Early in the Syrian conflict, the Islamic State of Iraq sent key leaders across the border to organize for jihadist insurgency. Over the next several years, the interaction between the Syrian and Iraqi theaters magnified its capabilities and impact, as it gained access to cross-border sanctuaries and growing flows of money, guns, and foreign fighters. Its political revival in Iraq was galvanized by Maliki's bloody crackdown on a protest encampment in Hawija, which infuriated many non-jihadist Iraqi Sunnis. In 2012, the Islamic State of Iraq reemerged in Anbar, with each violent response by the Iraqi security forces further angering and alienating Sunnis (Sowell 2014).

The Islamic State's dramatic seizure of Mosul came in the wake of years of alienation of the Sunni community, growing sectarian polarization, and interaction effects with the Syrian insurgency. The Iraqi government had lost effective sovereignty long before ISIS's military gains and the declaration of a Caliphate. The Islamic State's expansion was facilitated by Sunnis who had come to fear and hate what they viewed as dangerously sectarian, Shi'ite-dominated Iraqi military and police. The Iraqi government's growing reliance on Shi'ite militias to fight in the place of the Iraqi military only accelerated these hostilities. With U.S. support, the Iraqi military has made steady progress in retaking territory from the Islamic State, liberating a string of cities from Tikrit to Fallujah and moving toward Mosul.

Support to the Iraqi government in recapturing its territory should not lead the United States to embark on another large-scale deployment of military forces to Iraq. Where the United States does increase its military role, this should be kept as limited as possible and tightly connected to political objectives. The Obama administration deftly conditioned its military support to the Iraqi government on serious political changes. Maliki's replacement by Hayder al-Abadi offered the possibility of overcoming the legacies of nearly a decade of political mismanagement. The pathologies of a sectarian, corrupt, and autocratic state ran deeper than one man, however, and efforts to build a legitimate and functional Iraqi state run against more than a decade of postinvasion trends. Only by addressing those deeper pathologies and finding a formula for the full integration of Sunnis into the Iraqi political system can the conditions enabling ISIS's survival be ended. The Shi'ite Popular Mobilization Units (the Hashd) must be prevented from carrying out sectarian attacks and, ultimately, must be institutionalized within the Iraqi Security Forces under the control of the government.

Local insurgencies and state retraction

Even if the Islamic State were defeated in Iraq and Syria, it would continue to find opportunities to establish itself wherever state failure and regime abuses create openings. The pathologies of state failure and insurgency can also be seen at a more local level in discrete territories within otherwise still robust states. Libya's war, for instance, has spread instability across its borders into Tunisia, Algeria, and Mali. Perhaps the most urgent such case is Egypt's Sinai Peninsula, where the acceleration of a local insurgency in an area of collapsed governance has allowed the consolidation of an Islamic State affiliate.

Sinai has long challenged the control of the central Egyptian state (Ashour 2015; Sabry 2015). From the Mubarak years through the revolution, local tribal networks resisted state authority and periodically engaged in violent resistance. The Egyptian state typically responded with security crackdowns rather than with efforts to grapple with local economic and political grievances. During the first year following the Arab uprising, conditions in Sinai deteriorated rapidly. Cairo, consumed by political crisis, paid little attention to the evolving challenge as weapons and fighters flowed in from Libya and Gaza.

The Egyptian state's response only made things worse. Several years of heavy-handed state repression since a dramatic escalation in September 2013 only strengthened the evolving insurgency (Awad and Hashem 2015; Goodman 2014). The Sinai insurgency became of wider international significance when the insurgency group Ansar Bayt al-Maqdis declared its fealty to the Islamic State in November 2014 and the establishment of a "wilayat Sinai." U.S. efforts to help with this challenge have worked at cross purposes with other trends in the U.S.-Egyptian relationship linked to the fallout of the July 2013 military coup. This offers a useful window into how these adaptive and resilient jihadist movements can take advantage of state retreat and can be helped rather than hindered by aggressive military responses.

In such cases, international military assistance can make a more immediate and direct impact due to the existence of a potential state partner. Such assistance should be closely tied to an effective political strategy, however, to avoid simply fueling counterproductive cycles of punishment and repression. Provisions for the protection of human rights and the rule of law should be central pillars of assistance to U.S. partners as they seek to reassert state control over such areas.

Implications for the Next Administration

The horrifying consequences of the state failures and proxy wars that followed the Arab uprising will weigh heavily on the next administration. Even if the Obama administration managed to broker ceasefires in these countries that brought the immediate fighting to an end, this would only be the starting point for addressing the challenges that remain. Heavily armed spoilers will remain ready to strike. And the legacies of destruction, hatred, revenge, and polarization will not soon fade. Enforcement of ceasefires, support for transitional governments, and the repatriation of refugees will require significant resources. The costs of reconstruction and repatriation will be huge, of course, but not greater than the costs of prolonged military intervention.

There are some common lessons from these cases. Increased military involvement without corresponding political reforms has consistently failed to produce enduring results. Escalated American military support, especially in Syria, is unlikely to be decisive if it is not tied to an active diplomatic process coordinated with the other states deeply involved in the conflict such as Russia, Iran, the GCC states, and Turkey. All three wars have continued as long as they have precisely because opposing forces have not had the military power to defeat the other side, and because the external backers of each side are prepared to increase their support when needed. Thus, the further arming of Syria's rebels is more likely to produce an increase in Russian and Iranian support of the Assad regime than a decisive outcome. More than a year of a massive air campaign by the Saudi-led coalition in Yemen has produced few strategic gains or political progress.

The absence of viable military options points to the importance of negotiations toward a political solution. The increased levels of outside intervention have created greater dependence as well, which could in principle be used by those outside powers to impose a solution on local actors who might prefer to continue the fight. Enforcing such an agreement, if it could be found, typically requires significant external peacekeeping forces to guarantee commitments and provide security. In none of the cases discussed here is a significant external peacekeeping force likely, however. The focus thus far has, appropriately, been on efforts to build competent local forces to play such a role: the training of the Iraqi security forces, the efforts to build the Libyan national army, and the efforts to forge a unified Syrian opposition army.

All of these have foundered because of deeply entrenched political polarization and institutional pathologies, and greater success will require close attention to the politics (Sayigh 2015). Building security forces should not be undertaken in a military vacuum. The focus on military and security solutions has too often allowed embattled leaders to avoid significant political reforms and to instead double down on autocratic repression. Military aid should therefore always be heavily conditional, even in urgent situations, to ensure that the provision of assistance does not go to waste or even make matters worse.

None of this offers great grounds for optimism. We are far into the domain of loss on these conflicts. It may be premature in the short term to seek the final resolution of the deep political conflicts at the heart of these wars. Instead, the best chance may be the consolidation of long-term ceasefires and the de facto, but not de jure, partition of countries into self-governing areas. Syria might then see opposition-controlled areas, regime-controlled areas, and Kurdish-controlled areas rebuilding themselves under a very loose federal government. The same might be a temporary solution for north and south Yemen and for east and west Libya. Such arrangements would not satisfy any of the warring parties, but they would allow for a desperately needed return to normalcy, repatriation and rehabilitation of refugees, and the rebuilding of shattered economies, all in the interest of achieving a long-term resolution that is, at the current time, unidentifiable.

The emphasis for the next administration should be on de-escalating the wars and rebuilding these shattered states. It is vital to help rebuild state sovereignty without enabling a new authoritarianism, which means not allowing the exigencies of counterinsurgency to drive out human rights considerations. Again and again it has been the prioritization of security solutions over political accommodations that has accelerated insurgency and state failure. Efforts should prioritize the rehabilitation and repatriation of refugees, the breaking of war economies, and the normalization of everyday life (Yahya 2015). Such steps are an essential starting point for the urgently needed restoration of any form of regional order and alleviation of the tremendous suffering of the region's civilians.

References

Abboud, Samer. 2016. *Syria*. New York NY: Wiley and Sons.

Al-Ali, Zaid. 2014. *The struggle for Iraq's future: How corruption, incompetence, and sectarianism have undermined democracy*. New Haven, CT: Yale University Press.

Ashour, Omar. 8 November 2015. Sinai's stubborn insurgency. *Foreign Affairs*.

Awad, Mokhtar, and Mustafa Hashem. 2015. *Egypt's escalating Islamist insurgency*. Washington, DC: Carnegie Endowment for International Peace.

Goodman, Joshua. 2014. *Egypt's assault on Sinai*. Washington, DC: Carnegie Endowment for International Peace.

Haddad, Fanar. 2016. *Shia-centric state building and Sunni rejection in post-2003 Iraq*. Washington, DC: Carnegie Endowment for International Peace.

Hokayem, Emile. 2013. *Syria's war and the fracturing of the Levant*. New York, NY: Routledge.

International Crisis Group. 2015a. *Libya: Getting Geneva right*. Middle East and North Africa Report No. 157. New York, NY: International Crisis Group.

International Crisis Group. 2015b. *Yemen at war*. Middle East Briefing 45. New York, NY: International Crisis Group.

International Crisis Group. 2016. *Yemen: Is peace possible?* Middle East Report No. 157. New York, NY: International Crisis Group.

Lister, Charles. 2015. *The Syrian jihad*. London: Hurst Publishers.

Lynch, Marc, ed. 2013. *The political science of Syria's war*. Project on Middle East Political Science (POMEPS) Briefing 22. Washington, DC: Institute for Middle East Studies, the George Washington University.

Lynch, Marc. 2016. *The new Arab wars: Anarchy and uprising in the Middle East*. New York, NY: Public Affairs.

Pack, Jason, Karim Mezran, and Mohammad Eljarh. 2014. *Libya's Faustian bargain: Breaking the appeasement cycle*. Washington, DC: Atlantic Council.

Sabry, Mohannad. 2015. *Sinai: Egypt's linchpin, Gaza's lifeline, Israel's nightmare*. London: Oxford University Press.

Sayigh, Yezid. 2015. *Crumbling states: Security sector reform in Libya and Yemen*. Riad El Solh, Lebanon: Carnegie Middle East Center.

Sowell, Kirk. 9 August 2014. *Iraq's second Sunni insurgency*. Current Trends in Islamist Ideology. Washington, DC: Hudson Institute.

Syrian Center for Policy Research. 11 February 2016. *Confronting fragmentation*. Beirut: Syrian Center for Policy Research. Available from http://scpr-syria.org/publications/policy-reports/confronting-frag-men tation/

Wehrey, Fred. 3 March 2016 (2016a). The path forward in Libya. Testimony to Senate Foreign Relations Committee.

Wehrey, Fred. 17 February 2016 (2016b). Why Libya's transition to democracy failed. *Washington Post*.

Yahya, Maha. 2015. *Refugees and the making of an Arab regional disorder*. Riad El Solh, Lebanon: Carnegie Middle East Center.

Working toward a Stable Regional Order

By

PAUL SALEM

Conditions in the Arab world since 2011 have brought about a perfect storm of national and regional instability: the Arab revolts challenged the authoritarian order in six Arab countries, and intense competition among regional powers has flared into an open proxy war. The combination has caused four Arab states to fully or partially fail. Their failure has created the ungoverned space and sociopolitical chaos that has allowed al-Qaeda to resurge and enabled the formation and spread of ISIS. This article examines the elements of today's unstable Middle East regional order and suggests steps that the next U.S. president can take to help re-create a stable and less conflictual regional order, including in key states such as Saudi Arabia, Turkey, and Iran. This is key to ending civil wars, rebuilding failed states, and reclaiming ungoverned space from terrorist groups and denying ungoverned space to them in the future.

Keywords: Middle East; regional order; Iran; Turkey; Saudi Arabia; regional architecture

Although violent jihadi ideology has been present since the late 1960s, it has materialized as effective terrorist organizations only in spaces where states have failed, either fully or partially. This is true of 1980s Afghanistan and today's Somalia, Libya, Syria, Yemen, and Iraq. The causes of state failure can be internal or external—or a combination of both: internal, as a result of a massive breakdown of state-society relations and governance capacity; external, as a result of intervention by, or intensive competition between, external powers.

Conditions in the Arab world since 2011 brought about a perfect storm of internal and

Paul Salem is vice president for policy and research at The Middle East Institute in Washington, D.C. He is the author of numerous books, reports, and articles on issues of political change, transition, and conflict, as well as the regional and international relations of the Middle East.

Correspondence: psalem@mei.edu

DOI: 10.1177/0002716216666263

external factors: the Arab revolts challenged the authoritarian order in six Arab countries; intense external competition among regional powers exacerbated these tensions. The combination caused four Arab states to fully or partially fail. Their failure created the ungoverned space and social chaos that has allowed al-Qaeda to resurge and enabled the formation and spread of ISIS (also known as the Islamic State or ISIL).

In an unstable regional order, countries' internal and external conflicts are mutually exacerbating: internal tensions in one country draw in external alignments and contribute to regional proxy conflict, and regional conflict is more likely to impose itself onto domestic contests and push states toward failure and civil war. In a stable region, on the other hand, domestic tensions within one state are not likely to stimulate wider regional conflict, and the absence of intense regional conflict will reduce the divisive pressures on struggling states and societies, reducing the likelihood of state failure (see, e.g., Wolff 2011; Iqbal and Starr 2008; Mincheva 2005).

This article examines the elements of today's unstable Middle East regional order and suggests a path toward building a more stable and prosperous order. Building a stable regional order is key to ending civil wars and rebuilding failed states. And reconstituting states is key to reclaiming ungoverned space from terrorist groups and denying ungoverned space to them in the future.[1]

U.S. Involvement in Impacting Regional Order

The United States has been involved in impacting Middle East order and disorder for many decades. It was a key protagonist in the Cold War and the Arab-Israeli conflict that drove divisions and animated conflicts in the region for many years, and it was a key protagonist in the confrontation with post-1979 Iran that created many of today's regional battle lines (see, e.g., Pillar 2015; Hudson 1996).

The George W. Bush administration's invasion of Iraq decisively shattered the precarious Arab order, empowered Iran, and helped to unleash al-Qaeda in Iraq and the Arab Middle East. The Obama administration's relative retreat from the region created political vacuums that mutually hostile regional players as well as al-Qaeda and ISIS have rushed to fill. What the United States does or does not do in the Middle East has had great impacts on the region.

The United States has also played constructive roles at important junctures. After 1973 the United States was key in negotiating peace between Egypt and Israel, truce between Israel and Syria, and an eventual peace with Jordan. After the first gulf war, the United States led a wider effort—launched at the Madrid Peace Conference—to try to settle the Arab-Israeli conflict and create a stable regional architecture including the Arab countries and Israel, with working groups on security, economics, water, refugees, and the environment. In 2015 the United States got Iran to suspend key elements of its nuclear program, thus denying Iran a pathway to nuclear weapons for the next decade or more and, thus, avoiding the risk of wider nuclear proliferation in the region or an imminent Israeli-Iranian confrontation.

In the run up to the 2016 presidential election, the debate among candidates has focused largely on who will do more—or less—in defeating ISIS, monitoring and containing Iran, and standing with allies, all while keeping U.S. boots largely off the ground. While these debates about how much the United States will or will not do within a deeply unstable regional order are important, the more important and strategic question is what the United States can do to render the regional system more stable, less conflictual, more self-regulating, and thus less needy of direct U.S. intervention. The strategic question for the next U.S. president is not how much to do, but what to do.

The Bush administration developed a hegemonic understanding of creating Middle East order. Through use of overwhelming American military force, changing regimes in Iraq and Afghanistan—and potentially, after that, in Syria and Iran—the Bush administration hoped to create stable democratic and allied regional state systems (see Gordon 2003). In some ways, this goal echoed the achievements of U.S. power in creating stable, democratic, and allied orders after World War II in Western Europe and parts of East Asia. That vision for the Middle East ran aground in the hills of Afghanistan and the sands of Iraq.

The Obama administration's "strategic vision"—to the degree there was an articulated one—was to eschew hegemonic ambitions and return the United States to the role of an external balancer, similar to what had prevailed to some degree during the Nixon and Clinton years. But external balancing is a "system-preserving" strategy, not a "system-creating" one. In other words, an external balancer works for regions where a static standoff and power balance—however precarious—between self-interested states has already emerged. Balancing states that are in open conflict does not bring or preserve stability but, rather, usually prolongs the conflict. Trying to pursue "external balancing" when major terrorist and nonstate actors are also part of the regional mix does not work at all.

The Middle East's main conflict axis today is the open conflict between Iran and its allies on one side and Saudi Arabia and its allies on the other. The United States was instrumental in blocking Iran from acquiring a nuclear weapon, but otherwise it has left the conflict between Iran and the Gulf countries to grow and metastasize (Krauthammer 2015). The United States stands by its Gulf allies, helping them to maintain a "balance of power" with Iran. But in an open conflict system, this balance largely means that the two sides will sustain their conflict for years or decades to come, which will contribute to the further devastation of the region and the delight of terrorist and nonstate actors. Without a political breakthrough between the region's states, from open hostility and conflict to some measure of communication, cooperation, and respect for regional order, there will be no balance to preserve and no state order to maintain.

Other regions around the world have made the difficult transition from conflict to some measure of regional order and cooperation—in Europe, Africa, Latin America, and Asia. The Middle East can do so as well. Fifty years ago, Saudi Arabia and Egypt were engaged in a fierce struggle for dominance over the region, which led to direct war in Yemen and the toppling of governments in Iraq, Syria, Libya, and Sudan; yet the two states moved past their differences. Israel and the Arab states engaged in multiple wars between the 1950s and

1970s, but Egypt and Israel found peace, and the Arab states proposed a comprehensive peace initiative in 2002 (see, e.g., Kurtzer and Lasesnky 2008). The current conflict between the Iran-led and Gulf Cooperation Council (GCC)–led axes might seem inevitable and unstoppable today, but an understanding of the interests of the states involved and the ability of strategic vision and effective leadership to bring about change will indicate that there is an alternative future available.

The challenge for the next U.S. president is not to ponder what actions to take within a broken and conflictual regional order but, rather, what steps to take to bring about a more stable state order that is less conflictual and more self-regulating. President Obama used a robust combination of international sanctions and diplomacy to get Iran to accept norms and limits on its nuclear program—an important prerequisite for regional stabilization. Similarly, the next president will have to consider how to use the various levers of U.S. power and diplomacy to get Iran to accept international norms and limits on its regional policies as well as to get Iran and other major players in the region to de-escalate conflict and agree on respecting and strengthening a rules-based Westphalian regional state order.

As Zalmay Khalilzad argued in a recent article (2016), "Washington has sought to manage different crises in the Middle East without thinking more fundamentally about how U.S. diplomacy can catalyze a new, sustainable order for the region." This will require "hard-headed engagement" that includes measures that create "a balance of power in the region that checks Iran's bid for regional hegemony" and hardball diplomacy—such as that over the nuclear issue— "designed to bring Tehran onboard behind a new regional order that is consistent with U.S. interests." While U.S. influence "has declined in the region, the United States is the only power that can broker such an understanding. Just as the United States invested resources, energy and time in 'normalizing' the geopolitics of Europe and East Asia during the Cold War, we must make a generational commitment to do so in the Middle East."

Zbigniew Brzezinski (2016) makes a similar case, arguing that the United States "will require patient persistence in forging cooperative relationships with some new partners (particularly Russia and China) as well as joint efforts with more established and historically rooted Muslim states (Turkey, Iran, Egypt, and Saudi Arabia ...) in shaping a wider framework of regional stability. Our European allies, previously dominant in the region, can still be helpful in that regard."

Secretary Kerry has echoed this approach. In statements to GCC leaders in April 2016, he said that if Iran was willing to help end the conflicts in Syria and Yemen and to "cease ... activities that raise questions about credibility ... and intention," the United States "would welcome Iran to be part of a genuine security arrangement for the region" (Goodenough 2016). Even Saudi foreign minister Adel Jubeir declared that what the region needed was agreement among regional powers, including Iran, to—in his words—"abide by the good neighborhood principle and to refrain from interfering into the affairs" of neighboring states.[2] It is this line of thinking that should be the strategic focus of the next administration's Middle East policy.

The Evolution of a Broken Regional Order

The Middle East today has no regional order in any positive sense. It is the least ordered or governed regional subsystem in the world. The region we call the Middle East today is contested by the Gulf states, Iran, Turkey, Egypt and Israel. The Gulf states have created a regional architecture among themselves under the GCC; and the Gulf states, Egypt, and other Arab countries are grouped within the weak League of Arab States. The countries of North Africa established the Arab Maghreb Union, which is stymied by Algerian-Moroccan tension over the western Sahara and the collapse of Libya. The Organization of Islamic Cooperation includes the Arab countries with Turkey, Iran, and other Muslim-majority countries in Asia, but it has been an arena of tension between the Sunni powers and Iran more than an arena of cooperation. OPEC (Organization of the Petroleum Exporting Countries) includes the Gulf states and Iran and has seen periods of cooperation on oil production and pricing as well as periods of competition. The Madrid peace process was designed to lead to the development of regional security and economic cooperation between Israel and the Arab countries, but the process failed. Most recently, the International Syria Support Group has been one of the only venues where Saudi, Turkish, and Iranian leaders have met in a political context.

Unlike in East Asia, Africa, the Americas, or Western Europe, there is no dedicated forum or institutionalized mechanism for the main regional powers to communicate, identify concerns, defuse conflicts, build on common interests, and work toward establishing a set of principles for regional interaction other than direct or proxy war. Working toward establishing such a functioning order is essential to rebuilding regional stability and a fundamental necessity in the broader campaign to deny space to terrorist organizations. The United States has a clear interest in a more stable region with less proxy conflict, more stable states, and less ungoverned space for terrorist groups; and as in the campaign to counter Iran's nuclear weapons program, the United States is the only truly global power that can marshal enough international and regional influence to bring about lasting systemic changes. The United States needs to play a leading role in that arena.

The challenge of building a stable regional order in the modern Middle East is not a new one. For five centuries the Ottoman Empire was the regional order, as it governed—directly or indirectly—the bulk of Arab lands. The interwar period postponed the question of regional order, as the region was managed from Europe, but precarious new Arab states were created—particularly in the Levant—with fresh borders and no recent legacy of indigenous government. World War II brought independence from European control and the establishment of the League of Arab States.

The idea of an Arab order took deeper root after the Arab-Israeli war of 1948 and subsequent wars in 1967 and 1973. It had a strong Arab nationalist ethos. The Arab order had its own cold war between Saudi Arabia and Nasser's Egypt that raged from the late 1950s to the late 1960s and impacted security and politics from Yemen to Iraq, Syria, Lebanon, and Libya (Kerr 1971). After the death of Nasser, Egypt and Saudi Arabia came together around the 1973 war against Israel. Between the end of World War II and the late 1970s, both Iran and Turkey were oriented westward with little interest in getting greatly involved in the Arab Middle East.

The global U.S.-Soviet Cold War impinged upon this Arab order from the 1950s onward, with Arab states aligning with one global power or another. The West tried to create an anti-Soviet regional order through the Baghdad Pact of 1955, which included Iraq, Turkey, Iran, and Pakistan, and hoped that other Arab states would follow. Iraq withdrew from the pact after the overthrow of the monarchy there in 1958, and Nasser opposed it vehemently. The Soviet Union meanwhile made rapid headway, establishing strong political and military relations with Egypt, Iraq, Syria, Libya, Somalia, and the People's Democratic Republic of Yemen. Nasser built strong relations with the U.S.S.R. but tried to keep Egypt and his Arab allies away from direct Cold War alignments; he was a key member of the nonaligned movement.[3]

Rise of the Iranian-Saudi rivalry

The years 1973 and 1979 were watershed years in regional power patterns. The 1973 war set Egypt and Israel on the path to an eventual peace treaty that effectively ended the state-to-state Arab-Israeli conflict. That separate Egyptian peace with Israel also isolated Egypt and ended its leadership position in the Arab world. In 1973, the Saudi-led oil embargo against the United States and other countries triggered an enormous oil price surge: prices climbed from $3 per barrel at the beginning of 1973 to $38 per barrel by the end of the decade.[4] Regional power decidedly shifted away from Egypt to the petro-states of Saudi Arabia and Iran. They are still the beneficiaries of that power shift.

Until 1979, Iran and Saudi Arabia were on the same general strategic page: two conservative monarchies aligned with the United States against Communist expansion and revolutionary change. The Islamic Revolution in Iran in 1979 changed all that. It pitted the two petro states against each other for decades and helped to bring about the regional conflict system that persists as of this writing.

Revolutionary Iran challenged the regional order at several levels: it proclaimed that it was a pan-Islamic revolutionary movement, not a strictly Iranian one, whose goals included the overthrow of conservative monarchies, the overthrow of regimes aligned with the United States, the championing of Islamist causes, and bringing about an Islamic regional order effectively under Iranian leadership.

Iraq responded immediately by invading Iran. The resulting eight-year war was effectively the first Arab-Iranian war of modern times, as Saudi Arabia and the majority of Arab states backed Iraq; only Syria sided with Iran, an alliance that still stands as of this writing. The war ended inconclusively in 1988; the Saddam Hussein regime that prosecuted it is no more, but a generation of Iranians—and the majority of Iran's current leadership—were shaped by the events of that war. It underlies the deep hostility, anxiety, and distrust with which most of Iran's current leaders regard the Arab and Sunni states to their south and west.

Saudi Arabia responded to Khomeini's attempt to claim the mantle of pan-Islamic leadership and use that against Iran by pivoting to a much more Islamic profile of the Saudi monarchy (the king was retitled "Custodian of the Two Holy Mosques"), emphasizing the centrality of Mecca and Medina in the annual Hajj and Islamic gatherings, and using its resources to spread the influence of its own Wahhabi religious establishment throughout the Muslim world.

The Saudi pivot toward a more religious profile was also motivated by the 1979 armed takeover of the Grand Mosque in Mecca by Islamist extremists calling for the overthrow of the ruling family. During the 1950s and 1960s, the Saudis faced challenges from Arab nationalists and various secular leftists and communists; from 1979 onward, the main challenges would come from both Shiite and Sunni Islamists. The kingdom adopted a more religious profile in both its domestic and foreign policy to shore up its legitimacy.

While Iran proceeded to "weaponize" its religious foreign policy by creating the radical Shiite armed nonstate actor Hezbollah in the early 1980s and reaching out to other groups in the region, Saudi Arabia and the United States proceeded to weaponize radical Sunni nonstate actors in the war against the 1979 Soviet invasion of Afghanistan. The conditions unleashed by the momentous events of 1979 are still with us today: conflict between Iran and its neighbors, the instrumentalization and weaponization of sectarian proxy groups, and the empowerment of armed nonstate actors.

The Middle East today is locked in deep conflict between Iran and its allies on one side and Saudi Arabia and its allies on the other. The conflict has helped to rip Syria, Iraq, and Yemen apart and has provided ideal conditions for sectarian radicalization and the spread of armed nonstate actors and terrorist super groups. Defusing this region-wide conflict system, which could rage on for decades more, and replacing it with a stable regional order needs to be a top priority in the fight against terror.

The Paradox of Threat Perceptions

Iran, Turkey, and the GCC countries actually have many core interests in common. These potentially include regime and state security, regional stability, economic cooperation, and regional prosperity. But so far this potential positive interdependence has been overshadowed by the negative interdependence of security fears, conflict, and sectarian violence. While all the region's states and societies would benefit from a stable and cooperative regional order, they are stuck in what might be best described as a violence trap. Part of the problem are patterns of threat perception that fuel the ongoing conflict but need to be unpacked and disentangled.

Iran's conflictual approach to dealing with its region is perhaps the linchpin of the current violence trap. Its foreign policy is a toxic mix of haughty ambition linked to lofty revolutionary goals and a proud history of imperial grandeur, with the paranoid security fears of a regime that was attacked at birth and has a long history of foreign intervention and invasion—from the U.S.-engineered over-throw of Mossadegh in 1953 to the Anglo-Russian invasion of 1941. Its mix of ambition and paranoia has driven it to challenge the prevailing state order in the region, seek out sectarian allies, and build up armed nonstate actors; this policy triggered a mirror response from some of the GCC countries, and recently Turkey as well. Seeking to change Iranian policy in the region will be central in defusing the current violence trap and rebuilding stability and order in the region.

In the section on foreign policy in the Iranian constitution, Article 154 states that the Islamic Republic "supports the just struggles of the oppressed against the oppressors in every corner of the globe." The same article tries impossibly to square the circle by stating that this (support of the struggles) will be pursued "while scrupulously refraining from all forms of interference in the internal affairs of other nations." This contradiction illustrates Kissinger's view that "Iran has to decide whether it is a nation or a cause"; and "If Iran thinks of itself as a nation or can be brought to do so, it can be accorded a respected place in the international system" (Kissinger 2008). No doubt, getting Iranian leaders to emphasize the former over the latter will be key to stabilizing the region.

But despite the constitution and much ideological rhetoric, much of Iran's regional policy is driven by traditional concerns for regime and national security. Much of the Iranian leadership might be described as paranoid, but even para-noiacs sometimes have cause for their fears. Most cannot forget that the Gulf countries backed Iraq in its long and devastating war against Iran, or more recently that WikiLeaks revealed that some Gulf leaders privately urged Washington to bomb Iran (Black and Tisdall 2010). And the leadership interprets firebrand pronouncements from some Saudi Wahhabi preachers against Shiites as an existential threat.

Further afield, both Washington and Moscow backed Baghdad in the Iran-Iraq war, and regime change has been—on and off—part of official U.S. policy even under the Clinton administration. The Bush administration invaded Iran's two neighbors and declared Iran a member of the "Axis of Evil," implying that it could be next. The Obama administration has changed that narrative, but Iranian skeptics still hear enough hardline rhetoric from Members of Congress and the political parties to fear that, despite the Obama interlude, regime change could easily return as a theme in future U.S. administrations. Of course Iran and Israel are locked in confrontation, with Iran threatening to wipe Israel off the map, and Israel repeatedly threatening to bomb Iran.

Under sanctions for several decades and lacking the conventional capacities of the United States and Israel, Iran invested in asymmetric warfare. It built up

Hezbollah— a powerful entity "parked" off of Israel's northern border—to deter Israeli or U.S. attack against Iran. It built up relations with Iraqi anti-Saddam groups to weaken Saddam and neutralize the threat from Iraq. It rushed to the support of Bashar Assad after the uprising in Syria in 2011 for fear that if Damascus fell to what Iran perceived as an American-Sunni alliance, Hezbollah would also fall, the friendly regime in Baghdad would be vulnerable, and the threat would reach directly to the security of the regime in Tehran. The opportunity to exploit the Houthi rebellion in Yemen was seized to weaken Saudi Arabia on its vulnerable flank and deter it from progress in Syria and the Levant.

The Iranian regime not only feels vulnerable to regional and international enemies; it also feels internally vulnerable. Like other Middle Eastern autocracies, it sits uneasily over a young and restive population that revolted once already in 2009 and might do so again.

Iranian fears are matched by Gulf fears. While Iran sees existential enemies everywhere, Gulf leaders see an Iranian quest for regional hegemony everywhere. And Iranian actions in Lebanon, Syria, and Yemen have triggered strong reactions from the Gulf countries. Like two boxers in a darkened ring, the two sides are bloodying each other to no one's benefit.

The point is that, constitutional and ideological pronouncements aside, the Iranian leadership is motivated first and foremost by concern for its regime's security and survival, and second by concern for Iranian national security. It interprets recent events in the region within its own prism, perceives serious threats to regime and national security, and has intervened accordingly. Interestingly, the Gulf leadership has similar fears. It interprets recent events as directed against its own security and intervenes accordingly.

Power Balancing and Building Regional Order

Pushing back against Iranian intervention in the region, and convincing Iran's hardliners and the Supreme Leader that regional hegemony is impossible and its pursuit enormously costly to Iran, are keys to bringing Iran to seriously reconsider its regional policy. International sanctions and the P5+1 talks[5] got Iran to accept international norms and limits on its nuclear program; but in the meantime it felt free to escalate its intervention in Syria, Iraq, and Yemen and encouraged its proxy, Hezbollah, to expand its deployment from Lebanon to Syria.

The United States has established an annual summit with its GCC partners and is building up GCC military capacities to counterbalance and defend against any direct Iranian military threats, but the United States has done very little to push back on Iran's asymmetric and proxy interventions in the region. Indeed, after the rise of ISIS, the United States has indirectly cooperated with some Iranian forces and proxies, seeing them as enemy-of-my-enemy friends in the fight against ISIS.

In the absence of robust U.S. action in this area, Saudi Arabia has assembled a regional coalition of Arab and Muslim states. It has severed relations with Iran, intervened in Yemen, doubled down on support for the anti-Assad opposition in Syria, and suspended military aid and travel to Lebanon.

Power balancing and pushback are necessary, but the desired end point is not an open war for the Middle East that leaves more societies in ruins and more communities radicalized. The end point will require a diplomatic process in which all countries, including Iran, Saudi Arabia, and Turkey, agree on the need to rebuild a state-based order; defuse regional conflict; end proxy wars; build on common interests of security and economic development; and coexist in the region on the basis of respect for international law, good neighborhood, and non-interference in the affairs of other states.

While President Obama showed what American leadership can achieve in assembling a global coalition to get Iran to change its nuclear weapons policy, his administration has shown little confidence and energy in going much further toward dealing with the collapse of regional order. Indeed, Obama exasperatedly urged the Gulf countries to find a way to "share" the Middle East with Iran (Goldberg 2016). But what the Middle East does not need is another round of war ending with another Sykes-Picot agreement divvying up the region between Iran and Saudi Arabia; rather, it needs a political process that ends these regional wars and creates mutually agreed-upon principles and rules for a stable and prosperous Middle East. In that process, there is no substitute for U.S. leadership.

Outlines of a Transformative Policy

The point of robust and intelligent diplomacy is to disentangle all of the parties' legitimate concerns for regime and national security from the prevalent patterns of regional proxy wars and interventions. These proxy wars are not enhancing any state's regime or national security; quite the contrary, they are devastating the region and draining valuable resources.

A robust diplomatic effort would have to be sustained over several years. It would require leadership from the new U.S. president to lay out the vision and marshal the international and regional engagement to move it forward. It is not a costly strategy as it does not involve military or economic outlays but, rather, intelligent and sustained political and diplomatic effort. Nor is it a risky strategy, in that even if attempts at regional cooperation move slowly—or fail—we would be no worse off than we already are today.

In the sections below, I suggest a three-track approach for such an initiative. These tracks are not meant to be necessarily sequential and could—indeed, ideally, should—be pursued simultaneously. The first track would focus on the macro issue of working toward an agreement of principles on regional order and gradually building a regional institutional framework. The second track would focus on disentangling current proxy wars in a phased approach. The third would work on boosting cooperation on economic development, trade, investment, labor movement, water, energy, and cultural exchange, as well as considering some form of the Marshall Plan for the region.

Of course, there is more than one way to design a diplomatic initiative. The tracks suggested here certainly could be adapted or revised in various ways. And, as I mentioned, there is little guarantee of success. Even if the United States were able to lead and sustain such a diplomatic initiative—as it did in the nuclear talks with Iran—there is little to guarantee that decision-makers in Tehran, Riyadh, and Ankara—to name a few key capitals—would have the political vision, will, and capacity to engage in an impactful way and deliver the commitments and policy changes that progress in such talks would entail. On the other hand, top officials from all three capitals have at various times emphasized the need for a stable and cooperative regional order (Davutoglu 2007; Zarif 2015).[6] And the current disorder in the region is a lose-lose gambit that is costing all states dearly in terms of their national security and economic prospects.

Track one: Regional contact group

Track one could begin with establishing a regional contact group or consultation forum, which would include officials from the GCC, Egypt, Turkey, and Iran. This group could be chaired by the United Nations (UN) but facilitated and backed by the United States and Russia, with backing from the European Union and China. This group would not grapple directly with the ongoing conflicts in the region but would work to build agreement among regional states on a core set of long-term common principles for regional order. Learning from the experience of other regions, this declaration of principles could include something along the lines of

- affirmation of the Westphalian principles of respect for the sovereignty and territorial integrity of signatory states;
- respect for the national security of signatory states and refraining from the threat or use of force against each other;
- de-escalation and de-militarization of relations;
- commitment to the eradication of armed nonstate actors;
- commitment to helping failed and failing states reach internal political agreement and rebuild state sovereignty; and
- commitment to regular consultation and discussion.

A more ambitious set of core principles might also include

- a shift from conflict management to conflict prevention and peace-building;
- confidence-building measures and pilot initiatives for security cooperation;
- acceptance of cultural, religious, and ethnic diversity;
- phasing out religious and sectarian proselytizing and propaganda as a tool of foreign policy;
- building social and cultural interchange and ties;
- encouraging economic relations, trade, investment, and joint projects; and
- exploring the establishment of a permanent and structured cooperation framework.

Iranian Foreign Minister Muhammad Zarif proposed something very much along these lines in an op-ed in the *New York Times* in April 2015, where he called for "regional dialogue ... based on generally recognized principles and shared objectives, notably respect for sovereignty, territorial integrity and political independence of all states; inviolability of international boundaries; noninterference in internal affairs; peaceful settlement of disputes; impermissibility of threat or use of force; and promotion of peace, stability, progress and prosperity in the region."

Unfortunately, Mr. Zarif does not control Iran's foreign policy in the Middle East, and those who do—General Qasim Suleimani and the Revolutionary Guards—regularly violate almost every one of these necessary principles. Nevertheless, Zarif's position, along with Saudi Foreign Minister Adel Jubeir's position welcoming regional agreement to "abide by the good neighborhood principle and to refrain from interfering into the affairs"[7] of neighboring states, creates an important opening for such a regional contact group.

Turkey has proposed such frameworks for the Caucasus and the Black Sea area, and it had established the outlines of a cooperative economic framework in 2010 that included Turkey, Syria, Jordan, and Lebanon before the Syrian uprising broke out (Kucukkosum 2010). In an article in 2007, Turkish Foreign Minister Ahmet Davutoglu outlined four principles for building regional order in the Middle East: "First of all, security for everyone, not only for this group or that group, this country or that country, but common security for the entire region. Second, priority must be given to dialogue as a means of solving crises. . . . The third principle is economic interdependence. Order in the Middle East cannot be achieved in an atmosphere of isolated economies. . . . The fourth principle is cultural coexistence and plurality" (Davutoglu 2007).

The UN can bring to the table the experiences of other regions around the world that transformed from places of regional conflict to stable and cooperative regions with some institutional regional architecture. Europe's turning from continent-wide wars that killed more than 80 million in the first half of twentieth century to a cooperative framework is an important guide. There, the path from the Treaty of Paris of 1951 that created the European Coal and Steel Community to the Treaties of Rome in 1957 that established the European Economic Community, and so on, is instructive. So too might be the experience of the Organization of Security and Cooperation in Europe, which emerged from the Helsinki talks and created a platform in the mid-1970s that brought together eastern and western bloc countries, including the Soviet Union and the United States. Likewise the creation of the Association of South East Asian Nations (ASEAN), the Organization of American States, the African Union, the Arctic Council, Mercosur, the Southern African Development Community, and other regional and subregional frameworks would also provide important guides.

The goal of this track would be to seek an agreement on principles by the main Arab countries, Turkey, and Iran and to begin discussions on some form of regional communication and cooperation architecture. It should be clear that this trilateral Arab-Turkish-Iranian forum would not supplant or necessarily run counter to other regional forums and frameworks of which the various countries are part. The League of Arab States would remain the principle forum among Arab states, and Turkey and Iran are part of various other regional frameworks.

   This framework would also be separate from any eventual or potential Arab-Israeli peace and regional framework. Currently the prospects for Israeli-Palestinian peace are very dim. However, if that were to happen, the Arab states and Israel could find agreement based on the Arab peace initiative of 2002. And Israel and the Arab countries could establish a regional framework such as that proposed during the Madrid peace process. Turkey could possibly be included in such a framework, but it is hard to imagine Israel and Iran in any joint forum in the foreseeable future.

Track two: De-confliction and de-escalation

   The second track should be a quieter behind-the-scenes diplomatic track that tries to disentangle the regional players from the ongoing proxy arenas in the region. This track would concern itself with regional involvements in Syria, Yemen, Iraq, and Lebanon.

   Moving forward in Syria will still hinge on the regime and the opposition negotiating some form of political transition. If and when that happens, this track would focus on getting the commitment of regional players to support the new government and help it to reestablish authority over Syria. More importantly, this track would have to manage and phase the withdrawal of Iranian, Hezbollah, and other Shiite militias from Syria; the withdrawal of support by Turkey and the GCC from armed opposition groups; and the transfer of that support to the new authorities and their reconstituted security forces.

   In Yemen, the challenge might be not as complex as in Syria. Iran has no significant direct or proxy forces imported to Yemen from abroad. There are ongoing UN-led Yemeni peace talks among the main parties. If and when they reach agreement, the regional players must be brought to commit to supporting the new government and its state institutions. This track would also need to ensure the withdrawal of Saudi and coalition forces, the withdrawal of support by Iran to the Houthi rebel movement, and the transfer of that support to the new authorities.

   In Iraq, there already is a constitutional and state structure—albeit somewhat dysfunctional—to support. However, there are two regionally problematic challenges. The Arab Sunni community continues to feel excluded from representation and power sharing in the new order, and the rise of the Iranian-dominated Popular Mobilization Units (PMUs) is a cause of great concern. This track should get regional players to help the Iraqi government and the Arab Sunni leadership in Iraq to find an inclusive way forward in government and should get regional players to transfer their support from the PMUs or other irregular armed groups to the Iraqi armed forces.

   The issue of Hezbollah in Lebanon might be the hardest of all. Its existence predates the current crises in the other three countries. Although it was born in the midst of civil and regional conflict in the 1980s, it remains a permanent fixture in Lebanon 26 years after the end of the civil war there and 16 years after the end of the Israeli occupation. Hezbollah violates the simplest principles of Westphalian international or regional order—one state (Iran) openly and officially supports and maintains the world's largest nonstate army (Hezbollah) in another country

(Lebanon). In the long run, if no solution is found for Hezbollah, there can be no agreement on regional order and little hope for regional stability.

The challenge on this issue will be complex. Some phases of the work would include ensuring Hezbollah's withdrawal from Syria—if and when a transition deal were reached—and the withdrawal of its trainers and support from other arenas such as those in Yemen and Iraq. A second phase is dealing with its presence in Lebanon. This might initially include a gradual diminution of its forces and deployments in the country but will have to eventually broach the subject of its integration into the armed forces of the Lebanese state. In Iraq, the fear is that the PMUs will become a permanent nonstate army like Hezbollah in Lebanon; the hope is, rather, that the PMUs and Hezbollah could be integrated into the armed forces of their inclusive state structures.

What this track would also have to grapple with is the explosively high tension among Israel, Hezbollah, and Iran. Hezbollah does not want to start another war with Israel; nor does Israel want to get into one; but the tension on both sides could easily lead to another major war. UN, U.S., and Russian diplomacy could do more to reinforce the UN Security Council 1701 agreement that has maintained the precarious peace after the 2006 war and also to resolve the fairly minor border disputes that still exist between Lebanon and Israel.

More importantly, now that the Iranian nuclear weapons program has been dealt with, at least for the next 10 to 15 years, there should be renewed back-channel efforts to de-escalate tension between Iran and Israel—perhaps to reach some form of detente. If Iran is not moving toward a nuclear weapon, Israel has no interest in attacking Iran. And if Iran does not fear an attack from Israel, it has less reason to maintain a large proxy army on Israel's northern border. The United States and Iran have managed to de-escalate their 30-year open confrontation into something akin to a cold and cautious wariness, even though both sides still call each other names for public consumption. Israel and Iran might be able to arrive at the same state. That would be key in helping to resolve the keystone issue of Hezbollah.

Track three: Regional economic integration

The third track should focus on building intraregional economic ties and interdependence. Levels of intraregional trade and economic exchange in the region remain low by international standards. Intelligent country-level reforms and better intraregional economic integration could boost gross domestic product (GDP) growth in Middle Eastern countries from the 3.0–4.5 percent a year range to the 5–8 percent a year range (similar to the performance of developing countries in Asia) (Fardoust 2016, 31). This is a valuable goal in and of itself, but creating common economic interests will also raise the cost of conflict and encourage governments toward cooperation. The reference point here is not the 1648 Treaty of Westphalia but the 1951 Treaty of Paris, which created the European Coal and Steel Community (ECSC) between longtime regional enemies, France and (West) Germany, as well as Belgium, Italy, the Netherlands, and Luxembourg. Its aim was to build on the deep common economic interests within the European region and make war less attractive and much costlier.

This track could encourage a piecemeal cumulative bottom-up approach as well as a region-wide top-down approach. In the former category, the track could encourage sectoral cooperation among two or more countries in the region. This could come in the form of cooperation over energy, water, trade, labor, investment, information technology (IT), or any number of other sectors. As sectoral and bilateral ties grow among countries in the region, this should help to boost region-wide economic interdependence. Governments could take up bottom-up initiatives; but other economic actors in the private sector, chambers of commerce, and sector-specific interest groups could also work to boost economic cooperation between two or more countries in the region.

A formal top-down approach implies working toward region-wide economic agreements. It will not be easy. Attempts at economic integration even among the Arab countries has met with resistance from entrenched government and business interests. It will require a patient and phased approach, beginning with an agreement on principles, moving toward pilot projects, and establishing sector-specific working groups.

Given the magnitude of the region's humanitarian, postconflict, and economic challenges, many observers have rightly suggested launching something akin to the Marshall Plan for the Middle East (Frattini 2011; Yaacoubian 2012; Demirjian 2016). This is all the more relevant as many of the problems of today's Middle East stem from underlying factors such as high unemployment and strained land and water resources. If current trends continue, and if one also factors in the likely effects of climate change, these problems are likely to get significantly worse (Frangoul 2016).

In this track, U.S. leadership will need to bring together regional and international players to establish a Middle East Refugee, Reconstruction, and Development fund. Regional players such as the GCC, Iran, and Turkey should be principal contributors, but the United States, Europe, Russia, China, Japan, and others should play important roles as well. The fund will have to move quickly to respond to the urgent needs of Syrian refugees in the region. Policies and resources will also have to be organized for reconstruction in Yemen, Syria, parts of Iraq, and Libya. On the development side, the track should focus its investments on infrastructure and connectivity investments that would assist strained economies like those in Egypt, Tunisia, Jordan, Yemen, and Lebanon, but it should also lay the foundation for intraregional connectivity and interdependence. Such an initiative could build strong positive linkages with the ambitious Chinese One Belt, One Road program announced in 2013 and the Asian Infrastructure Investment Bank (AIIB) that started operations in January 2016.[8] It is important to note that Turkey, Iran, Saudi Arabia, and other GCC states are founding members of the AIIB.

In Closing

What I have outlined here seeks to grapple with the underlying regional conflict that has fueled much of the instability of the Middle East, brought down states, and created the conditions for the rise of major terrorist groups. This article proposes a broad initiative for U.S. leadership and the next president, which should be aimed at defusing regional conflict and building a stable and sustainable regional state order in the Middle East.

Achieving these goals will require cooperation with other global players such as Russia, the European Union (EU), and China but also serious engagement with and buy-in by the main regional players including Saudi Arabia, Turkey, Iran, and Egypt. It aims to build on the P5+1 nuclear deal with Iran that showed how robust U.S. leadership and coordinated political power and intelligent diplomacy could have a transformative role in the Middle East, even with a difficult player such as Iran.

The challenge for the next president is to work with key global and regional states toward a sustainable, stable, and inclusive state-based regional order. Only by finding a way to reaffirm and rebuild a Westphalian state order in the Middle East can armed nonstate actors and terrorist groups be decisively disenfranchised and defeated.

Notes

1. This article builds on previous work I have published on this topic (see Salem 2008, 2010, 2015, 2016) and on the work of my Middle East Institute colleague Ross Harrison (see Harrison 2015).

2. Remarks of Saudi Foreign Minister Adel Al-Jubeir (7 April 2016, U.S. Department of State), available from www.state.gov.

3. The Non Aligned Movement was a group of states that came together in the 1950s and 1960s that were not formally aligned with one side or the other of the U.S.-Soviet Cold War. India, Indonesia, Egypt, Ghana, and Yugoslavia were key members of the movement. The movement still exists, with headquarters in New York, and includes 120 member states.

4. "Crude Oil Prices Historical Chart," available from www.macrotrends.net.

5. This refers to the round of talks between the five permanent UN Security Council members (plus Germany) and Iran that started in 2013 and concluded with the Joint Comprehensive Plan of Action agreement on Iran's nuclear program, concluded in July 2015.

6. Remarks of Saudi Foreign Minister Adel Al-Jubeir.

7. Ibid.

8. The One Belt, One Road program is an ambitious program proposed by Chinese president Xi Jinping in 2013 to link China and sixty other countries in Asia, Europe, and Africa through over $4 trillion of investment in transport, trade, and infrastructure. The AIIB was established to help organize the finances of this venture. By increasing economic interdependence and win-win economic relations among countries in West Asia, the program should raise the opportunity costs of conflict and encourage decision-makers toward more cooperative regional policies.

References

Black, Ian, and Simon Tisdall. 28 November 2010. Saudi Arabia urges U.S. attack on Iran to stop nuclear programme. *The Guardian*. Available from www.theguardian.com.

Brzezinski, Zbigniew. 17 April 2016. Toward a global realignment. *The American Interest* 11 (6). Available from www.the-american-interest.com.

Davutoglu, Ahmet. 2007. Turkey's foreign policy vision. *Insight Turkey* 10 (1). Available from www.arsiv
    .setav.org.
Demirjian, Karoun. 8 April 2016. Lindsey Graham wants a Marshall Plan for the Middle East. *The
    Washington Post*.
Fardoust, Shahrokh. June 2016. *Economic integration in the Middle East: Prospects for development and
    stability*. Middle East Institute Policy Paper 2016-5. Washington, DC: The Middle East Institute.
    Available from www.mei.edu.
Frangoul, Anmar. 4 May 2016. Climate change could make North Africa and Middle East "uninhabitable."
    CNBC. Available from www.cnbc.com.
Frattini, Franco. 11 June 2011. Marshall Plan for the Arab world. *Europe's World*. Available from europe-
    sworld.org.
Goldberg, Jeffrey. April 2016. The Obama doctrine. *The Atlantic*.
Goodenough, Patrick. 8 April 2016. Kerry, in Bahrain, mentions possibility of "new arrangement" with
    Iran. CNS News. Available from cnsnews.com.
Gordon, Philip. 2003. Bush's Middle East vision. *Survival* 45 (1): 155–65.
Harrison, Ross. 2015. *Defying gravity: Working toward a regional strategy for a stable Middle East*.
    Middle East Institute Policy Paper. Washington, DC: The Middle East Institute. Available at www.mei
    .edu.
Hudson, Michael C. 1996. Playing the hegemon: Fifty years of U.S. policy toward the Middle East. *Middle
    East Journal* 50 (3): 329–43.
Iqbal, Zaryab, and Harvey Starr. 2008. Bad neighbors: Failed states and their consequences. *Conflict
    Management and Peace Science* 25 (4): 315–31.
Kerr, Malcom. 1971. *The Arab cold war*. 3rd ed. New York, NY: Oxford University Press.
Khalilzad, Zalmay. 28 March 2016. The neoconservative case for negotiating with Iran. *Politico*. Available
    from www.politico.com.
Kissinger, Henry. 24 May 2008. Lunch with the FT: Henry Kissinger. *Financial Times*. Available from
    www.henryakissinger.com.
Krauthammer, Charles. 23 January 2015. Obama looks away as Iran plows ahead. *The Chicago Tribune*.
Kucukkosum, Sevil. 11 June 2010. As EU vision fades, "MEI vision" emerges among Turkey, neighbors.
    Hürriyet Daily News. Available at www.hurriyetdailynews.com.
Kurtzer, Daniel C., and Scott B. Lasensky. 2008. *Negotiating Arab-Israeli peace*. Washington DC: United
    States Institute of Peace.
Mincheva, Ljubov G. 2005. Dissolving boundaries between domestic and regional/international conflict.
    New Balkan Politics 9. Available from www.newbalkanpolitics.org.mk.
Pillar, Paul. 8 July 2015. The heavy historical baggage of U.S. policy toward the Middle East. *The National
    Interest*. Available from www.nationalinterest.org.
Salem, Paul. June 2008. *The Middle East: Evolution of a broken regional order*. Carnegie Middle East
    Center Policy Paper. Washington, DC: Carnegie Middle East Center. Available from carnegieendow-
    ment.org.
Salem, Paul. June 2010. *Building cooperation in the eastern Middle East*. Carnegie Middle East Center
    Policy Paper. Washington, DC: Carnegie Middle East Center. Available from carnegieendowment.org.
Salem, Paul. 30 April 2015. *A response to Iranian Foreign Minister Zarif*. Washington, DC: The Middle
    East Institute. Available from www.mei.edu.
Salem, Paul. 20 April 2016. Obama's GCC Summit: Think outside the box. *The National Interest*. Available
    from www.nationalinterest.org.
Wolff, Stefan. 2011. State failure in a regional context. *Review of International Studies* 27 (3): 951–72.
Yaacoubian, Mona. 11 January 2012. Middle East "Marshall Plan" will sustain Arab Spring. *The Hill*.
    Available from www.thehill.com.
Zarif, Mohammad Javad. 20 April 2015. A message from Iran. *The New York Times*.

Competition among Violent Islamist Extremists: Combating an Unprecedented Threat

By
CHARLES LISTER

The jihadist threat emanating from the Middle East has transformed dramatically in the past five years due to unprecedented levels of sociopolitical instability. While the region and much of the world around it previously faced a threat dominated by al-Qaeda, developments in the heart of the Middle East since 2014 have given birth to a new and more dangerous dynamic—two international jihadist movements competing to outdo each other on an increasingly brutal and complex world stage. In recent years, al-Qaeda has undergone a consequential strategic evolution: increasingly autonomous affiliates have begun to adopt a patient, long-game approach to operations, while ISIS has sought to attain rapid results. As two divergent models of jihad develop, different threats result, with the one universal factor being the exploitation of political failure, failing states, and sociopolitical instability to further extremist narratives. It is now more important than ever to develop tailor-made policies designed not just to combat jihadism itself but to ameliorate underlying conditions that have allowed it to thrive.

Keywords: al-Qaeda; Syria; ISIS; Iraq; jihad; Libya; jihadist

The jihadist threat[1] emanating from the Middle East has transformed dramatically in the past five years, due in large part to unprecedented levels of sociopolitical instability spreading across the region. Prior to the so-called Arab Spring, the region and much of the world around it had spent nearly a decade

Charles Lister is a senior fellow at the Middle East Institute and a senior project consultant to The Shaikh Group's Syria Track II Dialogue Initiative. He was formerly a visiting fellow at the Brookings Institution's Doha Center in Qatar, and before that, he was head of MENA at IHS Jane's Terrorism and Insurgency Centre in London. He recently published The Syrian Jihad: Al-Qaeda, the Islamic State and the Evolution of an Insurgency (Oxford 2016) and The Islamic State: A Brief Introduction (Brookings Institution Press 2015).

Correspondence: clister@mei.edu

DOI: 10.1177/0002716216668500

combating the activities of a single jihadist organization—al-Qaeda. Since 2014, however, developments in the heart of the Middle East have given birth to a new and more dangerous dynamic—two international jihadist movements competing to outdo each other on an increasingly brutal and complex world stage. The rise to prominence of the so-called Islamic State (or ISIS) through its conquering of Mosul and subsequent Caliphate proclamation in the summer of 2014 set in motion a revolution within the world's jihadist community. Al-Qaeda's established global preeminence and credibility were fundamentally challenged, and an era of escalatory intra-jihadist competition was born.

The political protest in the Middle East and North Africa that began with Tunisia's uprising in late 2010 shattered the region's long-held acceptance of single-party, strong-armed government. While frequently deadly, the visible explosion of "people power" and the resulting widespread demand for democracy and representative government lent this outburst of instability the hopeful epithet of the Arab Spring. However, few countries struck by these hopeful revolutions can be said five years later in 2016 to have met their hoped-for objectives. Syria is being torn apart in what is perhaps modern history's most destructive civil war; Iraq virtually imploded in 2014 and continues to suffer from debilitating political fragility, all the while wrestling back territory from ISIS; Libya and Yemen lie in chaos, riddled by internecine conflict; and Egypt has reverted to dictatorial military rule and faces a powerful insurgency in the Sinai Peninsula. Only Tunisia can be said to have emerged close to better off.

The one thing unifying all of these examples is the role that jihadist militants have played in exploiting political failure, the weakening or failure of states, and the sociopolitical instability to further their extremist objectives. At the outset of the Arab Spring, it seemed that a popular trend toward democracy symbolized a comprehensive defeat to the jihadist ideology espoused most at the time by al-Qaeda. Even the resulting rise to prominence of political Islamist parties saw the likes of the Muslim Brotherhood demonstrate significant commitment to working within competitive electoral democratic systems.

The converse became true, however, as instability, macrolevel societal change, and political uncertainty all represented opportunities for jihadist exploitation. Senior al-Qaeda operatives began planning the deployment of key figures to Libya, Tunisia, Syria, and Yemen almost as soon as 2011 began (Ignatius 2015). For example, al-Qaeda's then–general manager, Attiyah Abd al-Rahman, suggested in a letter to Osama Bin Laden that key operative Yunes al-Mouritani "send his brothers to Tunisia and Syria and other places" (Joscelyn 2015). Bin Laden himself urged his followers to be "patient" and wait to exploit what he saw as the inevitable—that political Islamist bodies would fill emerging political vacuums:

> It would be nice to remind our brothers in the regions to be patient and deliberate, and warn them of entering into confrontations with the parties belonging to Islam, and it is probable that most of the areas will have governments established on the remnants of the previous governments, and most probably these governments will belong to the Islamic parties and groups, like the Brotherhood and the like. . . . Our duty at this stage is to pay attention to the call among Muslims and win over the supporters and spread the correct understanding. (Joscelyn 2015)

Al-Qaeda's strategic patience would be a major determinant of how it would exploit the Middle East's instability in the years that followed.

What became known in 2013 as ISIS had existed as a solely Iraq-based movement when Mohammed Bouazizi self-immolated in Tunisia on December 17, 2010. Known then as the Islamic State in Iraq (ISI), the jihadist movement had been founded by Abu Musab al-Zarqawi and had roots as far back as the late 1990s in Jordan and Afghanistan (Lister 2014); but it had been decimated in the final months of the U.S. occupation of Iraq, with thirty-four of the group's top forty-two leadership figures dead or in prison by mid-2010 (Shanker 2010).

By exploiting the U.S. withdrawal from Iraq, Prime Minister Nouri al-Maliki's divisive and sectarian-influenced domestic agenda, and neighboring Syria's collapse into civil war, the ISI rocketed back to prominence. By mid-2013 it had formally expanded into Syria and become ISIS; by mid-2014, it had definitively split from al-Qaeda and established a Caliphate; and by mid-2016, it maintained a formal presence in a dozen countries around the world, from Syria-Iraq to Afghanistan and to Nigeria. In growing and expanding so dramatically, ISIS sparked the biggest inflow of foreign jihadist fighters in history, with tens of thousands joining its cause in Syria and Iraq between 2013 and 2016.

Jihadist groups and cells had of course been active across the Middle East far before 2011, but the rise in political instability and conflict provided a swathe of opportunities for jihadist exploitation. The destabilization of multiple states across the region and their transformation into failing or failed states also catalyzed an intensification of efforts by rival regional great powers to further their respective influence. That conflicts in Syria, Iraq, and Yemen all devolved down sectarian lines encouraged this regional competition to adopt particularly divisive dynamics, which by extension provided the kind of societal cleavages that jihadists thrived on.

By 2016, al-Qaeda and ISIS had established a dynamic of intra-jihadist competition, whereby each movement sought to outplay the other on local, regional, and international levels. This rivalry intensified efforts by both movements to plan terrorist attacks in the West. But more importantly, it stimulated the necessity to demonstrate expansive international reach and a rapid momentum of operations. In short, both al-Qaeda and ISIS—through their rivalry—have encouraged the other to invest more heavily in securing more frequent and significant results.

This is a dangerous and difficult dynamic to defeat. It is now more necessary than ever to develop counterterrorism policies designed not just to combat the organizations and their modes of operation but to ameliorate the underlying conditions that have allowed them to thrive. Debilitating instability, societal breakdown, and state collapse are common themes in all countries and regions where both al-Qaeda and ISIS have maintained or established newly active operational presences since 2011. But over and above everything, the groups themselves need to be understood for the phenomena that they are. It is only by understanding those who pose the threats we face that we stand a chance of durably defeating them and addressing the vulnerabilities that they exploit to survive and thrive.

Rapid Expansion: The "Islamic State"

When ISIS proclaimed its self-styled Caliphate project on June 29, 2014, its territorial control and operational activities were limited solely to portions of Iraq and Syria. Answering a call by its leader Abu Bakr al-Baghdadi, ISIS subsequently acquired and accepted pledges of allegiance from existing and active jihadist groups in Libya, Egypt, Algeria, Saudi Arabia, and Yemen in November 2014. By June 2015, ISIS had also acquired affiliates in Afghanistan, Pakistan, Nigeria, and Russia's North Caucasus. Although not formally accepted and integrated into the Caliphate, ISIS had by early 2016 acquired additional affiliates or active and supportive cells in Lebanon, Turkey, the Philippines, Gaza, Indonesia, Tunisia, Bangladesh, and Bosnia-Herzegovina (Yourish, Watkins, and Giratikanon 2016).

In comparison, it had taken al-Qaeda six years following the 9/11 attacks to formalize its first two affiliates, in Iraq and North Africa. ISIS's dramatic expansion into nine countries within 12 months of announcing its Caliphate was therefore a significant accomplishment, which was won largely through a campaign of unforgiving terror against its enemies. Demonstrative brutality had played a key role in suppressing opposition to ISIS's growth in Syria and Iraq and deterring further dissent, while it also appeared to attract recruits and supporters from a new generation of more bloodthirsty jihadis. After Syrian opposition forces launched offensive operations against ISIS in early 2014, ISIS spokesman Abu Mohammed al-Adnani left little to the imagination:

> Learn from those who stood against the Mujahideen in Iraq. They are either under the ground, enslaved by the Rafidah or on the run. You stabbed us from the back while our positions were occupied by few guards. . . . If you repent we promise you safety, otherwise, know that we have armies in Iraq and an army in Sham composed of hungry lions. Their drink is blood and their favorite companions are dismembered body parts. They never tasted a drink more delicious than the blood of the Sahwas. We swear to God, we will bring a thousand then a thousand then another. None of you will remain and we will make you an example. (Lister 2015c)

While ISIS launched counterattacks against opposition groups in Syria, it later suppressed a localized tribal uprising by killing nine hundred men and boys over a three-day period (*Al-Akhbar* 2014).

Clearly, the emergence of a jihadist alternative to al-Qaeda that was even more brutal, even more sectarian, and intensely focused on achieving all of its objectives as fast as possible was an attractive proposition for portions of the jihadist community around the world. That ISIS proved capable of inspiring supporters and directing members to conduct attacks on its behalf in at least seven Western countries between September 2014 and July 2016[2] underlines ISIS's jihadist appeal. Though ISIS is now thought to be centrally directing attack plots in Europe, the roots of its call for "lone-wolf" attacks lie in another speech by ISIS spokesman, Adnani, from September 2014:

> If you can kill a disbelieving American or European—especially the spiteful and filthy French—or an Australian, or a Canadian, or any other disbeliever from the disbelievers

waging war, including the citizens of the countries that entered into a coalition against the Islamic State, then rely upon Allah, and kill him in any manner or way however it may be. Do not ask for anyone's advice and do not seek anyone's verdict. Kill the disbeliever whether he is civilian or military, for they have the same ruling. Both of them are disbelievers. . . .

If you are not able to find an IED or a bullet, then single out the disbelieving American, Frenchman, or any of their allies. Smash his head with a rock, or slaughter him with a knife, or run him over with your car, or throw him down from a high place, or choke him, or poison him. Do not lack. Do not be contemptible. . . . If you are unable to do so, then burn his home, car, or business. Or destroy his crops. . . . If you are unable to do so, then spit in his face. (al-Adnani 2014)

Exploiting its twisted claims of Islamic legitimacy, ISIS has operationalized an ink spot strategy of expansionism by way of its *wilayat* (province) model. Expanding beyond Syria and Iraq, ISIS sought to subsume active jihadist groups and disenfranchised subfactions of al-Qaeda affiliates with proven operational track records as individual *wilayat* within its "state" structure (Lister 2016b). As stated in its English-language magazine *Dabiq*, emphasis was placed clearly on accepting pledges of allegiance only from those groups with discernible and stable leaderships that maintained solid lines of communication with ISIS's senior leaders (*Dabiq* 2014). Many of these acquisitions benefited from preexisting contacts ISI had managed since its fight with the U.S.-led occupation of Iraq between 2003 and 2010, many of whom were foreign recruits who had fought in Iraq but had since returned to their countries of origin.

Syria and Iraq

ISIS's beating heart continues to be in Syria and Iraq, where much of the organization's key leadership remains and in which it maintains its two major capital cities of Raqqa and Mosul. It is there that ISIS first tested and developed its "state" model of territorial control and jihadist "governance"—which it would seek to replicate around the world, beginning in September 2014. By infiltrating territory and undermining those in control or by capturing territory through brute military force, ISIS acquired and consolidated its rule through force of arms and psychological intimidation. All behavior and social activities were strictly controlled and violating ISIS law meant severe punishment.

Since late 2015, coalition operations against ISIS (that began in August 2014) have demonstrated discernible progress. By that time, much of the jihadist organization's peripheral territories had been recaptured by indigenous forces, equating to approximately 40 percent of its territory held in Iraq in mid-2014 and 20 percent in Syria (*Reuters* 2016a). Additional pressure on ISIS's finances, primarily by targeting hard cash and the group's ability to extract, distribute, and sell oil and gas, has had a further detrimental impact on the group's operational capabilities. As much as $800 million of ISIS's cash and gold reserves had been destroyed (BBC News 2016), the group's oil incomes had been reduced by at least 30 percent (Hartogs 2016), fighter incomes had been cut by 50 percent (Pagliery 2016), and its foreign fighter recruitment rate had declined by at least

75 percent (*Reuters* 2016b). However, ISIS's control of populated territory will continue to provide it with a source of income, by way of heavy taxation and extortion of both individuals and business.

Taken together, these signs of progress had significantly degraded ISIS's capacity to demonstrate to its members and supporters a sense of consistent offensive momentum on the battlefield. While the organization had not yet been substantively challenged in its most strategically valuable territories—like the cities of Raqqa and Mosul, and in Syria's eastern Deir ez Zour governorate—a decline in operational momentum paired with a degenerated capacity to compensate existing fighters and recruit additional ones has weakened the movement, particularly in terms of morale. Moreover, an increased reliance on local recruits and a likely minimized provision of military training contributed toward a decline in individual fighter capability (Gibbons-Neff 2016).

While progress is clearly being made against ISIS in Syria and Iraq, there are significant obstacles that lie ahead for continued progress in confronting it in its most valuable areas. Political divisions are rising again in Iraq, while the problematic nature of Iranian-backed Shia militias within broader security dynamics across the country threatens to undermine the integrity and sustainability of gains made against ISIS. Moreover, the economic struggles of the Kurdistan Regional Government will have a deleterious impact upon the ability of the Kurdish Peshmerga to contribute effectively to the fight for Mosul, which by extension will result in an ethnic imbalance of forces involved in its hoped-for eventual capture.

In Syria, continued civil conflict and brutal violence, the increasing confidence of the Assad regime, the emerging hostilities between the mainstream opposition and the Kurdish YPG in the north, and ISIS's formal emergence in the south of the country all look set to provide the jihadi group with opportunities to exacerbate societal divisions and renew its momentum.

Egypt

ISIS acquired a formal presence in Egypt's Sinai Peninsula in November 2014, after accepting a pledge of allegiance from the already formidable jihadist group Jamaat Ansar Bayt al-Maqdis (JABM). Heavily tribally based and rooted within the Sinai's long disenfranchised and restless Bedouin community, ISIS's Wilayat Sina (Sinai Province) clearly benefits from the intense societal-level discontent with Egypt's central government and a society-wide antagonism toward state authority. Operationally, Wilayat Sina is heavily focused within Egypt's North Sinai Governorate, although it has a demonstrated capacity to reach into South Sinai as far as Sharm al-Sheikh. Consequently, Wilayat Sina has since emerged as one of ISIS's most promising international affiliates that has proven itself capable of sustaining a considerable insurgency against the Egyptian armed forces, while carrying out spectacular attacks with international repercussions, such as the downing of a Russian commercial airliner in October 2015 and the near-sinking of an Egyptian naval vessel a few months earlier in July 2015.

With several of its founding leaders having fought for ISIS's predecessor factions in Iraq, JABM's affiliation with ISIS was born out of strong structural links. Shortly after proclaiming its Caliphate, ISIS actively sought out JABM's allegiance twice: first by dispatching a message from a Libya-based commander, Abu Ahmed al-Libi, in the summer of 2014 (Gartenstein-Ross 2015); and then by dispatching a senior figure from Syria-Iraq, Musa'id Abu Qatmah, to the Sinai in September 2014 (Lahoud 2015). Concurrently, JABM was in need of supplementary sources of finance and, following a string of leadership losses, a united source of leadership (Gartenstein-Ross 2015). That Wilayat Sina subsequently transformed its operational strategy from primarily attacking Israel (until summer 2013) to targeting the Egyptian state for its overthrow of Mohammed Morsi (until November 2014), and then focused its attention on the Egyptian military as a model insurgency and on hitting other international targets from the Sinai as part of ISISs' broader global jihad, demonstrates the extent to which it identified closely with and was loyal to Abu Bakr al-Baghdadi's vision.

Wilayat Sina has revealed a heightened capacity to threaten both the Egyptian state and broader security dynamics since integrating into ISIS's global movement. Notwithstanding its spectacular attacks, Wilayat Sina militants have demonstrated an expanded operational reach, including into the capital Cairo and the nearby city of Giza. Wilayat Sina operations and media releases have shown that the group has access to advanced weaponry, including antitank guided missiles and man-portable air-defense systems (MANPADS), while the group's effective use of complex urban assault tactics has been demonstrated on a number of occasions, including in the attack on Sheikh Zuweid on July 1, 2015 (Faruki, Gowell, and Hoffman 2015). Given that its predominant zone of operation is in the Sinai, Wilayat Sina's operations have frequently threatened the Multinational Force and Observers (MFO) peacekeeping mission, which includes U.S. troops. Finally, and perhaps most significantly, Wilayat Sina has replicated ISIS-style attempts at territorial control and jihadist rule. As is the case in Syria and Iraq, these attempts at governance have assumed a particularly aggressive posture more accurately described as control than service.

Libya

As in Egypt, ISIS sought to exploit existing ungoverned space in Libya, to acquire itself another durable zone of operations from which it could realize its transnational vision and undermine cross-border security. Again, it sent influential figures—Abu Nabil al-Anbari (Iraqi), Abu Habib al-Jazrawi (Saudi), and Abu Bara al-Azdi (Yemeni)—to consolidate existing lines of communication into structurally sound relationships. Beginning in October 2014, ISIS began receiving small-scale pledges of allegiance from Libya-based militant movements, including Majlis Shura al-Shabab al-Islam (the Shura Council of Islamic Youth), a jihadist faction present primarily in the eastern city of Dernah. The following month, Majlis Shura al-Shabab al-Islam issued a unified pledge of allegiance alongside several smaller jihadist factions to Abu Bakr al-Baghdadi, and the assumption of ISIS status was formalized. By December 2014, ISIS had claimed three *wilayat* in Libya—"Barqa" in the east; "Tripoli" in the capital, Sirte, and Misrata; and "Fezzan" in the south (Lister 2016b).

The coastal city of Sirte soon assumed central importance to ISIS's operations in Libya. Situated in the middle of Libya's Mediterranean coast, Sirte was a key intersection between the east and west of the country and between north and south. By early 2016, ISIS had also acquired overwhelming influence over 190 kilometers eastward along the coast to the town of Al-Sidra. ISIS also maintained a substantial presence in the city of Benghazi, 385 kilometers further along the coast from Al-Sidra. By August 2016, ISIS had held out in several districts of Sirte against a sizable Libyan ground offensive backed by some number of U.S. airstrikes.

To acquire influence in Libya, ISIS cells invariably had to compete with complex local dynamics in which multiple rival armed groups held sway. As was similarly the case in Syria in 2013–2014, ISIS sought to exploit a lack of governance, service provision, or rule of law to demonstrate a certain minimal value to local populations. In Sirte—the hometown of Muammar Qadaffi—several local tribes and clans were widely distrusted for their former links to Qadaffi rule; ISIS offered them a "comeback" in exchange for their loyalty (Malsin 2015). Meanwhile, powerful militias from Misrata bearing down on Sirte had gained a reputation for violence and corruption. ISIS played its competitors against one another to establish its rule.

In Libya, ISIS has primarily relied on the taxation of people under its control as well as on local smuggling networks, extortion, and kidnapping for ransom as ways to finance its operations. By mid-2016, oil had not become a viable source of income for ISIS in Libya. Meanwhile, ISIS's Libyan contingents have steadily escalated their imposition of harsh forms of Sharia law. However, any popular backlash against their rule has been outweighed by the sheer chaos throughout Libya. As in Egypt, ISIS attacks in Libya have also demonstrated an international agenda, through the execution of Egyptian Coptic Christians in February 2015 and of Ethiopian Christians in April 2015, the bombing of multiple foreign embassies in Tripoli, and repeated attacks on major oil facilities.

Despite some progress on the political front, including most notably the establishment of the Government of National Accord (GNA), continued national-level political divisions and the acute levels of rivalry and distrust between various tribes and militias make a substantive and sustainable advance against ISIS's most valuable areas of control unlikely in the near-term. Particular attention must necessarily be devoted to forming a unified military command—gathering together militia forces from western Libya aligned to the GNA and the Libyan National Army (LNA) under General Khalifa Haftar. The deployment of U.S. Special Operations Forces "contact teams" to vet prospective local anti-ISIS partners is a needed first step, but a durable and reliable train and equip program takes time. Any policy that seeks fast results against ISIS without forming sufficient foundations to ensure an effective "hold" phase of operations will provide too many opportunities for ISIS and other extremist forces to exploit.

ISIS will always seek to leverage Libya's extensive instability to ensure that it has the greatest chance possible to withstand any future assault on its de facto

Libyan capital in Sirte or elsewhere. A truly effective counterstrategy must work more broadly than simply "fighting" ISIS on the battlefield. Libya's structural weaknesses, social divides, and economic shortcomings must necessarily be tackled to ensure that a centralized Libyan state and government represents something worth choosing over continued factionalism and instability.

Al-Qaeda's Long Game

Al-Qaeda has undergone a substantial phase of organizational learning and structural evolution since the death of its founding leader Osama Bin Laden in May 2011. ISIS's declaration of a Caliphate in mid-2014 laid down a considerable gauntlet to al-Qaeda to prove its jihadi credibility and compete with ISIS's clearly discernible and expanding "state" project. In response, al-Qaeda has sought to more strictly operationalize a new level of strategic thinking that first emerged out of its senior strategic thinkers in 2009. Al-Qaeda's new "long-game" strategy has focused on building alliances, avoiding making new enemies, and temporarily restricting the level of Sharia law imposed on the people (Lister 2015c).

Despite initial attempts at operationalizing this strategy of controlled pragmatism in Yemen (2011) and Mali (2012), the first successful test case has emerged in Syria, where Jabhat al-Nusra (named Jabhat Fateh al-Sham, or JFS, since July 28, 2016) employed the approach to grow deep and durable roots within an intensely chaotic environment. Al-Qaeda in the Arabian Peninsula (AQAP) appears to have replicated this model in Yemen following on from Saudi Arabian–led military intervention there in March 2015.

Al-Qaeda appears to have survived the challenge posed by ISIS as well as the loss of Nasir al-Wuhayshi—the leader of AQAP and al-Qaeda's deputy leader—in June 2015 and the public revelation of Taliban leader Mullah Mohammed Omar's April 2013 death. Though less eye-catching than ISIS's dramatic expansion and its inspiration for numerous attacks in the West, al-Qaeda's long-game strategy and its effective exploitation of the most unstable conflict-ridden zones of the Middle East look likely to provide the jihadist movement with the durable "safe zones" from which to launch al-Qaeda's global ambitions that Ayman al-Zawahiri ordered in 2013. Those objectives include most notably to "target America . . . to exhaust her and bleed her to death" by way of "targeting the interests of the western Zionist-Crusader alliance in any part of the world" (al-Zawahiri 2013).

Ultimately, al-Qaeda aims to achieve the very same objectives as ISIS—namely, the establishment of a global Islamic state. The fact that it is willing to take its time to get there and to establish zones of influence and territorial control that are far more sustainable and viable into the long-term should necessitate an acute level of attention from policy-makers. While certain al-Qaeda affiliates may appear locally focused for a time, the adoption of localism is merely a strategic mechanism for achieving durable roots within unstable societies, from which operations may one day assume a more transnational nature.

Syria

Initially established as a Syrian wing of the Islamic State in Iraq (ISI), Jabhat al-Nusra employed al-Qaeda's long-game strategy to great effect. Although unpopular in its first months of publicly acknowledged operations in Syria, Jabhat al-Nusra began gaining popular acceptance from mid- to late 2012 onward, by establishing coalitions and military operations with a wide array of mainstream Syrian opposition forces. Gone was al-Qaeda's traditional distrust of "nationalists" and insufficiently conservative Islamic movements. By making friends and avoiding enemies on the battlefield, Jabhat al-Nusra opened up space for similar cooperation on the civil governance side of territory "liberated" from the Assad regime. Beginning in the winter of 2012–2013, Jabhat al-Nusra entered into opposition-wide governance initiatives, which generally proved superior and more reliable than the more secular attempts made by the early forms of the Free Syrian Army (FSA).

Writing in December 2012, Jabhat al-Nusra's leader, Abu Mohammed al-Jolani, made clear his intended approach:

> Day after day, you're getting closer to the people and you have conquered their hearts and become trusted by them. . . . Beware of being hard on them, begin with the priorities and fundamentals of Islam and be flexible on the minor parts of religion. (Hassan 2013)

The challenge posed by ISIS's Caliphate proclamation was felt particularly intensely by Jabhat al-Nusra in Syria, especially because its more "pragmatic" approach meant that it had, by mid-2014, avoided unilaterally controlling any territory. Jabhat al-Nusra consequently began to step up the extent to which it sought to be the preeminent influence in Syria's northwestern Idlib governorate, where it had invested most of its efforts.

Since at least mid-2013, the group had already begun receiving senior and experienced al-Qaeda veterans from Afghanistan, Pakistan, Yemen, Iran, and elsewhere. Al-Qaeda's central leadership sought to bolster the standing of its Syrian affiliate. Some of these individuals were targeted in U.S. airstrikes from September 2014, after being accused of plotting external attacks, potentially in coordination with AQAP's chief bomb maker Ibrahim al-Asiri (CBS News 2014). This so-called Khorasan Group was largely decimated in targeted U.S. strikes and then instructed to dissolve back into Jabhat al-Nusra by Zawahiri in early 2015 (Lister 2015a).

Despite being temporarily challenged by the initiation of a near-nationwide cessation of hostilities in February 2016 in support of a political process launched in Geneva, Jabhat al-Nusra continues to demonstrate the power of the interdependent relationship it has established with the mainstream opposition and its civilian support base. Despite widespread Syrian unease regarding Jabhat al-Nusra's long-term intentions for Syria, this relationship is predicated on the jihadi group's powerful capabilities on the battlefield being of existential value to a Syrian opposition starved of sufficient support to defend itself independently.

Within this context, senior al-Qaeda figures have continued to flock to Syria through 2015 and into 2016, including the highly influential leader Saif al-Adel,[3] who had been released from "house arrest" in Iran (Callimachi and Schmitt 2015). Most of the group's senior leaders based in southern Syria were also redeployed to the north in late 2015, including Jordanian deputy leader Sami al-Oraydi and founding member Iyad Toubasi (Abu Julaybib). The resulting "weight" of Jabhat al-Nusra's jihadist contingent in Idlib in particular has catalyzed an intense internal discussion regarding the need to establish the group's first Emirate in Syria, in Idlib.

Given the stakes behind such a move, Jabhat al-Nusra has struggled to acquire consensus, while Islamic bodies representing the mainstream Syrian opposition across the country that would necessarily have to be consulted have strongly opposed the idea. Therefore, a process of internal debate was put into place in early 2016, frequently mediated and facilitated by technically independent, but al-Qaeda–linked, senior figures.[4] Two of these—Al-Gamaa al-Islamiyya founder Rifai Taha and veteran Chechnya-based commander Abu Omar al-Masri—were killed in a U.S. drone strike in April 2016 (al-Shafey 2016), which may in fact have been intended to target another jihadi figure, Ahmed Salameh Mabrouk (Abu Faraj al-Masri) (Lister 2016a). The purpose of this process was to solve differences between Jabhat al-Nusra and al-Qaeda's circles in Syria and between Jabhat al-Nusra and other influential Syrian Islamist opposition groups such as Ahrar al-Sham, which were pressing the group to break its ties to al-Qaeda.

Debate over the latter issue of al-Qaeda ties continued throughout the months that followed and gained particular intensity when nearly a dozen senior Jabhat al-Nusra leadership figures began preparing to splinter away and form a new independent group, Harakat al-Islamiya al-Souriya. Perceived as an ultimatum and a major threat to the unity of his project, Jabhat al-Nusra leader Jolani called a series of meetings of the group's Shura Council. After a week of leaks and rumor, Jabhat al-Nusra announced on July 28, 2016, the dissolution of all "external ties" and a rebranding under the JFS name. Perceived by many Syrians as a concession, Jabhat al-Nusra's attempt to demonstrate more overtly its localist focus looked likely to have further cemented its accepted status in Syria.

Given the definitive breakdown of the cessation of hostilities by late April 2016 and a sustained escalation in fighting through the summer, JFS's reassumption of an advantageous position of influence made its chances of success that much greater.

Yemen

By mid-2011, Ansar al-Sharia, which was rebranded as such in 2011 in an attempt to soften AQAP's image, had established strong control over much of southern Yemen's Abyan and Shabwah governorates, establishing their Islamic Emirate and initiating the limited provision of social services like food, water, electricity, education, and law and order. A whole media wing known as Madad News Agency was established to publicize Ansar al-Sharia's efforts in civil affairs, which also included the repairing and maintenance of core infrastructure and the provision of care to the poor and elderly (Zelin 2012).

Despite its best attempts to limit the extent to which it aggressively controlled the people, Ansar al-Sharia's unilateral assertion of power and rule did engender popular discontent, which contributed to an eventual military offensive in summer 2012. This offensive was backed by local tribes that effectively destroyed any semblance of an "Emirate." AQAP has been the instigator of the majority of al-Qaeda's post-9/11 plots to attack the West. The comprehensive defeat of AQAP's Emirate project in southern Yemen in mid- to late 2012 represented, then, a damaging blow to al-Qaeda's search for long-term territorial control.

However, the gradual breakdown of the Yemeni state amid the methodical seizure of power by the Houthis through 2014 and early 2015 provided AQAP with a second chance. When Saudi Arabia led a military intervention in March 2015 against the advancing Houthis, it removed the most effective anti-AQAP force from much of the battlefield. Until then, it had been Houthi forces keeping AQAP in check. AQAP pounced, seizing the southern city of Al-Mukalla—Yemen's third-largest port—in early April, freeing hundreds of its members and senior commanders (Johnsen 2015) and looting the provincial capital central bank's roughly $100 million in cash reserves (al-Batati and Fahim 2015). In June, another 1,200 prisoners were broken out of the central prison in the city of Taiz, with many suspected to have been AQAP operatives (*Reuters* 2015). The following month, AQAP began expanding its presence in the major city of Aden.

As with Ansar al-Sharia's first attempt at an Emirate in 2011 and with Jabhat al-Nusra's activities in Syria, AQAP embedded itself within broader revolutionary dynamics in southern Yemen, fighting alongside tribal factions opposed to Houthi rule. Once in joint control of populated territory like Al-Mukalla, AQAP began basic attempts at providing local services, from repairing bridges and roads to delivering free medical equipment for kidney dialysis and cancer treatment, while sharing governance responsibilities with Sunni tribal coalitions. AQAP sought again to rebrand its image, adopting names like Guardians of Sharia or Sons of Hadramaut (Bayoumy, Browning, and Ghobari 2016).

While earning substantial sums through the extraction and sale of oil and large extortion operations against major oil companies, AQAP even entered into negotiations—which were ultimately unsuccessful—with the Yemeni government to share profits from the country's oil trade. Making use of Al-Mukalla's vast port, AQAP fighters operated speedboats to impose fees on all shipping traffic, earning as much as $2 million per day (Bayoumy, Browning, and Ghobari 2016). That the Saudi-led Arab coalition recaptured the city from AQAP in April 2016 was therefore a significant blow to the recovering al-Qaeda affiliate.

That AQAP has not yet declared an Emirate in southern Yemen despite the scale of its territorial influence and financial clout underlines that it has learned the same lessons that Jabhat al-Nusra and now JFS has been demonstrating in Syria. By adopting a long-game strategy, AQAP seeks to socialize communities not only into accepting its increasingly clear influence, but ultimately into supporting it. Only then will the conditions be ripe for the establishment of what it would see as a durable Emirate. As the Saudi-led Arab coalition now seeks to escalate its ground fight against AQAP, the effectiveness of AQAP's efforts to root itself in southern Yemeni society will be definitively put to the test.

Policy Recommendations

The dramatic destabilization of the Middle East since 2011, and in particular the demise of a number of countries into failed or failing states, has provided invaluable opportunities to jihadist militants to establish footholds in seemingly intractable conflicts. Political failure, weak and insufficient governance, societal divides, regional great power politics, and sectarianism and societies increasingly confident in expressing the expectations they have from government have all contributed to creating conditions that jihadists in general could only have dreamt of.

Furthermore, Syria's catastrophic breakdown into civil war and ISIS's extraordinary recovery following the U.S. withdrawal from Iraq in 2010 have allowed for a new international jihadist movement to emerge—one in competition with al-Qaeda. Although both al-Qaeda and ISIS have the same ultimate objective— the establishment of a global Caliphate—they have adopted and refined markedly different strategies for reaching that point.

Because al-Qaeda and ISIS operate along divergent strategies, the United States and its allies need to develop a broader range of policies that not only counter terrorist threats but ameliorate instability across the Middle East and pull the rug from under the jihadists' feet. This argues for a kinetic, military approach, and also a set of tailor-made short- and long-term policies designed to weaken and eventually remove the sociopolitical cleavages that extremists can step into and exploit.

Exercise U.S. power more confidently

Al-Qaeda and ISIS have been emboldened by a perceived reduction in U.S. willingness to assert its power in the Middle East—whether through a premature withdrawal from Iraq, a refusal to more definitively intervene in Syria, a failure to act when the chemical weapons "red line" was crossed in August 2013, or in allowing Saudi Arabia to launch a poorly planned intervention in Yemen that empowered al-Qaeda and destroyed what was already a weak state. In an era of unprecedented Middle Eastern instability, in which rival great powers continually seek to undermine the other, thereby causing further destabilization, only a firm and assertive United States stand can hope to bring some sense of recovery to a flailing region. Despite the reputational blow incurred from the 2003 invasion of Iraq, the United States is still viewed by many in the Middle East region as the necessary arbiter of peace to situations like those in Syria, Iraq, Yemen, and Libya.

For well-known reasons, assertive U.S. power in the Middle East has not always been interpreted as a valuable activity. However, perceptions across the region that the United States has become increasingly disengaged in the Middle East have revealed a vacuum into which more troublesome state and nonstate actors have stepped. The United States should not use military or diplomatic hard power for the sake of asserting one's powerful status but, rather, to help deter spoilers, to restrain those seeking to instill divisions, and to prevent the resulting rise of extremist narratives and behaviors. In conflict zones such as Syria and Iraq, actors such as ISIS and Jabhat al-Nusra were provided with the space to rise to prominence in large part because the collective Western world, perceived as being led by the United States, refused and failed to prevent state-led mass killing and to support more definitively moderate or mainstream actors working to challenge the deadly status quo. This is as much about helping to shape a more moderate alternative to dictatorial rule as it is about confronting the dictators and extremists. Being perceived as averting one's eyes to mass suffering and war crimes only plays into extremist narratives, which both ISIS and al-Qaeda have invaluably tapped into since 2011.

The United States must urgently recover its status as *the* actor capable of discernibly asserting its power—political, financial, or military—upon those governments and nonstate actors deemed to be purposely destabilizing. This assertion of power must also expand beyond the Middle East, with, for example, the Russian government's military intervention in Syria. That intervention has significantly transformed the Syrian conflict's balance of power, degrading the chances of attaining a durable political settlement there.

Build and empower credible and representative local partners

In areas where al-Qaeda and ISIS have emerged as powerful nonstate actors, either militarily confronting a viable central government or further destabilizing a civil war, the United States must urgently seek out genuinely credible and socially representative local partners. This necessitates a deep understanding of microlevel dynamics and drivers behind village, town, and city dynamics both favorable and unfavorable to extremism. These local actors would be of political value—they could provide a viable social alternative to extremist rule—and of military value—they could provide effective armed forces to confront jihadists on the battlefield. Ultimately, jihadists have managed to benefit as they have in the Middle East since 2011 only because of the relative lack of better alternatives for civilians living in collapsed states and within intense conflicts.

These local actors would be of particular military value in undermining ISIS's claim to represent a viable and territorially contiguous "state" in Syria and Iraq and its self-described status as an organization founded on continuous momentum. Challenging this idealized status, as has been done already in parts of Syria and Iraq, is the most effective mechanism for minimizing ISIS's potential support base. Dramatically weakening its potential zones of strategic depth in the Egyptian Sinai and in Libya will also ensure that ISIS cannot switch attention elsewhere while experiencing losses in its founding heartlands.

The threat posed by al-Qaeda is qualitatively different, given the extensive roots it has in societies in Syria and Yemen, for example. In the case of al-Qaeda, empowering credible and representative local partners has a societal value and can present people with an attractive alternative to jihadist rule. As Jabhat al-Nusra and AQAP look to hold overwhelming influence over communities in northwestern Syria and southern Yemen for extensive periods of time, al-Qaeda will eventually seek to establish formal Emirates in those places. Only empowered and strongly supported Sunni Arab local partners will be capable of diminishing al-Qaeda's potential to do so.

Target jihadist leaderships

Individual al-Qaeda and ISIS affiliates across the Middle East rely heavily on a sense of internal cohesion and a senior leadership that is credible and capable. Just as killing tens of thousands of ISIS militants since late 2014 appears to have reduced the level of competence among individual ISIS fighters, so too will a degradation in leadership catalyze a degeneration of overall organizational capacity. Numerous ISIS leaders have been killed in targeted operations in Syria, Iraq, and Lebanon since 2015. This strategy should be sustained and, if possible, intensified. Similar operations should eventually be initiated against JFS in northern Syria, though during an internationally mediated period of calm, in which mainstream opposition groups may be kept from siding with their ally of military convenience. Such a strategy has become particularly important given attempts by al-Qaeda to revitalize its central global leadership on Syrian territory. The presence of dozens of veteran al-Qaeda figures is one especially important component of efforts to empower and eventually justify unilateral rule in an Idlib governorate.

Targeted strikes against jihadist leaders can also, importantly, induce a sense of paranoia within a jihadist group's ranks. Such strikes reveal a deep intelligence penetration into the organizations' most secretive lairs. The sense of paranoia can encourage unease and, potentially, internal divisions and friction; it is also likely to force many senior leaders to go "underground," minimizing their contact with others and feasibly diminishing the efficiency of the organization's operational capabilities.

Restrict access to finances and valuable resources

Money plays an existentially important role in keeping jihadist organizations operational, and given the intra-jihadist competitive dynamic existing today, both al-Qaeda and ISIS have sought to steadily increase their respective incomes to sustain steadily increasing operations.

ISIS has differentiated itself from al-Qaeda by establishing near-total independence from traditional private sources of jihadi, donation-based support. Whereas al-Qaeda affiliates remain heavily dependent on such external sources of finance, ISIS, and an increasing number of its *wilayats*, have sought to acquire local sources of income, including from taxation and extortion, natural resources, smuggling, and kidnapping for ransom. While taxation and extortion can only be durably restricted through the military recapture of ISIS territory, local, regional, and international states can play a role in severely restricting ISIS's capacity to access, extract, produce, distribute, and sell products such as oil, gas, and minerals. Through targeting key extraction and transport infrastructure; intensifying existing economic sanctions; and providing or subsidizing oil, gas, and other products to regions bordering ISIS territory, multinational efforts can successfully undermine the scale, scope, and durability of ISIS's access to significant sources of finance.

Al-Qaeda, on the other hand, continues to rely on affiliated individuals—many based in the Gulf—who operate alone or within covert charitable networks to collect money and transfer it to affiliate groups around the world. Whereas Syrian affiliate Jabhat al-Nusra earned substantial sums from its control of oil fields in eastern Syria until mid- to late 2014, the loss of those resources to ISIS saw the group revert primarily to external sources of funding. Existing UN and U.S. efforts to identify individuals outside Syria linked to this financial support should be intensified significantly. Likewise, the United States must urgently put more pressure on Gulf states to better enforce their legal expectations, by arresting and imprisoning those found to have assisted al-Qaeda.

Target potential and emerging ISIS affiliates

ISIS will come under increasing pressure throughout 2016 and into 2017, thanks to the slow but steady progress made by the U.S.-led coalition and its local partners in Iraq and parts of Syria. Counterterrorism forces at the local and international levels must urgently move to target and undermine the potential of existing, new, and potential future ISIS affiliates across the region. Doing so will prevent ISIS, as a transnational movement, from being able to present other areas of the region outside of Syria and Iraq as new sources of operational momentum and extensions of its Caliphate project. Algeria's effective neutralization of ISIS's affiliate by killing its leadership demonstrates how effective such a strategy can be. However, such a strategy not only requires local actors to take the initiative before a major threat presents itself but also requires an enhanced level of multinational intelligence sharing to ensure that the region's predictive capacity is in place and operating to its fullest.

Enhance multinational efforts to counter foreign fighter flows

Both al-Qaeda and ISIS rely on the recruitment of foreign fighters, though to differing extents. Al-Qaeda's current long-game strategy has focused less on presenting an international face to its operations in conflict zones such as Syria and Yemen, while a local face has become an intrinsic component of its temporarily "softer" strategy. However, al-Qaeda affiliates do continue to attract and recruit foreign fighters; in Syria, Jabhat al-Nusra is receiving a discernible number of al-Qaeda veterans from abroad. These flows must urgently be stemmed and such efforts should supplement efforts already made around Syria and Iraq, which have shown some success.

Some of the onus of responsibility here lies on individual states from which foreign fighters emanate, of which there are now more than one hundred (Norton-Taylor 2015). Domestic intelligence capabilities across the world must continue to be enhanced so as to quickly and effectively detect outward flows of foreign fighters, while border control measures should be adequately augmented to ensure potential jihadists do not slip through the cracks. Empowering families within at-risk communities, rather than criminalizing or stigmatizing them, is a proven mechanism for better detection and forming effective informant relationships (Lister 2015b).

In the Middle East, borders surrounding active zones of jihadist militancy require more effective reconnaissance and control to prevent the influx of extremist recruits. Counterterrorism and counterinsurgent strategies inside active zones of jihadist militancy should prioritize securing territories along borders, where groups linked to al-Qaeda or ISIS could otherwise receive recruits, supplies, finances, and other useful resources.

Facilitate regional dialogue to de-escalate rivalries

The political destabilization of the Middle East since 2011 was a consequence of a variety of deep underlying fissures that ruptured within the context of the so-called Arab Spring. The weakening of states and the emergence of a number of failed and failing states were dynamics that regional powers sought to take advantage of to further their own standing in the world and to undermine the standing of their rivals. While exacerbated by regional perceptions of shifting American priorities and relationships in the region, the intense rivalry between Iran and Saudi Arabia has added to the destabilization of states such as Syria, Yemen, and Iraq. While neither party is providing direct support to al-Qaeda or ISIS, their destructive policies have added to the already ripe conditions in which jihadist militancy thrive.

Therefore, the United States must leverage its political power to convene a series of closed-door dialogues between the leaderships of regional great powers such as Iran, Saudi Arabia, Turkey, and Egypt to begin to break down the climate of regional hostility that no party benefits from beyond the immediate term. A refocusing of these countries' diplomatic relations toward cultural and financial ties and away from sensitive political issues can help to de-escalate tensions and avoid extremist actors on all sides from exploiting them for sectarian reasons. This would be a massive undertaking that would in all likelihood take a good deal of time to achieve demonstrable results, but it must necessarily be initiated before hostile regional dynamics become permanently consolidated.

Notes

1. For the purpose of this article, "jihadists" will be taken to refer to adherents to transnational Salafi-jihadism and not to extremists emerging out of the Shia branch of Islam.
2. Those being Australia, Canada, France, Germany, Belgium, Denmark, and the United States.
3. Author interviews with multiple Syrian Islamists based in northern Syria.
4. Ibid.

References

al-Adnani, Abu Mohammed. 21 September 2014. Inn'a Rabaka la bil mirsad. *Al-Furqan Media*.

Al-Akhbar. 18 December 2014. Mass grave of 230 tribespeople found in Syria's Deir Ezzor: Monitoring group. *Al-Akhbar*.

al-Batati, Saeed, and Kareem Fahim. 16 April 2015. War in Yemen is allowing Qaeda group to expand. *New York Times*.

al-Shafey, Mohammed. 8 April 2016. US strike in Idlib kills the mastermind behind the assassination attempt on Mubarak. *Asharq al-Awsat*.

al-Zawahiri, Ayman. 14 September 2013. General guidelines for jihad. *As-Sahab Media*.

Bayoumy, Yara, Noah Browning, and Mohammed Ghobari. 8 April 2016. How Saudi Arabia's war in Yemen has made al-Qaeda stronger—and richer. *Reuters*.

BBC News. 26 April 2016. Islamic State: Up to $800m of funds "destroyed by strikes." *BBC News*.

Callimachi Rukmini, and Eric Schmitt. 17 September 2015. Iran released top members of Al Qaeda in a trade. *New York Times*.

CBS News. 18 September 2014. New Syrian Al Qaeda cell developing bomb plots against US flights. CBS News.

Dabiq. 21 November 2014. Remaining and expanding. *Dabiq*, issue 5.

Faruki Yasmin, Jenna Gowell, and Laura Hoffman. 2 July 2015. *ISIS's Wilayat Sinai launches largest offensive in Sheikh Zuweid*. Washington, DC: Institute for the Study of War.

Gartenstein-Ross, Daveed. 9 February 2015. *Ansar Bayt al-Maqdis' oath of allegiance to the Islamic State*. Washington, DC: Wikistrat.

Gibbons-Neff, Thomas. 27 April 2016. Watch Islamic State fighters attack Kurdish positions in a U.S.-made Humvee. *Washington Post*.

Hartogs, Jessica. 18 April 2016. ISIS oil production takes a hit: Study. *CNBC*.

Hassan, Hassan. 6 March 2013. Jihadis grow more dangerous as they conquer hearts in Syria. *The National*.

Ignatius, David. 6 May 2015. New bin Laden documents show how al-Qaeda prepared to exploit the Arab Spring. *Washington Post*.

Johnsen, Gregory D. 2 April 2015. Al-Qaeda commander freed in Yemen prison break. *Buzzfeed*.

Joscelyn, Thomas. 3 March 2015. Osama Bin Laden's files: The Arab revolutions. *The Long War Journal*.

Lahoud, Nelly. March 2015. The Province of Sinai: Why bother with Palestine if you can be part of the Islamic State? *Combating Terrorism Center Sentinel* 8(3). Available from https://www.ctc.usma.edu.

Lister, Charles. December 2014. *Profiling the Islamic State*. Washington, DC: Brookings Institution.

Lister, Charles. 31 May 2015 (2015a). *An internal struggle: Al Qaeda's Syrian affiliate is grappling with its identity*. Washington, DC: Brookings Institution.

Lister, Charles. 2015b. *Returning foreign fighters: Criminalization or reintegration?* Washington, DC: Brookings Institution.

Lister, Charles. 2015c. *The Syrian jihad: Al-Qaeda, the Islamic State and the evolution of an insurgency*. London: Hurst Publishers.

Lister, Charles 2016a. The dawn of mass jihad: Success fuels al-Qa'ida's evolution. *CTC Sentinel* 9 (9): 13–20.

Lister, Charles. 2016b. *Jihadi rivalry: The Islamic State challenges Al-Qaida*. Washington, DC: Brookings Institution.

Malsin, Jared. 19 August 2015. ISIS re-establish their hold on Qaddafi's home town after crushing a rebellion. *Time Magazine*.

Norton-Taylor, Richard. 17 November 2015. Up to 30,000 foreign fighters have gone to Syria and Iraq since 2011—Report. *The Guardian*.

Pagliery, Jose. 19 January 2016. ISIS cuts its fighters' salaries by 50%. *CNN Money*.

Reuters. 30 June 2015. Around 1,200 escape from Yemen prison, including Al-Qaeda suspects. *Reuters*.

Reuters. 5 January 2016 (2016a). ISIS lost 40 percent of territory in Iraq, 20 percent in Syria: Coalition spokesman. *Reuters*.

Reuters. 28 April 2016 (2016b). U.S. military softens claims on drop in Islamic State's foreign fighters. *Reuters*.

Shanker, Thom. 4 June 2010. Qaeda leaders in Iraq neutralized, U.S. says. *New York Times*.

Yourish, Karen, Derek Watkins, and Tom Giratikanon. 22 March 2016. Where ISIS has directed and inspired attacks around the world. *New York Times*.

Zelin, Aaron Y. 21 September 2012. Know your Ansar al-Sharia. *Foreign Policy*. Available from http://foreignpolicy.com/2012/09/21/.

The ideologies of al-Qaeda and the Islamic State are rooted in larger historical trends that have to do with the rise of Islamism in the Arab world and its authoritarian politics. This article provides the basic history and ideological composition of these two militant movements, how they differ from each other, and what accounts for their initial political success and more recent failure. It also offers policy recommendations for how to more effectively counter these groups.

Keywords: al-Qaeda; Islamic State; ISIS; ISIL; Islamism

ISIS and al-Qaeda—What Are They Thinking? Understanding the Adversary

By
BERNARD HAYKEL

The Origins of al-Qaeda and the Islamic State

The Jihadi-Salafi movements of al-Qaeda (AQ) and the so-called Islamic State (IS) are the product of a history of Sunni Islamic revivalist movements that have sought to empower Muslims against what they describe as Islam's enemies, both external and internal. Jihadi-Salafis are Muslims who claim to adhere to a strictly literalist interpretation of the Quran and the sayings of the Prophet Muhammad. They privilege armed struggle (*jihad*) as a means for implementing their austere, intolerant, and muscular vision of Islam. Salafis—not all of whom preach armed violence; only the Jihadi-Salafis do—have been an influential minority sect throughout the history of Islam. In premodern times, Salafis were associated with populist movements, such as when some of

Bernard Haykel is a professor of Near Eastern Studies and the director of the Institute for Transregional Studies at Princeton University. He is the author of Revival and Reform in Islam: The Legacy of Muhammad al-Shawkani (*Cambridge University Press 2003*) *and* coeditor of Saudi Arabia in Transition: Insights on Social, Political, Economic, and Religious Change (*Cambridge University Press 2015*).

Correspondence: haykel@princeton.edu

DOI: 10.1177/0002716216672649

their scholars were rabble-rousers in tenth-century Baghdad or when in eighteenth-century central Arabia they led a revivalist movement better known as Wahhabism (named after the founder of the movement, Muhammad ibn Abd al-Wahhab, who died in 1792) (Haykel 2009).

Despite some ideological and operational differences, both AQ and IS tap into a deep vein of resentment, disillusionment, and disenfranchisement, specifically among the Sunni Arabs. These movements offer up a fantasy vision of renewed power and glory that claims to reproduce the early history of Muslims, roughly the period from the seventh to ninth centuries, when the Islamic empires of the Umayyads and the Abbasids reigned supreme over huge swathes of the globe. AQ and IS identify the enemies of the Muslims with various groups and ideologies, the most important of which are (1) the West and the Jews, which are regarded as being engaged in a cultural, economic, and military onslaught that seeks to destroy the religion of Islam and to capture the strategically important resources of the Muslim World; and (2) apostates, or nominal Muslims, who are regarded as having abandoned the core tenets of the faith, the most important of which is to rule in accordance with God's law (*hakimiyya*). Such apostates must be fought and defeated, not least because they labor to subjugate Muslims on behalf of the West and the Jews.

For these religious revivalists, Muslim empowerment will come about by a "return" to the "true" message and teachings of Islam, which, of course, both AQ and IS claim to profess. Furthermore, Jihadi-Salafis claim that the global Muslim community finds itself in the current state of political and military weakness because many of its members, and certainly all of its political leaders, have abandoned the "authentic" teachings of the Quran and in so doing vitiated their faith and opened the door to the enemy. More specifically, they claim that many Muslims have forsaken, or corrupted, the doctrine of God's Oneness (*tawhid*) and abandoned the fundamental religious obligation to defend and propagate the faith through armed struggle (*jihad*). Both AQ's and IS's prescriptions involve the rediscovery of this doctrine of Oneness and the sanctification of the obligation to commit violence, which is the only means by which Muslims can be empowered (*tamkin*) and their enemies overcome (*nikaya bi-l-'aduww*). AQ and IS, however, differ significantly with respect to tactics and strategy or on how to achieve victory (McCants 2015; Bunzel 2015, 2016).

AQ and IS are not purely ideological constructs or the result of intellectual and political debates. They have arisen from specific and local political and material realities, despite being global in their ambitions, recruitment, and reach. AQ and IS are principally Arab movements and have emerged out of the failures and brutalities of Arab politics. The Arab world has been dominated by authoritarian regimes for well over half a century, and these governments are mostly unaccountable, repressive, and corrupt. The Arab military defeat by Israel in 1967 represented a watershed for the Arab political system, in particular its republican regimes, which were unable to deliver on promises of economic development, good governance, and military prowess. Beginning in the 1970s, this failure provided a renewed impetus for suppressed Islamic revivalist forces, otherwise known as Islamists. Islamists argued that Islam was a political ideology and not merely a spiritual system confined to rituals and beliefs, and they offered to deliver on the failed promises of the secular nationalist regimes. They used catchy slogans to sum up their message, such as "Islam is the solution," or "Sovereignty belongs to God." More specifically, Islamists promised to rule in accordance with God's law, which would ensure social justice and good rule, and restore sovereignty to God—theirs would be a regime based on God's rule, not man-made laws rooted in foreign concepts and ideologies such as nationalism, socialism, fascism, or liberal democracy.

This revival of religiously motivated political activists has been largely dominated by groups associated with the ideology of the Muslim Brotherhood (MB), a movement that began in Egypt in 1928, and whose program can be summed up in two ideas: (1) capture the apparatus of government in which the MB is active; and (2) use the state's institutions to impose Islamic law, which would signal that God is *the* sovereign and also make Islamist rule legitimate (Mitchell 1993; Wickham 2015). It is this particular feature of their program that has led many observers to argue that Islamists are antidemocratic and will use electoral processes to come to power but, once in power, will refuse to relinquish it to another party. This has often been summarized by the pithy maxim: one man, one vote, one time. The overall claim of the MB is that it is acting in defense of Islam against the religion's enemies, namely, the West. Yet what remains deliberately ambiguous with the MB are the modalities of how it will capture the state (i.e., through violent means or nonviolent activism), and how, and who, should interpret the Islamic law that the state will impose. The Sharia, or Islamic law, is an old and complex intellectual tradition that does not offer readymade answers, so the question of how it will be applied is apt.

The elites of the modern Arab state, whether in Algeria, Egypt, Syria, or Iraq, generally did not tolerate the rise of such Islamist groups, seeing in them an existential threat (Eickelman and Piscatori 2004). These states therefore resorted to repressing the MB and its more militant offshoots, not unlike the ongoing repression of the MB by the Egyptian military regime. Imprisonment and torture, and at times open warfare, were routinely practiced, and the Islamists were serially defeated by the repressive capacities of these governments (Eickelman and Piscatori 2004). Those Islamists who survived this brutal process became more radicalized and often fled into exile to such places as Pakistan, Afghanistan, Saudi Arabia, Qatar, and the UK among other countries. From here they called for, and often helped to organize, an armed struggle (*jihad*) as the means to effect political change. Thus, AQ's advocacy of violence, for example, can be understood as a response to this domestic repression experienced in countries from Algeria to Iraq.

The Rise of AQ

To understand more fully the story of Jihadi-Salafism, one also has to take into account broader events that transcend the geography of the Arab world. The

1970s witnessed a number of globally significant events that would give the radical Islamists much-needed vigor. The first was the Arab oil embargo of 1973, which transformed the monarchical and religiously conservative states of the Arabian Peninsula into financial powerhouses. These states injected money and influence into the Islamist project to bolster their own legitimacy against the hostile ideologies of Arab nationalism and socialism from states such as Egypt and Iraq. The second event was the 1979 Islamic Revolution in Iran, which illustrated that religious ideology—even if Shiite—could form the basis for political mobilization, revolutionary change, and Islamist rule. The third was the Soviet invasion of Afghanistan, which would galvanize Islamists to go to the aid of fellow Muslims against a non-Muslim invader. The experience of being engaged in a jihad in Afghanistan molded a generation of Islamist fighters and ideologues who became invested in global politics after the Soviets were defeated there in 1989. Filled with overweening pride, these men now formed a mobile army of fighters and activists who sought to resist non-Muslim forces whenever and wherever Muslims were under attack. Some of these so-called Afghan-Arabs or *mujahidin* went on to fight in Bosnia, Yemen, and Chechnya, and their undisputed leader was Osama Bin Laden, the scion of a wealthy Saudi-Yemeni business family and a leading organizer of the volunteer effort against the Soviets in the 1980s (Wright 2006).

The Saudi royals repeatedly rebuffed Bin Laden's entreaties, and the latter became convinced by the mid-1990s that it was not possible to co-opt the Saudi state to the cause of jihad. He also realized that it was equally impossible to defeat it militarily through direct action (Wright 2006). This was because the Saudi government was firmly supported, and protected, by the sole remaining superpower, the United States. Thus, Bin Laden developed the view that attacking the United States would be the only way to radicalize Muslim populations, which in turn would help to topple Arab governments such as the ones in Riyadh and Cairo. The U.S. reaction to direct attacks and the Arab regimes' defense of Washington would unmask these governments as puppets of America. Muslims would take the side of AQ in the struggle, and this would provide Bin Laden with the opportunity to seize power in the Kingdom. Saudi Arabia was the prize he sought because of its symbolic importance as Islam's holiest land, with its two grand mosques in Mecca and Medina, as well as its unparalleled hydrocarbon reserves that would enable the rise of a new global Islamic power. Bin Laden became convinced that with AQ's control over the massive oil supplies and the territory of Arabia, he could redress the imbalance of power in the world order (Haykel 2015, 138–42). For Bin Laden, as for many in AQ's leadership who see themselves as vanguards of the Islamic people, the struggle is geopolitical and the entire globe is a theatre of warfare—the enemy is America and its various vassals in the Arab world.

As an elitist movement seeking to foment revolution, Muslim lives matter for AQ in this war, and it is important for the masses not to be alienated by AQ's military operations and targeting. Experience illustrates that the principal chink in AQ's armor is the killing of fellow Muslims. For example, AQ lost the sympathy of the Saudi public when its campaign of attacks and bombings in the Kingdom from 2003 to 2007 resulted in the killing of mostly Muslim civilians (Hegghammer 2010). This is why the attacks on 9/11 represent the pinnacle of AQ's influence. Not only did these attacks show that America could be hurt badly on its own territory and by using its own culture and products against it, the targets were almost exclusively non-Muslim foreigners. Confining the struggle with AQ to Arab- and Muslim-majority lands and to use Muslim forces in this fight rather than a large number of Western troops is one way to diminish AQ's influence. Moreover, the wars in Afghanistan and Iraq disproved Bin Laden's theory about a mass radicalization of Muslims, the toppling of Arab states, and a rallying to AQ's cause. The key Arab state, Saudi Arabia, has proven resilient thus far; and the number of Muslim—mainly Sunni—deaths in AQ's attacks severely dented its image as a defender of Islam. As a result, AQ's appeal gradually diminished, and it was soon overtaken by IS.

The Rise of IS

There were ideologues and leaders affiliated with AQ from the 1990s who disagreed with Bin Laden's views on ideological, tactical, and strategic matters (McCants 2015). Some of these, such as Abu Musab al-Suri, argued that the 9/11 attacks were a blunder for the jihadists because Afghanistan was lost as a base of operations. Instead, al-Suri contends that jihadists should engage in attacks as disconnected cells, and in so doing wear down the enemy. AQ's most significant critic, however, was Abu Musab al-Zarqawi (d. 2006), a Jordanian who established an AQ affiliate in Iraq in 2004, which would eventually become the Islamic State (Bunzel 2015; McCants 2015). More exclusively inspired by Salafism, Zarqawi regarded the principal enemies of the jihadist project to be nominal Muslims, especially Shiites, as well as Sunni apostates, such as the Arab rulers and their agents (Haykel 2010). For Jihadi-Salafis like Zarqawi, the Shiites believed in false theological doctrines that put them beyond the pale of the Islamic faith, and had from time immemorial sought to undermine Islam from within. Because of this, Shiites needed to be terrorized, enslaved, and killed. In other words, the main enemy was "near" and not the more distant West, whose turn would come later. And the existing political order could be transformed by fomenting a civil war between Sunnis and Shiites, and only then could the jihadist Sunnis become the victors.

Zarqawi and his followers were able to draw on a rich vein of Sunni sectarianism, rooted mainly in the Wahhabi tradition of Arabia, and thereby focus on a familiar target, the Shiites, but also on those Sunnis who were deemed to have deviated from the truth, such as Sufis and "apostates." AQ's more abstract and elitist political arguments, about the nature and structure of global domination by the West, were less relevant to Zarqawi's followers. Zarqawi's movement consisted of fomenting a mass mobilization of the Sunni Muslims to his cause, whereas AQ's model of a vanguard group operating clandestinely increasingly appeared less relevant to the circumstances. More significantly, AQ's inability to reproduce spectacular feats of violence made the movement less appealing over time—the attacks of 9/11 were in a sense AQ's Achilles' heel since they could not be surpassed. By contrast, Zarqawi's Jihadi-Salafism was easier to understand by the masses and appeared relevant because it described more precisely the enfeebled state of the Sunni Arabs in the areas where they lived and how they could go about changing this condition. Zarqawi's group was also constantly in the news because of its endless attacks against soft targets, mainly Shiite civilians (Haykel 2010).

The U.S. invasion of Iraq proved a boon for Zarqawi and his worldview. The most significant result of the invasion was the disenfranchisement and marginalization of Iraq's Sunni minority. At the same time the majority Shiites, who had not ruled in Baghdad for at least a millennium, became the dominant political group, controlling the state and the massive oil reserves in Iraq's south (Nakash 2006). Because of this, Zarqawi was able to attract an endless number of recruits from among the Sunnis, including former Baathists, and embarked on an unrelenting campaign of suicide bombings against Shiite civilians.

AQ's central leadership, represented by Bin Laden and Ayman al-Zawahiri, sought to convince Zarqawi to stop this slaughter. In an exchange of letters, they argued that the wanton killing of Shiite civilians was not permitted by Islamic law, and, more importantly, this harmed the global jihadist cause since the broader Sunni public did not understand or condone such bloodletting. More specifically, AQ's argument—which is more in line with the MB's views rather than those of the Salafis—was that ordinary Shiites could not be punished for their false beliefs since they were religiously unlearned and simply followed what they were taught. Only Shiite scholars and leaders could be targeted. AQ's leadership went on to argue that most Sunnis did not regard Shiites as unbelievers and were therefore puzzled, even angered, by their killing. The mainstream Islamic religious tradition is categorical that Muslims should not kill one another.

Zarqawi refused the leadership's admonitions, arguing that as *the* commander in the field his decisions trumped theirs, and he continued to use terror as a signature tactic against Shiites and others he deemed to be enemies. He was to be proven correct that sectarian bloodletting did not estrange the Sunni population given the highly sectarian nature of politics after the U.S. invasion. The movement he founded, AQ in Iraq, became in 2006, soon after his death, the Islamic State of Iraq (ISI) (it relabeled itself in 2013 as the Islamic State of Iraq and the Levant [ISIL] and finally took on the name of the Islamic State [IS] under the guise of the caliphate in 2014) and continues as of this writing to target Shiites, through mass executions of captives and suicide attacks. The U.S. surge in Iraq in 2007, which combined military force against Zarqawi's group and financial payoffs to the Sunni tribes that had sided with ISI, appeared to have quelled the movement by 2010. However, ISI was able to resurrect itself in 2012 under a new leadership because Iraq's Prime Minister Nouri al-Maliki's policies of persecution and discrimination alienated the Sunni population, who again rallied to ISI.

The outbreak in 2011 of civil war in Syria pitted President Assad's Alawite-dominated regime against a majority Sunni population. The Alawites, who represent some 12 percent of Syria's population, are considered by Sunni Muslims to be a heretical branch of Shiite Islam (Reuters 2012). The war offered another opportunity for ISI to pursue its sectarian form of warfare. In August 2011, ISI's leader Abu Bakr al-Baghdadi sent a group to Syria to establish a branch of AQ there, which soon after called itself the Support Front for the People of Syria (aka the Nusra Front). By 2013, however, a split developed between the Nusra Front and ISI over the ultimate leadership of the global jihadist movement (McCants 2015). The Nusra Front remained loyal to AQ's central command under Ayman al-Zawahiri, whereas ISI—now ISIL—went into open defiance of AQ's world leader. In hindsight this split appears to have been inevitable because the ideological and operational differences between AQ and ISIL had become too great to ignore. ISIL soon began clashing militarily with the Nusra Front and quickly and decisively expanded its control over large swathes of territory in both Syria and Iraq. Raqqa in eastern Syria was conquered in late 2013, and Mosul, Iraq's second largest city, fell in June 2014.

With its conquests, ISIL ruled over nearly eight million people and occupied a territory the size of Great Britain. Claiming that these victories were a clear sign of divine sanction and support, and wanting to appropriate AQ's mantle of leadership, ISIL became exclusively referred to as *the* Islamic State (IS) and further raised the ante by declaring itself a caliphate—an imperial state with no fixed boundaries that purports to represent, and lead, the global Muslim community and to be in the mold of the classical model of the seventh century. IS established a professional media and public relations capacity, using catchy slogans such as "Enduring and Expanding" and presenting its numerous military victories in well-produced documentary-style videos that spread far and wide through social media channels on the Internet. Some of these videos were laden with heavy symbolic and political meaning, such as IS's orchestrated obliteration of the border posts between Iraq and Syria that had been delineated by Western colonial powers in the aftermath of the First World War.

IS quickly eclipsed AQ in the dissemination of jihadist propaganda and in appealing to a larger number of people. The tens of thousands of recruits to Syria and Iraq (estimated to be around thirty thousand) (Soufan Group 2015), for example, and the equally numerous Twitter accounts (estimated to be more than forty thousand) (Berger and Morgan 2015) that are associated with or sympathetic to IS's cause provide a measure of this success. Much of the appeal came from IS's masterful ability to use modern communication technologies to defy the international order and to trample on the concept of the territorial state, and to show its fighters doing this in vivid videos. In IS's ideology, identity and political belonging were to be defined in purely religious terms, and it constructed a fantasy world of virtuous and godly rule through cultural products such as poetry, a cappella chants, video games, ritual practices, modes of dress and etiquette, social work, military training, and ideological and political tracts and speeches (Creswell and Haykel 2015). The repertoire of IS's "soft power" is sophisticated and of high production quality and helped to galvanize a minority of Muslims from across the world to join the cause by emigrating to its territory (*hijra*). Not only does a promise to create a just political order drive recruitment, but it is also driven by a narrative that invokes apocalyptic stories about the End Times. IS claims that its actions are part of a sequence of events that will ultimately usher in victory for Islam and salvation for the faithful. It is a puritanical version of the faith that offers a redemptive narrative that is nonelitist and easy to comprehend. By contrast, AQ's narrative and ideology is elitist and comes across as less inspired, in particular because its leader, Ayman al-Zawahiri, lacks charisma and is not a gifted orator.

Despite IS's propaganda prowess, it has to keep delivering actual battlefield victories to remain relevant and popular. Military failure is its Achilles' heel, and the string of recent defeats to a combination of Kurdish and Iraqi-Shiite forces in Syria and Iraq is proving debilitating for its propaganda messaging. IS finds it difficult to explain how it can suffer reversals on the battlefield and yet be God's instrument in the world. Military success is the marker of divine anointment; it explains the success IS initially had at marginalizing other jihadist movements, most notably AQ. The desperation at military defeat can be gleaned not only from apologetic-sounding postings on Twitter and from IS's online radio bulletin that denies battlefield setbacks, but also from IS's interest in engaging in planned terrorist operations in Europe, such as the recent Paris and Brussels attacks. IS had shunned such attacks and even criticized AQ for advocating these kind of operations, arguing that the real battle was in Syria and Iraq. Other weaknesses for IS lie in its inability to deliver on the provision of social services, as well as order and justice, to the communities it governs. People are leaving IS's territory, including former fighters, and they describe a hellish reality that bears no resemblance to the propaganda videos and messages (De Freytas-Tamura 2015). Disseminating such accounts is important for undermining IS's narrative and marking it as yet another failed Islamist project.

The dispute between Zarqawi on one hand and Bin Laden and al-Zawahiri on the other reveals ideological differences between IS and AQ, but it also illustrates how jihadist movements are engaged in a competition that involves a continuous outbidding of one another. The currency of this rivalry is measured in terms of increased levels of violence and displays of military "success" against the enemy. Loss on the battlefield for IS and the inability of AQ to engage in spectacular terrorist attacks spell weakness for these movements. For example, should IS lose its territorial base in both Iraq and Syria, as seems to be the case, it will probably survive in pockets of Libya and the Sinai, but it will not enjoy the same aura of power.

It bears remembering that the number of recruits to these movements remains very small in proportion to the total number of Muslims in the world and that there is no coherent sociological or psychological profile that is common to these converts to the jihadist cause. In other words, the phenomenon, though dangerous, should not be overstated—it does not represent an existential threat to the West, although it is very destructive with regard to the societies of the Middle East. Moreover, while ideology plays a role in shaping the actions of these groups, jihadism is also a product of a history of misrule, brutal authoritarianism, and the recent marginalization of Sunni populations in the Arab world. Given these complex ideological processes and the sociopolitical origins of jihadism, completely defeating these movements will not be possible. Trying to contain and mitigate their harmful effects is perhaps a more effective way to think about this problem.

Policy Recommendations

The problem of jihadism stems principally from the long-standing failures of the Arab political system and societies, and as such this is a problem that does not have quick fixes. It will take a generation or more of internal reform—if and when it happens—before the appeal of Islamism, as a political ideology and system of rule, fades. Focusing on long-term solutions that involve better education and governance will help, but the effort has to come from within so as not to appear contrived and orchestrated by foreigners.

The United States cannot compete with jihadists on religious and cultural grounds because it has no religious authority and therefore no real standing in debates about what constitutes proper Islamic belief and practice. It should be conceded that jihadists, and more broadly Islamists, have been largely successful at portraying the United States as an enemy of Muslims. They use a number of claims to make this case: U.S. support for Israel and authoritarian Arab regimes, the massive military presence in the Persian Gulf to control oil resources, the 2003 invasion of Iraq, control of the global reserve currency, among many others. The resort to violence and terror is the only solution that jihadists offer to remedy these problems that allegedly keep Muslims weak. Jihadist violence requires that the United States remain vigilant and engage in a strategy of containing jihadists to regions of the Muslim World. As groups such as IS kill an increasing number of fellow Muslims and wreak havoc on these societies, their message will lose its luster, and other Muslim leaders will gain the courage to refute the jihadists' arguments. Some of this criticism is taking place, but the United States has to be careful not to openly cultivate the jihadists' Muslim opponents because of the risk of delegitimizing such leaders.

In addition to remaining vigilant, it is also crucial to be realistic about the threat the jihadists pose. They do not represent an existential threat to the United States, and they remain a very small minority among Muslims. Playing into the jihadist narrative by, for example, deploying U.S. troops to fight them on the ground would be counterproductive. It would confirm the United States as an enemy of the Muslims and would ultimately leave the United States with the problem of ruling over those territories and populations that are liberated from the jihadists. This does not represent a durable solution, and it might even further radicalize the region. Instead of direct and full engagement in warfare, continuing to contain and degrade IS and AQ militarily, especially through proxies, as has been the policy of the recent administration, is a better avenue to pursue. There is no silver bullet solution to this intractable problem. Instead, the selective use of special forces, drone attacks, and, more importantly, the deployment of local allies like the Kurds and certain factions of the Syrian rebel opposition represent better options. The more Sunni Muslims engage the jihadists in battle, and ideological debate, the better and the more durable the outcome. As such, it would be beneficial to exert additional pressure on countries such as Saudi Arabia, Qatar, the UAE, Egypt, and Morocco to ramp up their public fight against the jihadists, both militarily and ideologically.

While this long-term process is unfolding, the United States will unfortunately have to expect more terror attacks in the form of lone-wolf operations and perhaps also coordinated attacks such as the recent ones in Paris and Brussels. As the jihadists lose battles and ground in the Middle East, they will become desperate and resort to terror in the West to maintain the illusion of relevance and power. To prevent such attacks, it is important to maintain an excellent intelligence service as well as to cultivate good relations with members of the Muslim communities in the West who are overwhelmingly patriotic and see the jihadists as a threat to their own existence. Muslim citizens in the United States are the first line of defense against radical elements because they can help to identify potential terrorists. As such, policies of inclusiveness and better community relations with local government are crucial for obtaining their help against this scourge of the modern world.

References

Berger, J. M., and Jonathon Morgan. 2015. *The ISIS Twitter census: Defining and describing the population of ISIS supporters on Twitter*. Analysis Paper no. 20. Washington, DC: Brookings Institution. Available from https://www.brookings.edu/wp-content/uploads/2016/06/isis_twitter_census_berger_morgan.pdf.

Bunzel, Cole. 2015. *From paper state to Caliphate: The ideology of the Islamic State*. Analysis Paper no. 19. Washington, DC: Brookings Institution. Available from https://www.brookings.edu/research/from-paper-state-to-caliphate-the-ideology-of-the-islamic-state/.

Bunzel, Cole. 2016. *The Kingdom and the Caliphate: Duel of the Islamic States*. Washington, DC: Carnegie Endowment for International Peace. Available from http://carnegieendowment.org/2016/02/18/kingdom-and-caliphate-duel-of-islamic-states/iu4w.

Creswell, Robyn, and Bernard Haykel. 8 June 2015. Battle lines. *The New Yorker*.

De Freytas-Tamura, Kimiko. 20 September 2015. ISIS defectors reveal disillusionment. *New York Times*.

Eickelman, Dale F., and James Piscatori. 2004. *Muslim politics*. Princeton, NJ: Princeton University Press.

Haykel, Bernard. 2009. On the nature of Salafi thought and action. In *Global Salafism: Islam's new religious movement*, ed. Roel Meijer, 33–57. London: Hurst.

Haykel, Bernard. 2010. Jihadis and the Shi'a. In *Self-inflicted wounds: Debates and divisions within al-Qa'ida and its periphery*, eds. Assaf Moghaddam and Brian Fishman, 203–23. West Point, NY: Combating Terrorism Center.

Haykel, Bernard. 2015. Oil in Saudi Arabian culture and politics: From tribal poets to Al-Qaeda's ideologues. In *Saudi Arabia in transition*, eds. Bernard Haykel, Thomas Hegghammer, and Stephane Lacoix, 125–47. New York, NY: Cambridge University Press.

Hegghammer, Thomas. 2010. *Jihad in Saudi Arabia: Violence and Pan-Islamism since 1979*. Cambridge: Cambridge University Press.

McCants, William. 2015. *The ISIS apocalypse: The history, strategy, and doomsday vision of the Islamic State*. New York, NY: St. Martin's Press.

Mitchell, Richard P. 1993. *The Society of the Muslim Brothers*. Oxford: Oxford University Press.

Nakash, Yitzhak. 2006. *Reaching for power: The Shi'a in the modern Arab world*. Princeton, NJ: Princeton University Press.

Reuters. 31 January 2012. Syria's Alawites, a secretive and persecuted sect. Available from http://www
.reuters.com/article/us-syria-alawites-sect-idUSTRE80U1HK20120131 (accessed 1 September 2016).

The Soufan Group. 2015. *Foreign fighters: An updated assessment of the flow of foreign fighters into Syria
and Iraq*. New York, NY: The Soufan Group. Available from http://soufangroup.com/wp-content/
uploads/2015/12/TSG_ForeignFightersUpdate3.pdf (accessed 1 September 2016).

Wickham, Carrie R. 2015. *The Muslim Brotherhood: Evolution of an Islamist movement*. Princeton, NJ:
Princeton University Press.

Wright, Lawrence. 2006. *The looming tower: Al-Qaeda and the road to 9/11*. New York, NY: Knopf.

Grand Strategy versus Unending Extremism: Lessons from the United States and Coalition Experience

By
GEN. JOHN R. ALLEN (RET.)

This article focuses on the lessons learned from American and coalition experience in dealing with extremist groups such as al-Qaeda and the so-called Islamic State or ISIL. It also deals more generally with extremist networks, which increasingly have the capacity to function as nonstate actors, not only threatening the existence of a growing number of fragile states but increasingly acting as proto-states themselves. I raise issues that should be considered as the United States and its allies and partners gird themselves for the long-term struggle against violent extremism. I also address the challenges faced after long years of war, the general considerations in forming a coalition, the means for establishing and implementing a strategy, and thoughts on a way ahead in a negatively trending security environment. I focus on what needs to be done and avoid specifically praising or condemning successes and failures of the past.

Keywords: counter-ISIL; grand strategy; spheres of influence

The Challenge

As a people, a country, and a community of nations, we are emerging from a decade and a half of war since September 2001. For the United States, these wars have meant more than seven thousand dead, untold wounded, and trillions of dollars spent. Estimates of the dead among Iraqis and Afghans vary dramatically, but hundreds of thousands from these two countries perished in these wars, and the damage to their infrastructure will require

General John R. Allen is a retired four-star general who served as commander of the NATO International Security Assistance Force and commander of U.S. Forces Afghanistan from 2011 to 2013. After retirement, he served as President Obama's Special Envoy to the Global Coalition to Counter ISIL.

Correspondence: bsugg@brookings.edu

DOI: 10.1177/0002716216668813

decades to repair and cost additional hundreds of billions of dollars. It is important, however, to put these numbers into context.

We face today a growing menace in the form of unrelenting, violent extremism. For a variety of reasons, it is both spreading and gaining momentum. Much of the reason for the emergence of this threat has far less to do with religion, faith, or confession than it does with the massive and long-term corruption and predation of governments of the Middle East, which, when coupled with fundamental demographic changes—the emergence of the so-called youth bulge across North Africa, the traditional Middle East, and Asia—have provided the tinder for one wildfire after another. The so-called Arab Spring was one of the more recent conflagrations to engulf the region—it will not be the last. Unless sweeping and fundamental reform is undertaken in these states, Syria-like civil wars will be in our future for a long time to come, as one after another weak and fragile states goes down in turmoil and internal chaos.

Across the region, in state after state, the sense of intense dissatisfaction and hopelessness is on the rise. Weak and corrupt governments, failed judiciaries, collapsing economies, and an absence of human rights all add up to the widespread radicalization of untold thousands of young men and women whose options are few, and from whose ranks extremist groups find a ready-made source of adherents, foot soldiers, and suicide killers.

The so-called Islamic State (or the Islamic State in Iraq and the Levant [ISIL] or Daesh, the Arabic acronym for the same title) is the most recent manifestation of the growing menace of violent extremist organizations. Increasingly, organizations like these hold sway in ungoverned spaces. Indeed, the very term "ungoverned space" masks or dismisses the huge complexities of the regions plagued with extremism. In most cases where the United States and the West have consigned a people or region to being an ungoverned space, the reality is that there is indeed governance in that space, but that it functions in a way that is beyond our understanding of Westphalian order and, often, beyond our sensibilities and beyond the human pale.

The United States and its allies have experienced and learned much in the 15 years since September 11, 2001. Organizing to oppose al-Qaeda, ISIL, and a growing global network of extremist satellites has created one challenge after another. The principal challenge for the United States is not the application of force in a military sense but organizing a strategy to deal with these threats that does not exacerbate their effects, magnify their capabilities, or accelerate their spread.

Al-Qaeda and ISIL are not independent phenomena in and of themselves but, rather, are symptoms of a much more serious set of problems. And because the United States and the West have not systematically dealt with the underlying causal factors that have generated these entities, the West will be condemned to fight one group after another, ad infinitum. If a new administration in Washington, or if an alliance or coalition, desires to organize to oppose an existing or a newly emerging group, the factors presented in this article will be a useful roadmap to achieve a strategic outcome. The United States and the West cannot continue to deal with these extremist groups as one-off threats. They are spawn of horrendous human conditions across a vast swath of the globe. Failing to deal with the underlying conditions by adopting a generational, containment-like strategy with the features of a Marshall Plan means that the grandchildren of the current generation in Washington, Brussels, and elsewhere will be marching off to do battle and damning their grandparents for their lack of vision and irresolution. Thoughts on this long game are offered at the conclusion of the article.

On the Importance and Lifespan of Coalitions

During the years of war in the aftermath of September 2001, America would learn of the limits of its power in a number of unpleasant ways. While the United States has remained the preeminent global power, economic challenges at home and political polarization have created powerful headwinds against unilateralism. On the whole, this is probably a good thing, but these same forces have also been a debilitating brake on acting decisively in moments of peril. Under these circumstances, acting within a coalition, in concerted action within the community of nations, is the safer approach under nearly every scenario. Ideally, the optimal coalition is one buttressed by the force of international law or resolution. It was the case with the mature coalition in Afghanistan known as the NATO International Security Assistance Force or ISAF, which operated under the original UN Security Council Resolution or UNSCR 1386 as authorized on December 20, 2001, and later modified by subsequent authorizations. Not only did its mandate carry the force of law, but the structure was framed and organized by NATO, which gave immediate shape and form to the undertaking of fifty nations. In nearly every respect, this was the ideal confluent approach, but there are other factors inherent in wielding coalitions that must be considered.

Leadership

No nation on the planet has greater moral and practical convening power or a broader strategic reach than the United States. This places both an uncommon opportunity and responsibility for leadership that can be wielded as a vast instrument of power, or it can be wasted by inaction or indecisiveness.

In one crisis after another, the United States has not only convened powerful intersections of nations' common interests and values but has led their application at the strategic level. Having commanded ISAF, and having been at the heart of forming the global coalition to counter ISIL, I have seen firsthand the sense of exceptional trust conferred by coalition nations upon the United States. There are a number of reasons for this. At the practical level, few states, even most "old Europe" partners, can defend themselves from concerted attack. Witness the assault on the European heartland from the attack cells of ISIL. Only the United States can come from over the horizon with the capacity and combat power to fight nearly anywhere on the globe overnight, to defend partners or punish antagonists. Siding with the United States, as a practical matter, is a good decision.

But there is a more important reason: U.S. moral leadership. Yes, U.S. moral leadership has been dented of late by confused national policies and unfortunate campaign rhetoric on torture and human rights, but these policies or pronouncements do not represent who we are as a people and a nation, and most of the community of nations not only realize that, they seek to gravitate to the American example.

Finally, from my experiences leading NATO forces in Afghanistan, and in forming the Counter-ISIL Coalition, it is clear that many potential coalition members will join a coalition simply because the United States has assessed that the emergency of the moment requires U.S. action. Particularly among the Central European states, loyalty to the United States and its causes runs deep. Partly out of gratitude for U.S. perseverance during the Cold War, and partly out of U.S. support for membership in NATO, many states will bear the political and materiel burden of coalition membership simply because they see the United States moving to confront crisis.

Only the United States can form coalitions the magnitude of NATO, or ISAF, or the current global coalition to counter ISIL, and only the United States can lead these endeavors from the front. Where the United States leads purposefully and unambiguously, the strategic direction of the coalition is certain and compelling. Absent clear and decisive American leadership, the coalition will drift, fray, and falter. Members will depart or go their own way. If America convokes a coalition, then America must lead that coalition and be seen as its leader. There can be no ambiguity here. Convening the heads of state of the coalition early in the crisis, and periodically thereafter, will sustain the cohesion of the organization and the strategic commitment that are essential to achieving long-term goals.

Membership

Absent a UNSCR, membership in an ad hoc coalition will be more tentative. While some states will never join a coalition without a clear UN commitment, many will join because of U.S. leadership. While all members of a coalition both expect and deserve to be treated with the respect due a sovereign member, the reality is that many of the member states will have little to contribute to the strategic outcome other than the name of their state and their moral support. In most cases, this is enough; and wise U.S. leadership should celebrate this contribution—often the only resource a small or young nation can offer—rather than condemn its paucity.

As recent experience in Iraq, Afghanistan, and in countering ISIL has shown us, coalitions also contain members with significant resources, who join intent to participate in every dimension of the undertaking. Some will join with fixed resources or with a very focused intent, such as supporting police development or building the capacity of the judiciary, versus participating actively in combat operations. U.S. leaders should keep in mind that forming and shaping a coalition is akin to assembling a jigsaw puzzle. Some pieces will be larger than others. Some pieces will be multifaceted with ties into multiple aspects of the strategy.

Regardless of the size and the variation of shapes, each member of the coalition has a role to play in the larger strategy, and the challenge, indeed the privilege, for the United States is to fit the many pieces together to create the synergy and symbiosis necessary for the strategy. Only U.S. leadership can do this.

Transition

If the coalition is not a permanent, standing organization, early consideration must be given to transitioning the coalition's functions over time to permanent structures. On a daily basis in Iraq and in Afghanistan, coalitions performed hundreds of distinct and measurable functions. In closing the American and coalition involvement in both theaters, detailed plans were drawn up to transition the functions in a time-phased manner. Some functions went to the major standing headquarters at the U.S. Central Command or to NATO, such as continued training of Afghan security forces; and some went to national ministries or departments in capitals, such as ministerial capacity building. Some went to embassies in Baghdad and Kabul, respectively, such as helping civil society groups. And many, but not all, went to the host nations themselves, such as primary responsibility for security force training. Finally, some functions were phased out entirely. The point is an ad hoc coalition, formed in response to an emergency, cannot be a permanent organization unless the members choose to make it so, and without a UNSCR this is unlikely. Transitioning a coalition should be both planned and systematic, with a discernable horizon or "sunset"; this kind of careful planning is critical to both the coherence of the organization's purpose and the cohesion of the membership—coalitions should not go out with a whimper. If the United States led the formation of a coalition, the United States should lead its planned dissolution.

In this vein, the current global coalition to counter ISIL should be, as of this writing, under serious consideration for transition. In its second year of a three-year initial strategic horizon, the coalition should be enumerating its functions now, and beginning to build the transition timeline for moving these functions to long-term owners.

What Effective Strategy Looks Like

In most cases, organizations such as al-Qaeda and ISIL did not burst wholly made onto the scene because of military or security factors. These groups and their ilk emerged over time as the result of widespread social inequity and systematic predation over, in most cases, decades or generations. Strategies to deal with these violent entities must be whole-of-government affairs—and in the context of coalitions, whole-of-governments. And they must be grand strategies, that is, approaches that exist and are orchestrated at the highest echelons of the government.

When dealing with groups such as al-Qaeda or Daesh, the strategy must operate along multiple converging lines of effort and must seek to achieve effects by exploiting the weaknesses inherent in such asymmetric opponents. When Daesh declared itself a so-called Caliphate, it assumed the trappings of a proto state and, in so doing, exposed its multiple weaknesses. The need for the caliphate to pursue its dogma, to relentlessly expand, and to control ground and dominate human terrain has in fact created multiple weak points that can be exploited by a multifaceted strategy that leverages national and coalition power.

Spheres of engagement

Over the years, in dealing with threats such as al-Qaeda and other groups, it has become apparent that these groups operate simultaneously in multiple spheres. Thus, it is useful to think of the strategy as engaging threats (in this case extremist groups) simultaneously and in multiple spheres. Strategy in this case revolves principally around three spheres: the physical sphere, the economic sphere, and the information sphere. These are the battle spaces or mediums in which the strategy seeks to achieve decisive effect; and decisive engagement of the opponent may occur in any sphere from the effects of multiple lines of the strategy operating simultaneously and in combination. For example, while the defeat of ISIL may be measurable in the physical sphere, its demise can be hastened through strangulation in the economic sphere. That said, its true defeat can occur only in the information sphere when the idea of ISIL has been so utterly discredited that its recruiting collapses and its adherents and donors leave the group bereft of resources. Put differently, while all the spheres are crucial mediums of conflict, the information sphere will likely be the decisive battle space and the center of gravity of the overall coalition effort.

Multiple converging lines

The number of lines of effort and their function will vary by virtue of the target (today ISIL and al-Qaeda, tomorrow some other ideological or criminal nonstate actor); and the lines will likely evolve over time as pressure is exerted by them individually and collectively. The capacity to detect and assess change in the operational environment and in the target organization, and the way the strategy is implemented, will dictate the ways in which the lines of effort evolve over time. Indeed, some will run their course and conclude. Some will combine. Some will split. The more lines, the more complex the strategy, necessitating greater and greater attention to the technical implementation of the strategy itself. For the purposes of this article, the names of the lines of effort are generic and would address the following broad efforts: political stability, development, military operations, countering terrorist finance, countering foreign terrorist fighters, information, and defending the homeland. If the strategy has been properly derived from overarching political objectives, the lines of effort will converge over time to accomplish not just strategic but also political objectives.

Strategic logic

The logic of any strategy relies on the ability to integrate the ways and means to achieve the ends. More practically, it relies on the capacity to integrate resources: usually people, materiel and money, and time. A properly integrated and resourced strategy will create a horizon in time, or a combination of effects, that logically delivers the accomplishment of the strategy. If the strategy is sound, then so too is the logic of the undertaking; and remaining oriented on and committed to that horizon is vital, even though its achievement may be years away. Confidence is also important for resisting or staving off decisions during moments of urgency that may change the direction of the strategy. If the logic of a strategy is clear, it is possible to remain focused on the strategy, rather than reacting prematurely to the here and now. For example, when the city of Ar Ramadi fell to ISIL in the Al Anbar Province of Iraq, there were calls to change the counter-ISIL strategy. These calls were rejected, because the defeat in Ramadi, while an embarrassing setback for the Iraqi government at the tactical level, did not alter the operational or strategic conditions that would have necessitated a change in strategy.

Two important considerations emerge at this point. First, whoever owns the strategy must have the capacity to explain it, necessitating the early creation of a fully formed communications plan that resonates with the media, the Congress, the American people, and the members of the coalition. Second, preemptively removing one's own options and capacities early in a crisis virtually ensures confusion and fuels a churn of debate about the intent of the strategy. The most obvious example of this latter point was the current administration's assurance that it would not deploy U.S. conventional combat forces to Iraq to oppose ISIL. This commitment created an intense debate over the use of American "boots on the ground." This decision not only took many of the most useful options for the United States off the table at the outset of the crisis, it also assured ISIL that U.S. commitment was low or incremental and set the administration unnecessarily at odds with attentive audiences such as the Congress and the media. Over time, the administration would find it necessary to increase its commitments. Rather than focusing on the horizon, where all U.S. and coalition resources and capabilities would potentially be in play, deliberations about required or necessary forces on the ground centered on self-imposed troop caps and whether, with some small additional number of troops, the president would somehow have violated his own commitment. This distraction consumed many of what might have otherwise been important and objective requirements-based versus limitations-based conversations. In the end, the logic behind any strategy must create confidence.

Implementation

The greatest strategy poorly implemented will be for naught, but a mediocre strategy can have good effect if the implementation is comprehensive and aggressive. In recent years, our problems have not been the absence of strategy, but suboptimal implementation of the strategy. Put differently, it is not enough to envisage a strategy; success relies just as much on the leadership and processes to achieve the objectives of the strategy. Success requires thinking (the strategy) and doing (the implementation), and the two must exist in equilibrium.

Policy formulation processes versus campaign design/plan

Grand strategies—focusing most or all measures of national power—are not, and cannot be, implemented as policy processes. If the president of the United States were to create and pursue a grand strategy for the defeat of ISIL or al-Qaeda, it should logically be pursued with at least a campaign design—a broad, general outline of a campaign plan—if not a fully developed and comprehensive campaign plan that coordinates and integrates the actions of the lines of effort over time to achieve strategic objectives. The National Security Council (NSC) was never intended to run operations such as these and is neither equipped nor organized to achieve the unity of effort, purpose, and command necessary to achieve the overall coherence required for such strategic undertakings. Within the context of the NSC policy process, no number of meetings of the deputies or the principals committees (DC or PC) can substitute for a well-conceived strategy orchestrated through a comprehensive campaign plan. Key issues can be brought forward periodically for decision by the deputies, the principals, or the president, but that process, if substituted in lieu of an active and comprehensive campaign plan, will virtually ensure an absence of the synergy, agility, and flexibility necessary to be faster and more adaptable than the asymmetric nonstate actors being engaged now and in the future.

Implementation

If the administration chooses to pursue a grand strategy coordinated through a campaign, an early decision must be who or what will have the moment-to-moment responsibility to implement the plan and shepherd the strategy. This is best accomplished through the use of a functionally designed cell or task force in the form of a specifically constituted and standing Combined Joint Interagency Task Force (CJIATF) led either by a presidential appointee positioned in the NSC or a lead agency designated by the president. The moment-to-moment execution of the strategy can be led and managed through the cell or task force with periodic situation reporting through the deputy or national security advisors to the deputies or principals committees and on to the president. Previously agreed-on key decisions will be presented to the DC, PC, or NSC, but the daily management of the strategy, including target development, effects engagement, and assessment, will be handled specifically by a functionally oriented, long-standing task force with the authorities and permissions in place to run the campaign and accomplish the strategy.

Assessment

Assessing the strategy is one of the most important functions among the implementation measures. Assessments can be quantitative (objective), qualitative (subjective), or a combination of the two, but the strategy must be assessed. Without a means for assessment, it is not possible to know whether the strategy is succeeding and how to apply resources to accelerate success or arrest failure.

Ideally the assessment mechanism is purpose-built, with the support of analytical organizations (for example from the Center for Naval Analysis or the Center for Army Analysis). If the objectives of each of the lines of effort are properly derived from the overall objectives of the strategy, then each line should have its own measures of performance and effectiveness, which contribute logically and directly to an overall strategic assessment. When developed properly, measures of effectiveness are built uniformly across each line of effort, with each contributing to a mechanism for overall strategic assessment. Full strategy assessments are best conducted every six months. In that context, the overall trajectory of the strategy can be accurately assessed, and individual lines of efforts can be adjusted if necessary.

In the past, there was a reluctance to develop measures of effectiveness and performance, fearing they would be used as report cards for the various agencies involved. However, attempting to run a strategy without any means to assess its effectiveness leaves decision-makers guessing on strategic progress and the need for strategy adjustments or revision. In the end, through a comprehensive assessment process, the president and the coalition should know exactly how the lines of effort are progressing and the state of the grand strategy.

Targeting and effects platforms

In the absence of a coherent grand strategic campaign and leadership and management to implement the strategy, it is very difficult to integrate the lines of effort and the core requirements for success. Integrating intelligence into broader target development and into an accompanying effects strategy is nearly impossible. "Targets" are not purely military, and the effects we seek to achieve do not solely rely on defense resources. Without a campaign and an implementation cell, lines of effort are left largely to fend for themselves. In the case of the current counter-ISIL strategy, for example, some of the very best analysis and target development has been done within the counter-finance line of effort, but because there is no grand strategic targeting or effects strategy within this line, there were not many occasions where the results of the economic analysis could be presented to those within the U.S. government. While the military has a role to play here, this is not a military function. Ideally, lines of effort would periodically appear before an "effects board," which would consist of representatives of the various effects platforms from across the agencies.

The array of potential economic targets could span the gamut, from oil wellheads to modular refineries, from tanker trucks to border crossings and corrupt customs officials, from black marketers to money-laundering financial institutions. Elements from within the interagency that own specific capabilities to prosecute the targets developed by, in this case, the counter-finance line of effort would be present at the effects board. Wellheads, modular refineries, and tanker trucks could be targeted with kinetic fires (such as air strikes or artillery fires) or special operations forces. Border crossings could be disrupted with coordinated U.S. and host-nation law enforcement operations; corrupt officials and kingpins could be indicted, their assets frozen, and given over to foreign governments for extradition; and money-laundering institutions could be sanctioned to separate them from the international financial system. In just this scenario alone, the effects platforms, that is, those entities within the interagency capable of delivering effects, would be owned by the Department of Defense, the Department of State, elements of the intelligence community, the Treasury, the Department of Justice, and the Attorney General. Coordinating this process across this array of agencies and departments is essential. Engaging those targets in the right sequence and combination over time to achieve an overall strategic effect is nearly as important as assigning the right target to the right platform. It is not just about individual target engagement; it is about the aggregate and cumulative grand strategic targeting effect.

None of these kinds of activities can occur if the strategy, as individual lines of effort, is being managed through the day-to-day efforts of the NSC. The enormity and complexity of implementing a grand strategy cannot be overstated—in volume alone, it exceeds the capacity and experience of the NSC. The manner and the means for organizing the strategy will both drive the effectiveness of the strategy and signal to all involved the seriousness of the administration.

Intelligence and covert action

The importance of the role of intelligence and the importance of the U.S. and coalition intelligence communities (IC) cannot be overstated. They will touch nearly every aspect of the successful implementation of the strategy. Intelligence functions will play central roles within all the lines of effort; and from the outset of the strategy, the director of National Intelligence and the seventeen intelligence entities within the IC will need to consider what unique organizational approaches will be necessary to support the various components of the grand strategy.

Essential functions are more obvious within the physical and financial spheres and in support of the military line of effort, but there will be a vital role for the IC in ongoing target development for the individual lines of effort, in constantly assessing the effects of target engagement to facilitate subsequent actions, and in assessing the effectiveness and performance of the lines of effort and the overall strategy. Depending on the region and the host country(ies) wherein the strategy is being implemented, there could be unique intelligence functions associated with the political, economic, counter-finance, foreign fighter, and information lines of effort. Of all the entities within the interagency, the IC will be the one upon which the full weight of implementation of the strategy will fall; and the development of the strategy itself may in some manner be deeply affected by the capacity of the IC to accomplish its vital ongoing functions, and flex or pivot organizationally and functionally to support a focused long-term counter-extremist strategy.

Given the sensitivity of covert action, it will not be addressed in detail in this article. That said, it is vital to understand that organizations such as al-Qaeda and ISIL are waging unrestricted, total war on the United States and its partners. For the moment, these violent extremist groups may not pose an existential threat to the United States and many of its partners, but clearly the United States and the coalition are an existential threat to these groups. The strategies to defeat these organizations should consider every aspect of U.S. and coalition power, including covert action, which, if used carefully, could exploit the vulnerable underpinnings of these groups and accelerate their defeat. There is no question that al-Qaeda and ISIL are seeking weapons of mass destruction, including some nuclear capacity. Adding covert action to the full spectrum of the U.S. and coalition response, therefore, should be an early part of the grand strategy.

The Deep Horizon

In 1946 George F. Kennan formulated the seminal cable on the sources of Soviet conduct, which would form the basis for post–World War II thinking on the Soviet threat. Later, in 1947, writing in *Foreign Affairs* as "X," his thoughts would spawn the intellectual underpinnings of a grand U.S. and coalition strategy—one that would span decades and contain and limit the threat of the Soviet Union while shaping the political, diplomatic, and economic reality of the Free World (Kennan 1947). Had the United States not pursued a generational grand strategy, emanating from a small group of visionaries, the Cold War could have been an interminable series of crises and regional and postcolonial wars with the great potential for either a nuclear catastrophe or a prolonged, debilitating bipolar stalemate.

These visionaries saw the solution at the deep horizon, one where all aspects of American and coalition power would be needed, and they focused to achieve fundamental and tectonic change. As it was, the era was fraught. Wars were fought, and some policies failed spectacularly, but overall the strategic logic of the approach was sufficiently sound, and the strategic vision was sufficiently clear across nearly two generations, so that the idea and the strategy prevailed.

The lessons of this article underline the need to engage extremist organizations in the near term, in the near horizon. But near-term solutions will not resolve the long-term challenges, challenges that are very much on a negative trend line. Essential partners, beleaguered by increasing radicalization and expanding extremist movements, will need the full attention of the United States and the West in the medium term—at the distant horizon—to prevent their continued weakening and even their collapse. Tunisia, Egypt, Jordan, Iraq, and Pakistan come immediately to mind—especially Pakistan, a nuclear-armed state whose faltering or collapse would carry the gravest possible consequences. Yet a medium-term approach will still be insufficient: unless and until the United States and its coalition partners embrace the urgency of this moment, and together pivot toward the enormity of the changes and the reforms necessary at the deep horizon, the world of the mid-to-late twenty-first century will be a very different, and likely a very inhospitable, place. Here there is room to find common ground and common cause with major regional and emerging powers, whether democratic India or authoritarian Russia and China.

The time is now for the new Mr. X to step forward.

References

Kennan, George F. ["X," pseud.]. July 1947. The sources of Soviet conduct. *Foreign Affairs*.

Section II

Approaches for Countering Violent Extremism at Home and Abroad

By
GEORGE SELIM

As the struggle against violent extremism continues 15 years after 9/11, practitioners of counterterrorism note that law enforcement and military approaches alone cannot break the cycle of violence, and new threats emerge as existing threats are defeated. This article provides an overview of post-9/11 efforts related to countering violent extremism (CVE), or the prevention, intervention, and rehabilitative efforts to provide a noncoercive, nonkinetic pathway toward preventing recruitment and radicalization to extreme violence. Specifically, this article explores the spread of the ISIS ideology and the Obama administration's CVE efforts, and provides an overview of subsequent articles in this series that expand on particular CVE approaches.

Keywords: terrorism; countering violent extremism; CVE; psychology of terrorism; counterterrorism

The previous section of this volume revealed that trends in transnational terrorist threats are sobering—the threat from ISIL (also known as ISIS or Islamic State) has made radicalization to extreme violence a truly global phenomenon, differently and more broadly than threats from al-Qaeda and related groups. One might be tempted to think, "These trends are making it harder for us to *win*." An apt analogy is that "countering terrorism" as exemplified by military and law enforcement action is like an average person playing one-on-one basketball

George Selim has over a decade of public service, including serving as the first director of the Office for Community Partnerships at the U.S. Department of Homeland Security (DHS), serving as the lead of a new CVE Task Force, and serving for four years on the National Security Council staff at the White House. He is also a commissioned officer in the United States Navy Reserve.

NOTE: The opinions expressed by the writer are his alone and not necessarily those of the United States government or any of its departments.

Correspondence: george.selim@hq.dhs.gov

DOI: 10.1177/0002716216672866

against LeBron James, only the rules are that no matter how many points the average person scores, the only way to win is for the average person to block every shot LeBron attempts. In other words, it does not matter how many shots we make, or how many of the other team's we block, since the game lasts forever and each shot we fail to block is a victory for our foe. In the following articles, you will read myriad ways in which the international community has recognized that the struggle against terrorism is not only a question of blocking shots but of changing the rules of the game.

Counterterrorism tools have typically been applied to investigate, prosecute, and imprison individuals who have been radicalized and are acting with terroristic intent, or to capture or kill them on the battlefield. However, in many ways, fighting terrorists in this manner requires mechanisms—such as surveillance, military action, and so on—that also act as recruitment tools for terrorists who propagandize those efforts as evidence of a Western war with Islam, or of the deep divisions between local Muslim communities in the West and their non-Muslim community members. For every terrorist we arrest or take off the battlefield, their coconspirators may use our action to recruit and radicalize more. In short, in the struggle against violent extremism, we cannot arrest and kill our way to victory, or, as President Obama has said, "We cannot use force everywhere that a radical ideology takes root; and in the absence of a strategy that reduces the wellspring of extremism, a perpetual war . . . will prove self-defeating, and alter our country in troubling ways. . . . [We need a] strategy [that] involves addressing the underlying grievances and conflicts that feed extremism" (Obama 2013). Success requires developing comprehensive efforts aimed at preventing a new generation of recruits to violent extremist causes.

This recognition has led to the prioritization of a relatively new model, the prevention model of post-9/11 terrorism, known to many as countering violent extremism (CVE). Whereas "counterterrorism" implies countering an individual who, in the eyes of the law, has already taken steps toward committing a terrorist act or joining a terrorist group, CVE counters the ideological recruitment, focusing on the root causes of many terrorist motivations, and working to prevent those causes, or provide "off-ramps" for individuals who may have taken steps toward embracing ideologically motivated violence. There are already multiple definitions of CVE, typically noting that CVE is a collection of noncoercive, non-kinetic, and, most importantly, voluntary activities to prevent and intervene in the process of radicalization to violence (see, e.g., White House 2015a, 2015b; United Nations Security Council 2014).[1]

There is no one path for an individual to take in becoming radicalized. From what we know about people who have joined terrorist organizations, it is clear that there is some combination of ideological, psychological, and community-based factors that leads them in that direction (see e.g., Schmid 2013). Those factors could take the form of "push" factors, such as government oppression or a systematic dearth of livelihoods, or "pull" factors, the elements about violent extremism that attract someone to it, such as a feeling of brotherhood, or even a salary.

Those factors may be countered through a range of activities on the spectrum of preventing terrorism by countering the root causes of motivation:

- *Prevention*, which consists of assessing the push and pull factors and addressing their root causes, such as efforts to integrate disenfranchised communities into broader societies or to create opportunities for hope among those who have lost it;
- *Intervention* and *disengagement*, which involves working with an individual whose behavior may suggest an interest in violent extremism and providing an "off-ramp" through mental health or religious counseling or alternative means of self-expression; and
- *Rehabilitation* and *reintegration*, which, similar to intervention, entail working with individuals who have paid their debt to society and seek to reform from previous violent extremist behavior and be reintegrated into society.

In practice, these efforts might range from countering the recruitment narratives of terrorist organizations, to creating opportunities for livelihoods or engagement with disenfranchised communities and individuals, to increased access to mental health and social service resources. And successful outcomes are typically most effectively achieved through empowering local communities to create intracommunity dialogue, build trust, and offer alternatives.

When we first began looking at practices such as these, there was some debate as to what we should call the overarching concept. Immediately after 9/11, anger fueled blame, which sometimes led to profiling based on ethnicity or religion. As initial efforts to "win hearts and minds" were considered, they were sometimes referred to as efforts to "counter *Islamic* extremism" or "counter violent *Islamic* extremism." These were misnomers, and it is important that we recognize the implications of that inaccuracy. Today, we often see expressions of rage that sometimes use religion as an explanation or excuse. Yet compared to the 1.6 billion Muslims in the world (Pew 2015), the few who have turned to extremism are a minuscule percentage; moreover, some of ISIL's recruits only converted to Islam to join ISIL and be part of a larger, and, to them, appealing, cause. To almost all Muslims, these extremists do not represent the true faith, and their interpretation of Islam is rejected. Why then should we use such terminology with respect to Islam when the U.S. government does not label others who commit acts of violence out of extremist religious conviction as, for example, Christian or Jewish extremists?

Therefore, the global community of nations, largely led by the United States, has decided to call this type of work "Countering Violent Extremism." In so doing, we are all recognizing that linking a religion to the extremism inaccurately implies a broader responsibility and that our justice systems are based on objective standards—meaning it is the action of violence that is the problem, not an extreme ideological viewpoint. While this debate may continue, it is important to remember that words matter, that words can create divisions and isolate those whom we wish to divert from extremism, ultimately undermining our efforts to end recruitment and reduce violence. That said, you will note in the Introduction to this volume of *The ANNALS* that the editors use the term "violent Islamist extremism" and explain their rationale for using the term. While I understand their effort to add clarity and focus in academic discussions, the public dialogue may not appreciate the fully accurate distinction they are putting forward.

Following the attacks on 9/11, it took the U.S. government some time to put these concepts into practice, but slowly we have begun to stand them up. Since then, we have adapted to a community-based approach. In the 2011 *Empowering Local Partners to Prevent Violent Extremism in the United States* (The White House 2011) and its corresponding implementation plan, the U.S. government outlined an approach to CVE that would push the activities of preventing radicalization out of the government's hands and into those of local community partners. Building on lessons learned from public health, gang prevention, and community trust-building efforts, the government conveyed the need to engage communities that felt marginalized, or experienced a real or perceived discriminatory impact from post-9/11 law and policy. Internationally, we created the Center for Strategic Counterterrorism Communications (now renamed the Global Engagement Center) to counter the message of groups like al-Qaeda, and later ISIL, and help foreign partners to do so as well. We also increased foreign assistance to foreign partner governments and civil society to help reduce the likelihood of radicalization. Unfortunately, these overall efforts still paled in comparison to other issue areas our government prioritizes. In 2015, regarding overseas approaches to terrorism specifically, only 6 percent of funding related to terrorism goes to our diplomatic and development communities (Belasco 2014), and under 8 percent of that funding is used for prevention activities (Romaniuk 2015). Domestically, the ratio is similar.

More hopefully, however, in 2015 the policy community's approach to CVE dramatically shifted, at least in terms of its priority. Following the tragic attacks in Paris against staff of the *Charlie Hebdo* magazine and a related attack at a grocery market, and building on a year of engagement with local authorities within the United States, President Obama convened both local and global leaders for a CVE Summit in February of that year (White House 2015a). The summit and follow-on events around the world showcased approaches to preventing extremist violence at the highest levels, and conveyed the need that we do more on the side of prevention (White House 2015b). So far, that heightened look at the issue has galvanized further efforts and freed up some funding (White House 2015b; U.S. Department of Homeland Security 2016b), but much more has yet to be done (Rosand 2016).

Preventing the next generation of recruits to terrorism has become more important than ever. A generation ago, individuals may have been radicalized by members of their local communities over the course of several years; now, while that still takes place, it is far more common to self-radicalize online. One example of the older model in transition is Zachary Chesser, a Virginia native who has plead guilty to supporting Somali terrorists and crimes of violence. He was a typical suburban Virginia youth; growing up, he was a good student and a soccer fan. He radicalized between 2008 and 2010, integrating online sources of extremism with in-person relationships and the exchange of formal letters.[2]

By contrast more recently, we now see individuals like the two men who departed London to fight with ISIL in Syria no less than two weeks after purchasing *Islam for Dummies* so they could learn the basic information about their purported cause (Dodd 2014). ISIL's deft use of Internet propaganda, together with that content's wide availability, has broadened the population of potentially vulnerable individuals, and shortened the timespan of their recruitment. According to researchers at the University of Maryland, radicalization of foreign fighters from the United States in 2002 took an average of 16.3 months, compared to 9.8 months in 2015 (Jensen, James, and Tinsley 2016). George Washington University (GW) researchers note that the role of the Internet in particular has facilitated "grooming from afar," with recruiters able to disguise their true nature behind the veil of online identities and use of online resources to target those most vulnerable, regardless of location (Vidino and Hughes 2015). As the GW report outlines, ISIL supporters in America are an "incredibly heterogeneous group" that is spread out across the country and is younger than recruits to previous violent extremist causes. One example is that of Mohamed Hamza Khan, who was arrested in 2014 at age 19 and whose road to radicalization took place in a relatively short window of time, seemingly entirely through online sources (Sullivan 2014).

In September 2014, ISIL conveyed a message to the world that was unusual for a terrorist organization. Beyond conveying their views of ISIL's prowess on the international stage, ISIL's spokesman released an audio message calling for individuals from around the world to join the so-called Caliphate, or—in a break from typical statements by terrorist organizations—to kill Westerners in their home countries. "[S]ingle out the disbelieving American, Frenchman, or any of their allies," the spokesman urged. "Smash his head with a rock, or slaughter him with a knife, or run him over with your car, or throw him down from a high place, or choke him, or poison him. . . . If you are unable to do so, then burn his home, car, or business. Or destroy his crops. If you are unable to do so, then spit in his face" (Bayoumy 2014).

Since then, we have had "ISIL-inspired" attacks worldwide, including in San Bernardino, California; Garland, Texas; and Chattanooga, Tennessee. In this new era, terrorism is no longer perpetrated only by career terrorists secretly plotting "spectacular attacks" from safe havens. We now have to fear terrorist threats from anyone, anywhere, in any way. While attacks from untrained lone actors tend to be unsuccessful or result in fewer casualties than carefully plotted attacks, Paris and San Bernardino and Brussels provide little solace. While Western countries, particularly America, tend to have strong law enforcement and counterterrorism capabilities, attacks still occur. Nonetheless, our approach is evolving. ISIL is no longer expanding and is, in fact, contracting in Syria and Iraq. As of this writing, the Coalition to Counter ISIL has destroyed more than 26,000 targets (U.S. Department of Defense 2016), killed 45,000 ISIL members (Wong 2016), and reclaimed 45 percent of ISIL territory in Iraq and 20 percent in Syria (Michaels 2016). Affected nations are sharing intelligence and information as never before, such as a 400 percent increase in INTERPOL watch-listing of foreign terrorist fighters in a two-year period (White House 2016). And individual countries are beginning to be serious about CVE at the local level, such as Vilvoorde, Belgium, and Aarhus, Denmark, taking new approaches of integration and understanding to engage at-risk individuals (e.g., Rosin 2016; Cendrowicz 2015). In light of the truly globalized nature of radicalization and recruitment to ISIL's cause, the imperative for a truly whole-of-society and global approach has never been more paramount.

Today, the United States, and our partners and allies abroad, have significantly stepped up efforts. Notably, at home, we have begun to broaden our efforts beyond engagement between government and communities, and have begun to fund programs to address the root causes of potential disenfranchisement. The U.S. Department of Homeland Security (DHS) has set up a new office (Johnson 2015) reporting directly to the Secretary and the White House has created an interagency "task force" led by DHS to coordinate and synchronize interagency CVE efforts across a range of programs and priority initiatives (U.S. Department of Homeland Security 2016a). We have also expanded government partnerships with Silicon Valley (Kang and Apuzzo 2016). We have sought a strong commitment from social media companies to help prevent the manipulation of their services for recruitment and radicalization, such as Alphabet (formerly Google) support for Google ad-based countermessaging (Greenberg 2016). Abroad, we are also funding more programs (Epstein, Lawson, and Tiersky 2016) and working closely with foreign partners to help them stand up similar prevention efforts, such as through establishing a Strong Cities Network for municipal leaders to coordinate local approaches on a global scale (Temple-Raston 2016). But even as we do so, some of those efforts are undermined by the proliferation of domestic extremist messages, blaming Muslims for terrorism, spreading Islamophobia in a way that could very well make the problem worse. It will be critical in the coming years not only to expand our efforts but to ensure our policies and our politics support the prevention of radicalization, not exacerbate it.

In the following articles, you will read a range of viewpoints and experiences from top experts in the CVE field. In the first article, Jessica Stern—a research professor at Boston University, who is part of an interdisciplinary team based at Boston's Children's Hospital that has been studying attitudes among Somali refugee youth in the United States and Canada—explains what drives individuals to extremist violence and sets the scene for how we might counter it.

In the next three articles, John Cohen, Hedieh Mirahmadi, and Katie Moffet and Tony Sgro present a comprehensive overview of how the United States has wrestled with these challenges in the various levels of government, in local communities, and in educational institutions, and how we can learn from what has been done here in America. John Cohen is a distinguished professor of professional practice in criminal justice at Rutgers University. He also served as the acting Undersecretary for Intelligence and Analysis and the Counter-Terrorism Coordinator in the U.S. Department of Homeland Security. Hedieh Mirahmadi is founder and a board member of the World Organization for Resource Development and Education (WORDE) and a world-renowned expert in CVE; she is a consultant to several federal departments and local law enforcement agencies in the United States. Tony Sgro is the founder and CEO of EdVenture

Partners, which created and manages the P2P: Challenging Extremism program—an initiative that counters violent extremism through youth engagement. Katie Moffett is Content Marketing Manager for EdVenture Partners, where she develops the firm's overall content strategy and brand development. She leads the marketing efforts for the P2P: Challenging Extremism program.

Karen Greenberg is a noted expert on national security, terrorism, and civil liberties and director of the Center on National Security at Fordham University School of Law. In her article, Greenberg looks at Internet recruitment and the challenges in countering it.

The articles by Judy Korn and Maqsoud Kruse offer a chance at comparison; Korn and Kruse explore how European and Muslim World partners are building their CVE efforts. Korn is a longtime leader against extremism who has worked with radicalized individuals; she is also the founder of the Violence Prevention Network in Germany. Kruse has served as the executive director of Hedayah, the International Center of Excellence for Countering Violent Extremism, since it was established in December 2012.

The next generation of recruits to groups such as ISIL can be minimized. The next several examples from our experts help to guide understanding of these issues and offer suggestions for the future. As dismal as threat assessments may sound, there is cause for optimism that we are moving in a positive direction, identifying better approaches to preventing radicalization, and empowering communities to take greater responsibility for building solutions.

Notes

1. See also Club de Madrid (2015).
2. George Washington University. 2012. Court documents, *United States of America v. Zachary Adam Chesser*. Washington, DC.

References

Bayoumy, Yara. 22 September 2014. ISIS urges more attacks on Western "disbelievers." *The Independent*.
Belasco, Amy. 8 December 2014. *The cost of Iraq, Afghanistan, and other global war on terror operations since 9/11*. RL33110. Washington, DC: Congressional Research Service.
Cendrowicz, Leo. 30 December 2015. Vilvoorde: The Brussels district fighting radicalisation with kindness. *The Independent*.
Club de Madrid. 28 October 2015. *Statement on preventing and countering violent extremism*. Available from http://www.clubmadrid.org/en/programa/policy_dialogue_2015.
Dodd, Vikram. 8 July 2014. Two British men admit to linking up with extremist group in Syria. *The Guardian*.
Epstein, Susan, Marian Lawson, and Alex Tiersky. 19 February 2016. *FY2017 State, foreign operations and related programs budget request: In brief*. R44391. Washington, DC: Congressional Research Service.
Greenberg, Andy. 7 September 2016. Google's clever plan to stop aspiring ISIS recruits. *Wired*.
Jensen, Michael, Patrick James, and Herbert Tinsley. 2016. *Overview: Profiles of individual radicalization in the United States - foreign fighters*. College Park, MD: National Consortium for the Study of Terrorism and Responses to Terrorism.

Johnson, Secretary Jeh C. 28 September 2015. Statement by Secretary Jeh C. Johnson on DHS's New Office for Community Partnerships. Washington, DC: U.S. Department of Homeland Security.

Kang, Cecilia, and Matt Apuzzo. 24 February 2016. U.S. asks tech and entertainment industries help in fighting terrorism. *New York Times*.

Michaels, Jim. 17 May 2016. ISIS loses 45 percent of territory in Iraq, 20 percent in Syria. *Military Times*.

Obama, President Barack. 23 May 2013. Remarks by the President at the National Defense University, Fort McNair, Washington, DC.

Pew Research Center. 7 December 2015. *Muslims and Islam: Key findings in the U.S. and around the world*. Washington, DC: Pew Research Center.

Romaniuk, Peter. 2015. *Does CVE work? Lessons learned from the global effort to counter violent extremism*. Washington, DC: Global Center on Cooperative Security.

Rosand, Eric. 20 April 2016. *The global CVE agenda: Can we move from talk to walk?* Washington, DC: Brookings Institution.

Rosin, Hanna. 15 July 2016. How a Danish town helped young Muslims turn away from ISIS. National Public Radio.

Schmid, A. P. 2013. Radicalisation, de-radicalisation, counter-radicalisation: A conceptual discussion and literature review. ICCT Research Paper 4, no. 2. The Hague: The International Centre for Counter-Terrorism.

Sullivan, Kevin. 8 December 2014. Three American teens, recruited online, are caught trying to join the Islamic State. *Washington Post*.

Temple-Raston, Dina. 1 March 2016. Communities encouraged to share ways to combat extremists. National Public Radio.

United Nations Security Council. 2014. Resolution 2178. New York, NY: United Nations.

U.S. Department of Defense. 31 May 2016. *Operation inherent resolve: Targeted operations against ISIL terrorists*. Special Report. Washington, DC: Department of Defense. Available from www.defense.gov/Special-Reports.

U.S. Department of Homeland Security. 8 January 2016 (2016a). Countering violent extremism task force. Washington, DC: Department of Homeland Security. Available from www.dhs.gov.

U.S. Department of Homeland Security. 6 July 2016 (2016b). Fact sheet: FY 2016 Countering violent extremism (CVE) grants. Washington, DC: Department of Homeland Security. Available from www.dhs.gov.

Vidino, Lorenzo, and Seamus Hughes. 2015. *ISIS in America: From retweets to Raqqa*. Washington, DC: George Washington University.

The White House. August 2011. *Empowering local partners to prevent violent extremism in the United States*. Washington, DC: The White House. Available from https://www.whitehouse.gov/sites/default/files/empowering_local_partners.pdf.

The White House. 18 February 2015 (2015a). Fact Sheet: The White House summit on countering violent extremism. Washington, DC: The White House, Office of the Press Secretary.

The White House. 29 September 2015 (2015b). Leaders' summit on countering ISIL and violent extremism. Washington, DC: The White House, Office of the Press Secretary.

The White House. 15 January 2016. Fact Sheet: Maintaining momentum in the fight against ISIL. Washington, DC: The White House, Office of the Press Secretary.

Wong, Kristina. 11 August 2016. General: 45,000 ISIS fighters killed in two years. *The Hill*.

Radicalization to Extremism and Mobilization to Violence: What Have We Learned and What Can We Do about It?

By
JESSICA STERN

This article discusses individual mobilization to extremist violence from the perspective of a researcher and analyst, exploring what we know about the psychological and social factors motivating young people to join extremist groups and how that knowledge relates to the recruitment of individuals into ISIS. The biggest threat to the West, at least for now, is not core ISIS (or any jihadi group operating in the Middle East and North Africa region), but Westerners who self-mobilize for attacks at home or who return, trained to fight, from the "jihad" abroad. Finally, the article suggests specific ways for governments to respond to this threat, noting the limits of what government can do, and arguing that they join forces with the private sector. Mobilization to extremism must be addressed with broad, multi-institutional social strategies.

Keywords: radicalization; mobilization to violence; risk factors; terrorism

How are individuals mobilized to join terrorist groups (Kruglanski et al. 2014, 69–93)?[1] How can the U.S. government make use of what scholars have learned about the process of mobilization to develop better policy responses?

The field of terrorism studies, or "terrorology," as it is sometimes called, has exploded since the 9/11 attacks (Silke and Schmidt-Petersen 2015; McCauley and Moskalenko 2014; Sageman 2004). Research has improved, partly as a result of an increase in government funding, and because significantly more data are available. Scholars from many disciplines are now contributing to the

Jessica Stern is a research professor at Boston University's Pardee School of Global Studies and a member of the Aspen Homeland Security Advisory Group. She is the author of numerous books and articles on terrorism. She served on President Clinton's National Security Council Staff in 1994–1995.

NOTE: The author thanks the editors of this special edition and her two tireless research assistants, Justin O'Shea and Jaclyn Roache.

Correspondence: sternjes@bu.edu

DOI: 10.1177/0002716216673807

literature, but most of the government funding has been used to produce incident-level databases or quantitative analyses (Sageman 2004, 565–80; McCauley and Moskalenko 2011);[2] few studies have addressed the question of how individuals are mobilized to become terrorists. Although this article's focus is the relatively under-studied topic of individual mobilization, it is still helpful to begin with a review of societal conditions that correlate with terrorism.

We are not able definitively to identify so-called root causes of terrorism, whether top-down (from society) or bottom-up (from the individual), but schol-ars are beginning to find correlations at the level of groups and societies (Crenshaw 2000).[3] For example, high male/female ratios (Hudson and Den Boer 2002) and youth bulges (Urdal 2006) have been shown to be risk factors for inter-nal war or terrorism.

While democracy is often thought of as a panacea for terrorism, studies by econometrician Alberto Abadie show that this is not the case and that the transi-tion from autocracy to democracy is itself a risk factor (Abadie 2006). Economists have clearly demonstrated that low gross domestic product (GDP) per capita is not correlated with terrorism risk (Abadie 2006, 50–56; Krueger 2008). For transnational terrorism, there is a U-shaped curve: as per capita income increases from a very low level, nationals become more likely to become perpetrators of transnational terrorism. But as incomes increase further, it becomes more diffi-cult to mobilize perpetrators of transnational terrorism (Elbakidze and Jin 2015, 1520–35).

Education is a complicated variable. When socioeconomic conditions are good, education makes mobilization to terrorism more difficult. But when these conditions are unfavorable, education is a risk factor, according to several studies (Brockhoff, Krieger, and Meierrieks 2015, 1186–1215; Gambetta and Hertog 2016). Risk factors for the emergence of suicide bombing campaigns include military occupation (Pape 2005), intergroup competition (Bloom 2005), and a perceived need to demonstrate dedication to the cause both to wavering follow-ers and to victims (Gambetta 2005), among many others (Moghadam 2008, 46–78). Additionally, failed states or states with weak regimes are often more likely to be sources of transnational terrorism as well as victims of their own domestic terrorist attacks (Piazza 2008, 469–88). Such work helps to identify societal con-ditions that are associated with the rise of terrorist groups, but it does not explain much about individual mobilization.

In this article, I discuss individual mobilization to radicalism from the perspec-tive of a researcher and analyst, exploring what we know about the psychological and social factors that motivate young people to join extremist groups and how that knowledge relates to the recruitment of individuals into ISIS (also known as ISIL or Islamic State). I pay specific attention to the recruitment of Westerners to radicalism, because Western recruits are the most significant threat to U.S. security. Finally, I suggest specific ways for governments to respond, noting the limits of what government can do and arguing that mobilization to extremism must be addressed with broad, multi-institutional social strategies.

Extant Research on Individual Mobilization

Part of what makes individual mobilization difficult to study is that terrorism remains a rare phenomenon: very few people are willing to join terrorist groups, even when they agree with the terrorists' political goals or share their sacred values (Atran 2006). Far more individuals hold radical views than are willing to engage in violent action (McCauley and Moskalenko 2008, 415–33). Given the rarity of terrorist mobilization—even in societies where the terrorists' stated grievances are broadly shared—it stands to reason that there must be individual risk factors that explain why some members of an aggrieved group join terrorist groups while most do not. Still, as Jeffrey Victoroff argued in his comprehensive and instructive review of psychological theories of terrorism, "any effort to uncover 'the terrorist mind' will more likely result in uncovering a spectrum of terrorist minds" (2005, 7).[4] Victoroff provides a research agenda for studying these "terrorist minds," but he also outlines the difficulties of pursuing such a project, including the danger inherent in interviewing terrorists, the difficulties of obtaining human-subjects approval, and, most importantly, the lack of funding (2005, 35).

Added to these difficulties is that for many years, scholars have shied away from identifying personal qualities or needs that might lead individuals to join violent extremist groups, focusing, instead, on the terrorists' *instrumental* goals— the political grievances that terrorists claim to be addressing. For many years, it has been deemed "politically incorrect" to focus on risk factors for terrorism at the level of individual psychology or beliefs. Scholars who focused on individual factors were subject to the claim that their work was journalistic, or that they were trying to downplay the importance of political grievances by suggesting that individual psychology might also be relevant to mobilization. "Die-hard social scientists still claim that the mind-sets of extremists are irrelevant," Diego Gambetta and Steffen Hertog observe (2016, 129).[5]

I have been interviewing violent extremists for many years, and I have found that individuals are mobilized to join terrorist organizations as they would any other organization: They concur with the group's mission; or they are persuaded to join by friends or family members; or they are attracted by the spiritual, emotional, or material benefits of belonging. Individuals are influenced at several different levels—personal psychology or history, group dynamics, and social conditions.

I am part of an interdisciplinary team based at Boston's Children's Hospital that has been studying attitudes among Somali refugee youth in the United States and Canada. Our study builds on a decade-long community-based research program focused on understanding and supporting the mental health of young Somali refugees.[6] To assess individual factors associated with resistance to or support for radicalization, we developed a survey instrument by working together with community partners. We used the Activism and Radicalism Intention Scales (ARIS), but adapted it in response to the input provided by our community partners (McCauley and Moskalenko 2009).[7] The questionnaire has been administered to more than four hundred ethnic Somalis in the United States and Canada; the vast majority of these youth were opposed to any form of violence, including violent activism.

Our research found that some participants who held attitudes that were support-ive of violent activism also were highly civically and politically engaged; others were not. A third group was moderately supportive of violent activism and also likely to be involved in gangs and other types of delinquency. Despite these differences, some common predictors of both prosocial and antisocial forms of activism have emerged. Moderate levels of trauma exposure and discrimination tend to be associated with support for both nonviolent and violent activism. In addition, our research suggests that there is a correlation between support for violent activism and social marginaliza-tion. Time on the Internet is another risk factor. We have also found that strong social bonds, and in particular a sense of attachment to the United States or Canada, are protective (Ellis, Abdi, Lazarevic, et al. 2015).

A survey of nearly two hundred Muslim immigrants in the United States revealed that those who identify with neither their heritage culture nor American culture are most prone to feeling marginalized and insignificant. The experience of discrimination made marginalized immigrants more likely to support a "radical interpretation of Islam," which was defined as support for combative jihad, among other variables (Lyons-Padilla et al. 2015).

Interestingly, one study has shown empirically that jihadists living in Muslim-majority countries are significantly better educated than jihadists who live in the West; and engineers are overrepresented from everywhere except Saudi Arabia, where engineering skills are prized and engineers are far less likely to be under-employed (Gambetta and Hertog 2016). Engineers do not seem to be recruited for bomb making, as might be hypothesized (Gambetta and Hertog 2016, 33).[8] The authors, Diego Gambetta and Steffen Hertog, propose two possible explana-tions for why engineers are recruited in such high numbers: unmet professional expectations and personality types. Three personality traits have been linked to right-wing attitudes by political psychologists: a desire to draw rigid boundaries between insiders and outsiders, a need for cognitive closure, and proneness to disgust.[9] The authors argue, based on survey data, that these traits are stronger among engineers and weaker among humanities and social science graduates (Gambetta and Hertog 2016).

In short, individuals are influenced and radicalized at several different levels. Risk factors for radicalization and mobilization start with a grievance, more or less widely shared, often about some form of social injustice. But not every per-son, living in difficult social conditions, is willing to take up arms to aim at non-combatants. Individual traits are important, significantly complicating the study of mobilization.

The influence of groups

Individuals are influenced by the people who surround them. They sometimes join institutions or groups, not so much because they believe in the cause, but because their friends persuade them to, or they receive benefits—unrelated to the mission—that they find attractive. This applies to joining a terrorist group equally as much as it applies to joining the board of a nongovernmental organiza-tion. A neo-Nazi whom I interviewed over several days admitted to me that part of his attraction to the far right was based on his interest in Nazi uniforms (Stern 2014). William Pierce, the author of the *Turner Diaries* and the founder of the American neo-Nazi group National Alliance, bought a music company that produced recordings known to be attractive to neo-Nazis (Anti-Defamation League n.d.). Once individuals are inside a group, group dynamics likely play a role in their decision-making. Scott Atran (2010) has found that while sacred values are significant for jihadists, social bonds and "altruistically" killing and dying for a "band of brothers" are even more important. Marc Sageman (2004), similarly, has found that social bonds are critical to the mobilization of groups.

There is undeniable appeal to joining a group that is fired up with righteous indignation. Some people, moved to help others, join political parties, raise money for causes, or try to increase awareness of injustices around the world. Some risk their lives covering war zones as reporters or as physicians helping the sick. But some individuals are willing to kill civilians as part of their holy war against perceived oppression, even though all mainstream religions forbid this. Sura 5:32 in the Qur'an states, "Because of that, We decreed upon the Children of Israel that whoever kills a soul unless for a soul or for corruption [done] in the land—it is as if he had slain mankind entirely." Matthew 5:21 of the New International Version of the Bible states, "You have heard that it was said to those of old, 'You shall not murder; and whoever murders will be subject to judgment.'" Some individuals, sadly, see jihad as a cool way of expressing dissatisfaction with a power elite, whether that elite is real or imagined, whether power is held by totalitarian monarchs or by democratically elected leaders. Many seek redemption from a sense of deep humiliation, while still others may believe they are participating in the lead-up to the End of Times. Because there is such a wide variety of "wants" satisfied by terrorist organizations, prevention and counter-radicalization programs need to be tailored to individual needs.

Terrorists often claim to be seeking strategic goals, for example, to establish a caliphate and change the world. To survive, however, they cannot focus exclusively on achieving their stated goals; they must recognize that participants in organizations are mobilized by multiple interests, both disparate and common, instrumental and expressive. Some are mobilized by material benefits, especially over time (Rapoport 1992).[10] These maintenance goals are required to secure the capital and labor needed to keep the organization in business; they often "absorb much energy; and, in the extreme (but perhaps not rare) case, they become ends in themselves" (Scott 1981, 52). Over time, groups that survive tend to evolve from the cause-maximizing end of the spectrum to the incentive-maximizing end (Stern 2003; Stern and Modi 2008).

How These Factors Apply to ISIS

ISIS claims to be aiming to change the world—to maintain and spread its so-called Caliphate. But the individuals who join the group are often mobilized by more mundane or personal factors, including the chance to be a hero, to remake themselves, or to earn a higher salary.

A team of decision analysts, commissioned by the U.S. Special Operations Command Central to determine what ISIS wants, concluded, based on a comprehensive review of ISIS's statements and interviews with subject-matter experts, that ISIS's strategic objectives include establishing, running, and expanding their Caliphate, as well as re-creating the power and glory of Sunni Islam (Siebert, Winterfeldt, and John 2016).[11] We can distinguish here between the strategic goal of the organization, its "mission," and the maintenance goals discussed above, required to secure and maintain labor. Although there was overlap with the strategic objectives of leaders, the team determined that followers' were seeking emotional, spiritual, and material goals, not only re-creating the glory of Sunni Islam, but also giving meaning to their own lives by acquiring status and wealth, joining a worthy cause, or feeling empowered. [12]

A terrorist leader has to be "almost a psychologist," as a former neo-Nazi put it to me (Stern 2003, 9–31). Terrorist leaders exploit a basic human need—the need for meaning, achievement, or esteem. One way of putting this, put forward by political psychologist Arie Kruglanski and others, is that terrorists are on a quest for personal significance (Kruglanski et al. 2014, 69–93). The leader has to make followers feel that by pursuing the terrorist mission, their quest for significance will be satisfied. The quest for significance is awakened by a loss of self-esteem, which could occur for entire groups or for individuals.

Mobilizing Labor:[13] How ISIS Seduces Personnel with a Promise of Protection and Redemption

Those living in ISIS-controlled territory are often disenfranchised Sunnis who feel ill-protected by their own governments. Local recruits from Iraq and Syria have admitted that working for ISIS was the highest-paying job they could find. To such disenfranchised Sunnis, ISIS offers physical protection, free housing, sexual partners, and a sense of purpose. It also offers what it refers to as the only Sharia-based state anywhere on earth.

In examining ISIS recruitment, many of my colleagues have focused on ISIS's "winner's" narrative and the carefully choreographed branding whereby ISIS advertises—and attempts to create—a utopian state (Miller and Mekhennet 2015). But I would suggest that ISIS is not as different from al-Qaeda as many experts think (see, for example, Barr and Gartenstein-Ross 2015; Fernandez 2016). The narrative of victory most appeals to those who feel they have lost something. And ISIS deliberately appeals to disenfranchised Muslims, as well as to potential converts around the world, to those—as ISIS puts it—"drowning in oceans of disgrace, being nursed on the milk of humiliation, and being ruled by the vilest of all people" (Van Ostaeyen 2015). To those oppressed, ISIS promises the opportunity "to remove the garments of dishonor, and shake off the dust of humiliation and disgrace, for the era of lamenting and moaning has gone and the dawn of honor has emerged anew" (Van Ostaeyen 2015). ISIS proclaims that "the sun of jihad has risen." In the twelfth issue of its online magazine, *Dabiq*, ISIS refers to its followers as "the brothers who have refused to live a life of humiliation" (Al-Ushan 2015).

An essay in *Dabiq* Issue 9 further underscores the promised reversal of fortunes. The author gloats that ISIS has established a true Caliphate, with "honor and pride for the Muslim and humiliation and degradation for the kaffir (apostates)" (Al-Muhajirah 2015). The victory ISIS speaks of is the victory of the formerly oppressed.

There are many reasons why this narrative of humiliation and redemption resonates in the Middle East, sociopolitics among them. According to a study by the Carnegie Middle East Center, Arab youth are not being adequately prepared to compete in a globalized society (Faour 2011). And the Middle East Policy Council finds that labor markets in many Arab states are incapable of producing enough jobs to sustain their growing youth populations (Akacem 2010).

Borrowing from the secular anticolonialist Franz Fanon, jihadi ideologues argue that violence is a way to cure the pernicious effects of centuries of humiliation and a "cleansing force" that frees an oppressed youth from his "inferiority complex," "despair," and "inaction," and restores his self-respect (Fanon 1963). However, unlike al-Qaeda, ISIS is a populist organization. It is seeking to seduce anyone and everyone who might be willing to join. One of the unique features of the group is that it tailors its narrative to individual recruits. But the overarching "victory" narrative, in my view, is meant to seduce those who feel the need to rise up against the oppressors. I hypothesize that the theme of civilizational humiliation resonates most deeply with individuals who have been subject to extreme trauma and personal humiliations, such as torture, pederasty, and rape, a hypothesis that requires further study.

Poor governance creates the conditions under which extremist groups thrive and are able to spread their message that the West is responsible for Arab plight. Many economists believe that a "natural-resource curse" prevents oil-rich countries from achieving viable democracies (Leite and Weidman 1999; Sachs and Warner 1997). But as demonstrated by the U.S. attempt to impose Iraqi democracy, democratization is not necessarily the best way to fight Islamist extremism. To the contrary, where there is an absence of institutions to protect minorities, majoritarian rule can actually lead to an increase in violence (Byman 2013).

In the Middle East and North Africa there are simultaneously a "youth bulge," an established risk factor for terrorism (Urdal 2006 607–29), and frustration among youth about their socioeconomic prospects. A poll carried out in sixteen countries in the Middle East and North Africa revealed that only 44 percent of 18- to 24-year-olds feel optimistic about their chances of finding appropriate jobs, and 53 percent felt it was more important for the government to provide stability than democracy (Siebert, Winterfeldt, and John 2016).[14] And yet while terrorist groups capitalize on these socioeconomic frustrations, only a very small portion of those that feel aggrieved will join. Seventy-seven percent of the youth surveyed were concerned about the rise of ISIS, with 50 percent calling ISIS the biggest obstacle facing the Middle East. These youth are exposed to the same disappointing sociopolitical environment as those who join ISIS. And yet nearly

80 percent ruled out joining the group, even if it moderated its level of violence.[15] These are hopeful findings.

The National Combatting Terrorism Center's preliminary evaluation of entry forms for more than four thousand ISIS recruits shows that recruits were better educated than average for the population from which they were drawn, but underemployed for their level of education. These were obtained by NBC News from an ISIS defector and chronicled intake forms from 2013 and 2014. Only 5 percent of the recruits described themselves as having an advanced understanding of Sharia, while 70 percent said that they had only a basic understanding. Saudi Arabia was the most important source of those most educated in Sharia law (forty-seven of seventy) and also the source of 64 percent of recruits with military or police backgrounds. All recruits were male, and the average age was 26 to 27 (Dodwell, Milton, and Rassler 2016). Underemployment appears to be a risk factor in many of the studies cited.

Mobilizing Attacks in the West

Sophisticated attacks outside ISIS-controlled territory require trained fighters, as evidenced in the November 2015 attack in Paris. But such attacks are significantly easier to carry out with operational assistance of local personnel. For ISIS, finding labor is less taxing when they can recruit from an existing pool of disenfranchised Muslims.

ISIS and the jihadi movement are in some ways similar to earlier revolutionary movements, such as Communism. In the Middle East, ISIS is exploiting Sunni disenfranchisement. But in the West, where many of its recruits are converts, we can compare its seductive appeal to the antiestablishment youth movements of the 1960s and 1970s, although its goals and the values it represents are of course quite different. Jihadists express their dissatisfaction with the status quo by making war, not love. They are seduced by Thanatos rather than Eros. They "love death as much as you [in the West] love life," in Osama bin Laden's famous and often-paraphrased words.

Western Recruits: The Most Significant Threat to the United States

Western recruits represent the principal threat to the United States, at least for now. As of fall 2015, more than nine hundred Americans have been investigated for ISIS-related activities, and as we have seen in San Bernardino and Orlando, ISIS is capable of inspiring American sympathizers with no direct ties to the group to attack at home (Vidino and Hughes 2015, 11; Brennan 2016). Recruitment often begins on social media platforms, as a coauthor and I discussed at great length in a recent book, and has been widely acknowledged (Stern and Berger 2015; Vidino and Hughes 2015; Berger and Morgan 2015). ISIS would very much like to turn

Western Muslims against their homelands. For now, at least, this has proven more easily accomplished in Europe than in the United States.

One primary explanation may be that the pool of disenfranchised Muslim youth is larger in Europe. European Muslim youth describe themselves, often accurately, as victims of prejudice in the workplace and in society more generally. In the most recent European Union Minorities and Discrimination Survey, one in three Muslim respondents reported experiencing discrimination, with the effect greatest among Muslims aged 16 to 24 (overall discrimination rates decline with age) (European Union Agency for Fundamental Rights 2009). Muslims in Europe are far more likely to be unemployed and to receive lower pay for the same work than "native" Europeans. Consequently, Muslim immigrants in Europe are disproportionately impoverished. While 10 percent of native Belgians live below the poverty line, that number is 59 percent for Turks and 56 percent for Moroccans in Belgium. There are 4.7 million Muslims living in France, many of them in poverty. An estimated 1,550 French citizens have left for Syria or Iraq; some 11,400 citizens have been identified as radical Islamists in French surveillance data (Kirk 2016; Atran and Hamid 2015).

By contrast, a majority of American Muslims are deeply integrated into American society. There is little evidence that "Islam hates America." On the contrary, American Muslims, on average, are happy to be living here. A 2011 poll carried out by the Pew Research Center on U.S. Politics and Policy showed that a majority of American Muslims were concerned about Islamic extremism, both at home and abroad (Pew Research Center 2011). Muslim Americans were significantly more satisfied (56 percent) with the way things were going in the United States than the general public (23 percent). Nearly two-thirds (66 percent) said that the quality of life for Muslims living in the United States was better than in most Muslim-majority countries. A majority believes that most Muslims who immigrate to the United States want to adopt American customs and way of life (Pew Research Center 2011).

These findings were corroborated by a smaller but more recent poll carried out by the Institute for Social Policy and Understanding, which confirmed that Muslims are significantly more satisfied with the direction the country is going than are other religious groups in the United States (Mogahed and Pervez 2016). That sentiment could change, however, with discussion of patrolling and controlling Muslim neighborhoods, or requiring Muslims to register with the U.S. government. That type of draconian curtailment of rights could actually facilitate and catalyze ISIS's goals of American Muslim alienation. It is worth noting that some 40 percent of those charged in connection with ISIS-related crimes were American-born converts to Islam.[16]

While mobilizing European Muslims appears to be an easier task than mobilizing Americans, at least for now, there are several areas in the United States where recruitment of clusters of individuals has been successful. These include Minneapolis-Saint Paul, Minnesota; New York City, New York; and St. Louis, Missouri. In most cases, according to the George Washington University Program on Extremism, a mix of social media and personal relationships were used to recruit these clusters.[17]

Responding to ISIS's Propaganda and Mobilization of Youth

Others in this volume are addressing the military response to ISIS as well as the failure of governments to confront socioeconomic issues in the Middle East, which I and many others have addressed elsewhere. Here, I focus on responding to ISIS's mobilization of volunteers.

Individuals who escaped from ISIS-controlled territory told the *Washington Post* that the organization has recruited personnel, often from the West, with expertise in social media, film-making, magazine layout, story telling, and so on, and that the individuals involved in ISIS's psychological operations are paid more than its fighters (Miller and Mekhennet 2015). This suggests that we need to respond in kind, by devoting a lot more attention to story telling and what George Kennan called "political warfare."

During the Cold War, psychological operations were a critically important part of the strategy to defeat the Soviet Union. In George Kennan's 1946 "long tele-gram," later published in *Foreign Affairs* as "The Sources of Soviet Conduct," Kennan described the difficulties faced by the Marxists in attempting to spread their revolutionary movement in Russia, and urged that the West should contain the Soviets rather than attempt to defeat them. There, he wrote:

> Lacking wide popular support for the choice of bloody revolution as a means of social betterment, these revolutionists found in Marxist theory a highly convenient rationaliza-tion of their own instinctive desires. It afforded pseudo-scientific justification . . . for their yearning for power and revenge and for their inclination to cut corners in the pursuit of it. (Kennan 1947)

If we exchange "Salafi jihadist theory" for "Marxist theory," this description might equally apply to ISIS and the way it rules inside the territory it controls. Kennan argued that the establishment of dictatorial power becomes a necessity when the broader population does not share in the revolutionaries' zeal. And it is for this reason that ISIS has imposed dictatorial powers, as described by some who have managed to escape (Weiss 2015).

Kennan, the architect of containment, considered psychological operations, or "political warfare," to be even more important than military operations in the effort to defeat the Soviet regime and its false promises. In 1948, he argued that

> political warfare is the logical application of Clausewitz's doctrine in time of peace. In broadest definition, political warfare is the employment of all the means at a nation's command, short of war, to achieve its national objectives. Such operations are both overt and covert. They range from such overt actions as political alliances, economic measures (as ERP), and "white" propaganda to such covert operations as clandestine support of "friendly" foreign elements, "black" psychological warfare and even encouragement of underground resistance in hostile states. (Kennan 1948)

This argues for a significantly beefed-up containment effort against ISIS, one that could profitably be modeled on an updated version of Kennan's notion of political warfare. Initiating it will require input from business leaders, attorneys, philanthropists, and the government, just as was the case for political-warfare operations against the Soviet Union. Students and teachers should be brought into the effort. An effective political warfare operation will require, in the words of Bernard Haykel (2015), "engaging in cultural and educational efforts to defeat ISIS's ideology that sanctifies violence as the only means for Sunni empowerment and glory."

Western governments are not equipped to do this alone. Haykel (2015) notes that "it is an effort that must emerge from within the Arab and Muslim communities." Saudi Arabia, as the source of the "untamed Wahhabism" that underlies ISIS ideology, has an important role to play moving forward (Kirkpatrick 2014). Arab states need to offer more than military support; they need to lead the containment of ISIS ideology and to model alternative narratives.

ISIS is spreading a bad—but still seductive—idea that has dispersed way beyond the borders of its Caliphate, not only into areas of poor governance and weak states, but also into the West. We cannot deploy drones against an ideology, and we cannot deploy them against our ISIS-affiliated enemies in the West. Countering ISIS's propaganda is essential, and the foregoing leads me to offer this specific plan.

Amplify the stories of the real wives of ISIS and other defectors. We need to amplify the stories of defectors and refugees from the areas that ISIS controls. For example, one of the three British schoolgirls who left her East London home in February 2016, apparently to join ISIS, had been in contact with an infamous ISIS recruiter, Aqsa Mahmood, who specializes in recruiting young women to serve as "jihadi wives." Stories about the horrific real lives of jihadi wives need to be told, by women who manage to run away.

Take on ISIS's version of Islam in a way that appeals to potential ISIS recruits. ISIS has developed convoluted arguments about why it engages in war crimes that are forbidden by Islamic law. Thousands of religious scholars have taken on ISIS's interpretation of Islam, but the scholars' style of presenting their arguments is often boring to the kind of young people drawn to ISIS propaganda. They present their ideas in ways that appeal to those who share their mainstream views, not young adults who are ignorant about Islam. Duke University's Muslim chaplain, who is an expert at talking to kids, has sometimes been brought in to help "de-radicalize" kids converted to what he calls "ISIS Islam."[18] He said that having these youth read the Qur'an is an important first step; they often realize they have no interest in Islam at all. At least some of those potential recruits to "ISIS Islam" can be reached via social media, including via one-on-one conversations.

Highlight ISIS's hypocrisy. ISIS makes much of its supposed puritanical virtue and promotion of chastity, whipping women who do not wear attire ISIS considers appropriate, and executing gay men by throwing them off the tops of buildings. Yet according to the UN and ISIS's own propaganda, its fighters are involved in a wide range of horrifying acts of sexual abuse, from sexual slavery to the reported rape of men and women, including both adults and children. In this area and many others, ISIS's deranged double standards should be addressed head-on.

Publicize ISIS's atrocities against Sunnis. We need to fully exploit aerial and electronic surveillance and remote imaging to show what really happens in the belly of the beast. We should pay particular attention to documenting war crimes and atrocities against Sunni Muslims in regions controlled by ISIS. It is obvious that ISIS has no qualms about advertising its war crimes against certain classes of people—Shi'a Muslims primarily, and religious minorities like the Yazidis. ISIS claims to protect Sunnis from sectarian regimes in both Iraq and Syria. While ISIS is happy to flaunt its massacres of Shi'ites and Iraqi military personnel, it has been relatively quiet in regard to its massacres of uncooperative Sunni tribes. Our countermessaging should highlight the murder of Sunnis in particular.

Aggressively suspend ISIS social media accounts. There is a robust debate over the merits of suspending extremist social media accounts, which encompasses a complex set of issues including free speech and the question of who should decide what content is acceptable. What we do know, based on an analysis of tens of thousands of Twitter accounts, is that suspensions do limit the audience for ISIS's gruesome propaganda. The current rate of suspensions is damaging the ISIS social media machine. The practice should be maintained at the current rate at the very least, but it would be better for Twitter and other social media companies to get even more aggressive.

Conclusion

The nations fighting ISIS need a counternarrative campaign. The campaign should be led by individuals who know how to access at-risk youth. A commission needs to study how ISIS and related groups market themselves and develop a plan for competing directly in those markets, while at the same time developing a strategy for expanding into other markets.

One model that is helping experts access at-risk youth directly is called P2P: Challenging Extremism (see Moffett and Sgro, this volume). This ongoing initiative provides an opportunity for university students from the United States, Canada, the Middle East, North Africa, Europe, Australia, and Asia to create online communities whose goal is to counter the extremist narrative by becoming educated influencers. With support from the U.S. Department of State and Facebook, the effort is being run by a private organization called EdVenture Partners, which helps companies like Honda market to youth. After students conduct primary research, they compete to create the best products, tools, or digital initiatives to reach their peers and spread narratives against extremism.

Containing ISIS will take a multipronged approach, including, most importantly, pressure on its real-world components. But the presence of Western troops on the ground entails significant risk and could backfire by helping ISIS recruit additional personnel who buy into its false narrative about a Western crusade against Islam. While social media campaigns will not defeat ISIS, they can plant seeds of doubt, which former terrorists often describe as central to their decisions to leave terrorism behind. With a major effort, it has been possible to alter narratives in respect to other dangerous activities. Consider the Centers for Disease Control and Prevention's antismoking campaign involving tips from former smokers, which reportedly led 100,000 individuals to give up smoking in its first three-month-long effort. We need an analogous campaign of tips from former jihadists, spread widely over the ever-changing social media environment and beyond. Such a campaign, to be effective, will require money and effort. But the cost of such efforts is tiny compared to that of military force, whether counted in dollars, loss of life, or blowback on American streets. It is a smart investment.

Notes

1. In the U.S. government, the term "radicalization" is usually used to denote adherence to radical beliefs, while "mobilization" denotes the turn to violence in service of those beliefs. I use these terms in the way that it used by the U.S. government. For an excellent discussion of what "radicalization" entails, see Kruglanski et al. (2014).

2. John Monahan (2012) summarizes several (as yet untested) attempts to identify individual risk factors for terrorism, including McCauley and Moskalenko (2011).

3. Martha Crenshaw has been arguing for years that terrorism arises from a combination of social and individual factors.

4. For an excellent assessment of the difficulties of identifying individual risk factors for terrorism, see Monahan (2012). See also Lafree and Dugan (2009).

5. For example, over many years, Israeli psychologist Ariel Merari has attempted to identify some personality characteristics of Palestinian suicide attackers, including by systematically evaluating all of the failed suicide bombers held in Israeli prisons, and comparing them with controls. He found that a significant minority of the interviewees had at least some suicidal tendencies (40 percent) and that a "dependent/avoidant" personality might be a risk factor. His findings were tentative: he concluded that the number of failed bombers was too small to draw statistically significant conclusions, but still large enough to warrant further research. Still, his work was criticized as evincing "unconscious political interest" on the part of some of the interviewers, who hoped to "depoliticize and delegitimize the Palestinian national movement." See Merari, Diamant, et al. (2010); Merari, Fiugel, et al. (2010); Merari (2010); see also Brym and Araj (2012); Stern (2003).

6. Community-based participatory research (CBPR) is an approach to research that involves a partnership between academic and community stakeholders in which the needs, capacity, and knowledge of the community of study are central to the research. See Israel et al. (1998).

7. The original ARIS was designed (by Moskalenko and McCauley [2009]) to assess readiness to participate in legal or illegal/violent political action, and to be used as an indicator of radical intent among groups potentially vulnerable to terrorist recruitment. Ellis and colleagues adapted the scale to be used with Somali refugees after receiving detailed feedback from Somali community leaders (Ellis, Abdi, Horgan, et al. 2015). The scale includes four items assessing readiness to participate in legal political action (activism) and five items assessing readiness to participate in illegal and violent political action (radicalism).

8. The ratio of bomb makers among engineers is no higher than it is for jihadists with other degrees; see Gambetta and Hertog (2016, 33).

9. For a detailed discussion of sources, see Gambetta and Hertog (2016).

10. Very few terrorist groups get past identifying their collective cause or mission, to successfully secure the capital, labor, and brand that are required to persist. Indeed, according to a study by political scientist David Rapoport (1992), 90 percent of terrorist organizations survive less than a single year; and of those that manage to survive beyond the first year, more than half disappear within the following decade.

11. Findings were based on a comprehensive review of ISIS leaders' speeches, social media postings, as well as interviews with subject matter experts.

12. Twenty-four percent of youth believe that the primary reason that youth are attracted to ISIS is poor job prospects. (Another 24 percent could not understand why anyone would join ISIS.) See www .arabyouthsurvey.com.

13. ISIS needs both capital and labor. Here I only discuss labor.

14. Findings were based on a comprehensive review of ISIS leaders' speeches, social media postings, as well as interviews with subject matter experts. See www.arabyouthsurvey.com.

15. Concern about lack of job opportunities remains an issue across the sixteen countries polled, with fewer than half (44 percent) agreeing with the statement that there are good job opportunities in the areas they live in. Concern is particularly high in those countries where Daesh (ISIS) has actively recruited young people. Just 2 percent of young Yemenis, 7 percent of Libyans, 20 percent of Palestinians, 21 percent of Lebanese, 28 percent of Tunisians, and 39 percent of young Iraqis believe that they have good job opportunities available to them in their country.

16. According to analysis by George Washington University's Program on Extremism, approximately 38 percent of Americans charged in connection with ISIS-related crimes are converts. See https://cchs .gwu.edu/sites/cchs.gwu.edu/files/downloads/Snapshot_Update_March_0.pdf.

17. See https://cchs.gwu.edu/sites/cchs.gwu.edu/files/downloads/Snapshot_Update_March_0.pdf.

18. Imam Abdullah Antelepi, speaking at Ethics Policy Forum, March 15, 2016, http://eppc.org/publi cations/dr-jessica-stern-and-imam-abdullah-antepli-at-the-march-2016-faith-angle-forum/.

References

Abadie, Alberto. 2006. Poverty, political freedom, and the roots of terrorism. *American Economic Association* 2:50–56.

Akacem, Mohammed. 2010. Book review: *Arab economies in the twenty-first century* by Paul Rivlin. 17 (4) Washington, DC: Middle East Policy Council.

Al-Muhajirah, Umm Sumayyah. 21 May 2015. Slave-girls or prostitutes? *Dabiq* 9:46.

Al Ushan, Isa Ibn Sa'd. 2015. Advice to the Mujahidin: Listen and obey. *Dabiq* 12:9–10.

Anti-Defamation League. n.d. *The Turner diaries. Extremism in American.* Philadelphia, PA: Anti-Defamation League. Available from archive.adl.org.

Atran, Scott. 2006. The moral logic and growth of suicide terrorism. *Washington Quarterly* 29 (2): 127–47.

Atran, Scott. 2010. *Talking to the enemy: Violent extremism, sacred values, and what it means to be human.* New York, NY: Penguin.

Atran, Scott, and Nafees Hamid. 16 November 2015. Paris: The war ISIS wants. *The New York Review of Books.*

Barr, Nathaniel, and Daveed Gartenstein-Ross. 2015. *The winner's messaging strategy of the Islamic State.* Washington, DC: Foundation for Defense of Democracies. Available from http://www.defenddemoc racy.org/content/uploads/publications/The-Winner%E2%80%99s-Messaging-Strategy-of-the-Islamic-State-Wikistrat-report.pdf.

Berger, J. M., and Jonathan Morgan. 2015. *The ISIS Twitter census: Defining and describing the population of ISIS supporters on Twitter.* The Brookings Project on U.S. Relations with the Islamic World. Analysis Paper 20. Washington, DC: Center for Middle East Policy at Brookings Institution.

Bloom, Mia. 2005. *Dying to kill: The allure of suicide terror.* New York, NY: Columbia University Press.

Brennan, John. 16 June 2016. Statement as prepared for delivery before the Senate Select Committee on Intelligence. Washington, DC: Central Intelligence Agency.

Brockhoff, Sarah, Tim Krieger, and Daniel Meierrieks. 2015. Great expectations and hard times. *Journal of Conflict Resolution* 59 (7): 1186–1215.

Brym, Robert J., and Bader Araj. 2012. Are suicide bombers suicidal? *Studies in Conflict & Terrorism* 35:432–43.

Byman, Daniel. 12 December 2013. The Resurgence of al Qaeda in Iraq. Testimony before the House Committee on Foreign Relations. Available from https://www.brookings.edu/testimonies/the-resur gence-of-al-qaeda-in-iraq/.

Crenshaw, Martha. 2000. The psychology of terrorism: An agenda for the 21st century. *Political Psychology* 2:405–20.

Dodwell, Brian, Daniel Milton, and Don Rassler. 2016. *The Caliphate's global workforce: An inside look at the Islamic State's foreign fighter paper trail*. Westpoint, NY: Combating Terrorism Center at West Point, United States Military Academy.

Elbakidze, L., and Y. H. Jin. 2015. Are economic development and education improvement associated with participation in transnational terrorism? *Risk Analysis* 35 (8): 1520–35.

Ellis, B. Heidi, Saida M. Abdi, John Horgan, Alisa B. Miller, Glenn N. Saxe, and Emily Blood. 2015. Trauma and openness to legal and illegal activism among Somali refugees. *Terrorism and Political Violence* 27 (5): 857–83.

Ellis, B. Heidi, Saida M. Abdi, Vanja Lazarevic, Matthew T. White, Alisa K. Lincoln, Jessica E. Stern, and John G. Horgan. 2015. Relation of psychosocial factors to diverse behaviors and attitudes among somali refugees. *American Journal of Orthopsychiatry*. doi:10.1037/ort0000121.

European Union Agency for Fundamental Rights. 2009. *EU-MIDIS: European Union Minorities and Discrimination survey, main results report*. Vienna: European Union Agency for Fundamental Rights. Available from http://fra.europa.eu/sites/default/files/fra_uploads/664-eumidis_mainreport_conference-edition_en_.pdf.

Fanon, Frantz. 1963. *The wretched of the earth*. New York, NY: Grove Press.

Faour, Muhammad. 2011. *The importance of education in the Arab world*. Washington, DC: Carnegie Endowment for International Peace.

Fernandez, Alberto. 2016. *Here to stay and growing: Combating ISIS propaganda networks*. Washington, DC: The Brookings Institute. Available from https://www.brookings.edu/wp-content/uploads/2016/07/IS-Propaganda_Web_English_v2-1.pdf.

Gambetta, Diego. 2005. *Making sense of suicide missions*. Oxford: Oxford University Press.

Gambetta, Diego, and Steffen Hertog. 2016. *Engineers of jihad: The curious connection between violent extremism and education*. Princeton, NJ: Princeton University Press.

Haykel, Bernard. 19 November 2015. Paris confirms IS's weakness. *The Hindu*.

Hudson, Valerie, and Andrea Den Boer. 2002. A surplus of men, a deficit of peace: Security and sex ratios in Asia's largest states. *International Security* 4:5–38.

Israel, Barbara A., Amy J. Schulz, Edith A. Parker, and Adam B. Becker. 1998. Review of community-based research: Assessing partnership approaches to improve public health. *Annual Review of Public Health* 19:173–202.

Kennan, George. July 1947. The sources of Soviet conduct. *Foreign Affairs*.

Kennan, Goerge F. 30 April 1948. George F. Kennan on organizing political warfare. Wilson Center History and Public Policy Program Digital Archive. Available from http://digitalarchive.wilsoncenter.org/document/114320.

Kirk, Ashley. 24 March 2016. Iraq and Syria: How many foreign fighters are fighting for ISIL. *The Telegraph*.

Kirkpatrick, David D. 24 September 2014. ISIS' harsh brand of Islam is rooted in austere Saudi creed. *New York Times*.

Krueger, Alan B. 2008. *What makes a terrorist*. Princeton, NJ: Princeton University Press.

Kruglanski, Arie W., Michele J. Gelfand, Jocelyn J. Belanger, Anna Sheveland, Malkanthi Hetiarachchi, and Rohan Gunaratna. 2014. The psychology of radicalization and deradicalization: How significance quest impacts violent extremism. *Political Psychology* 35 (S1): 69–93.

Lafree, Gary, and Laura Dugan. 2009. Research on terrorism and countering terrorism. *Crime and Justice* 38:413–77.

Leite, Carlos, and Jens Weidman. 1999. *Does mother nature corrupt? Natural resources, corruption, and economic growth*. Washington, DC: International Monetary Fund.

Lyons-Padilla, Sarah, Michele J. Gelfand, Hedieh Mirahmadi, Mehreen Farooq, and Marieke van Egmond. 2015. Belonging nowhere: Marginalization & radicalization risk among Muslim immigrants. *Behavioral Science & Policy* 1 (2): 1–12.

McCauley, Clark, and Sophia Moskalenko. 2008. Mechanisms of political radicalization: Pathways toward terrorism. *Terrorism and Political Violence* 20 (3): 415–33.

McCauley, Clark, and Sophia Moskalenko 2011. *Friction: How radicalization happens to the them and to us*. New York: NY: Oxford University Press.

McCauley, Clark, and Sophia Moskalenko. 2014. Some things we think we've learned since 9/11: A commentary on Marc Sageman's "The stagnation in terrorism research." *Terrorism and Political Violence* 26 (4): 601–6.

Merari, Ariel. 2010. *Driven to death*. Oxford: Oxford University Press.

Merari, Ariel, Ilan Diamant, Arie Bibi, Yoav Broshi, and Gora Zakin. 2010. Personality characteristics of "self martyrs"/"suicide bombers" and organizers of suicide attacks. *Terrorism and Political Violence* 22:87–101.

Merari, Ariel, Jonathan Fiugel, Boaz Ganor, Ephraim Lavie, Yohanan Tzoreff, and Arie Livne. 2010. Making Palestinian "martyrdom operations"/"suicide attacks": Interviews with would-be perpetrators and organizers. *Terrorism and Political Violence* 22:102–19.

Miller, Greg, and Souad Mekhennet. 20 November 2015. Inside the surreal world of the ISIS propaganda machine. *The Washington Post*.

Mogahed, Dalia, and Fouad Pervez. 2016. *American Muslim poll: Participation, priorities, and facing prejudice in the 2016 elections*. Deerborn, MI: Institute For Social Policy and Understanding (ISPU). Available from http://www.ispu.org/pdfs/repository/amp2016.pdf.

Moghadam, Assaf. 2008. *The globalization of martyrdom*. Baltimore, MD: John Hopkins University Press.

Monahan, John. 2012. The individual risk assessment of terrorism. *Psychology, Public Policy and Law* 18 (2): 167–205.

Moskalenko, Sophia, and Clark McCauley. 2009. Measuring political mobilization: The distinction between activism and radicalism. *Terrorism and Political Violence* 21:239–60.

Pape, Robert A. 2005. *Dying to win: The strategic logic of suicide terrorism*. New York, NY: Random House.

Pew Research Center. 2011. *Muslim Americans: No signs of growth in alienation or support for extremism*. Washington, DC: Pew Research Center. Available from http://www.people-press.org/2011/08/30/muslim-americans-no-signs-of-growth-in-alienation-or-support-for-extremism/.

Piazza, James A. 2008. Incubators of terror: Do failed and failing states promote transnational terrorism? *International Studies Quarterly* 52:469–88.

Rapoport, David C. 1992. Terrorism. In *Routledge encyclopedia of government and politics*, vol. 2, eds. Mary Hawkesworth and Maurice Kogan. London: Routledge.

Sachs, Jeffrey D., and Andrew M. Warner. 1997. *Natural resource abundance and economic growth*. Cambridge, MA: Center for International Development and Harvard Institute for International Development.

Sageman, Marc. 2004. *Understanding terror networks*. Philadelphia, PA: University of Pennsylvania Press.

Scott, W. Richard. 1981. *Organizations: Rational, natural, and open systems*. 2nd ed. Englewood Cliffs, NJ: Prentice Hall.

Siebert, Johannes, Detlof von Winterfeldt, and Richard S. John. 2016. Identifying and structuring the objectives of the Islamic State of Iraq and the Levant (ISIL) and its followers. *Decision Analysis* 13 (1): 26–50.

Silke, Andrew, and Jennifer Schmidt-Petersen. 2015. The golden age? What the 100 most cited articles in terrorism studies tell us. *Terrorism and Political Violence*. doi:10.1080/09546553.2015.1064397.

Stern, Jessica. 2003. *Terror in the name of God: Why religious militants kill*. 1st ed. New York, NY: Ecco.

Stern, Jessica. 2008. Organizational forms of terrorism. In *Countering the financing of terrorism*, eds. Thomas Biersteker and Sue Eckert. With Amit Modi. New York, NY: Routledge.

Stern, Jessica. 2014. X: A case study of a Swedish Neo-Nazi. *Behavioral Sciences & the Law* 32 (3): 440–53.

Stern, Jessica, and J. M. Berger. 2015. *ISIS: The state of terror*. 1st ed. New York, NY: Ecco.

Urdal, Henrik. 2006. A clash of generations? Youth bulges and political violence. *International Studies Quarterly* 50:607–29.

Vanostaeyen, Pieter. 2015. The Islamic State restores the Caliphate. Available from https://pietervanostaeyen.wordpress.com/2014/06/.

Victoroff, Jeff. 2005. The mind of the terrorist: A review and critique of psychological approaches. *Journal of Conflict Resolution* 49 (1): 3–42.

Vidino, Lorenzo, and Seamus Hughes. 2015. *ISIS in America: From retweets to Raqqa*. Washington, DC: Program on Extremism, The George Washington University.

Weiss, Michael. 18 November 2015. How I escaped from ISIS. *The Daily Beast*.

The Next Generation of Government CVE Strategies at Home: Expanding Opportunities for Intervention

By
JOHN D. COHEN

Using social media and other Internet-based communication platforms, groups such as ISIS have become effective at influencing vulnerable, disaffected young people who are in search of some sense of social connection and greater life purpose and encouraging them to commit acts of violence on behalf of their extremist cause. Traditional counterterrorism-related investigative strategies are insufficient to prevent these acts of targeted violence by lone offenders. Accordingly, we must expand the use of behavioral risk assessment methodologies as part of investigative protocols. We must empower local partnerships among law enforcement; the communities they serve; and others such as mental health professionals, educators, and faith leaders. Countering the terrorist narrative is not enough; we must adapt our efforts and prioritize holistic and collaborative ways to detect, assess, and intervene in situations where individuals may exhibit the behaviors and indicators of violent extremism in order to prevent a violent attack.

Keywords: violence; extremism; mass casualty attacks; targeted violence; intervention

O n February 25, 2015, in a speech before the nation's state attorneys general, Federal Bureau of Investigation (FBI) Director James Comey raised concerns over the growing risk of a terrorist attack within the United States by self-radicalized individuals (Alpert 2015). The director's stark description of the domestic threat posed by independent, self-radicalized, ideologically motivated, violent extremists was consistent with the views held by a number of other law enforcement and

John D. Cohen is a distinguished professor of professional practice in criminal justice at Rutgers University. He has 32 years of experience in law enforcement and homeland security operations, including having served as the acting Undersecretary for Intelligence and Analysis and the Counter-Terrorism Coordinator in the United States Department of Homeland Security.

Correspondence: john.cohen@rutgers.edu

DOI: 10.1177/0002716216669933

security officials.[1] And while the threat posed by domestic violent extremists such as those inspired by antigovernment and white supremacist causes has existed for years, the director's comments reflected an increased level of concern over both the nature and the size of the threat and the fact that international terrorist groups such as the Islamic State in Iraq and Syria (ISIS, also known as the Islamic State or ISIL) were increasingly and effectively using sophisticated social media campaigns to inspire individuals to conduct attacks in furtherance of the group's global objectives. In the time that has passed since the director's comments, and notwithstanding extensive investigative efforts by law enforcement authorities,[2] the nation has experienced a number of violent incidents by ISIS-inspired individuals including attacks in Orlando, Florida; San Bernardino, California; Garland, Texas; and Chattanooga, Tennessee.[3] There have also been multiple mass casualty attacks by individuals motivated by non-ISIS-related ideological narratives, including the murder of nine congregants of a historic African American church in Charleston, South Carolina (Gumbel 2015). Accordingly, countering the threat posed by violent individuals motivated by extremist ideology, but who operate independent of designated terrorist organizations, has emerged as a top law enforcement and security concern for the United States government and local officials (Alpert 2015).

In many cases, an individual's journey from extremist thought to violent action may take only a matter of months. Violent extremists in the United States are mostly self-radicalized, self-trained, self-executing, and ideologically ignorant. Expanded use of social media and Internet forums by terrorist organizations (such as ISIS) and domestic extremist groups has dramatically expanded the ability of these groups to spread their extremist narrative and influence the behavior of a vulnerable subset of the U.S. population. A growing body of analysis and research by law enforcement and mental health professionals has revealed that there is no religious, ethnic, or socioeconomic profile even among those motivated by extremist ideologies such as those of terrorist groups like ISIS. However, a number of common behavioral and psychological characteristics are shared by this population of offenders. Once committed to the extremist cause, these individuals can acquire preoperational intelligence and materials to be used in an attack via the Internet and, more importantly, without ever having to meet with collaborators. Detection of these potential attackers is difficult for intelligence or law enforcement authorities, who are using traditional counterterrorism tools that were designed primarily to detect those communicating with or working under the direction and control of a foreign terrorist organization. However, this does not mean that individuals go unnoticed. In most cases, those radicalized to violence exhibit behaviors of concern that are observed by those who associate with that individual. This is why United States law enforcement and homeland security officials have sought to develop and employ locally based prevention strategies designed to aid authorities in detecting those on the verge of ideologically motivated violence. These programmatic efforts have become known as "countering violent extremism" (CVE).

Initially, efforts to prevent ideologically motivated violence was a matter to be handled by law enforcement authorities who leveraged traditional investigative strategies to disrupt or investigate after the acts of violence were committed. Over time and based on growing concerns over al-Qaeda- or ISIS-inspired attacks, national CVE efforts expanded to include engagement and outreach campaigns directed at mostly Muslim and Arab American community organizations. The goal of these outreach and engagement activities was to foster greater collaboration in an effort to better detect potential threats from within those communities. These outreach efforts were received with mixed reactions, in some cases elevating tensions between government authorities and the community members with which they sought to engage. Some communities viewed engagement efforts with suspicion, regarding these efforts as a way for law enforcement to recruit informants or mask domestic surveillance activities.

As the nation approaches the 2016 presidential election, the domestic threat posed by violent extremists has shown no sign of abating. However, there has been significant growth in research and analysis that has revealed much about the behavioral characteristics of violent extremists and how those characteristics relate to behaviors associated with mass casualty attacks based on nonideological motives. In 2016, based on this knowledge, a new model for preventing violent extremist attacks emerged. It is an operational model informed by long-standing behavioral risk assessment and threat management techniques employed by organizations such as the United States Secret Service and involves incorporating CVE into community-based, multidisciplinary activities intended to prevent targeted violent activity and mass casualty attacks more broadly. This article describes the evolution of national efforts to address violent extremism in the United States and recommends steps that should be taken to adapt that strategy.

Countering Violent Extremism: An Evolving Strategy

The national strategy

In August 2011, the While House released *The National Strategy for Empowering Local Partners to Prevent Extremism in the United States* (herein "the Strategy"), which outlined a national community-based approach for CVE and the federal government's role in empowering local stakeholders to build resilience against violent extremism (White House 2011a). The Strategy rightfully acknowledged that "(1) communities provide the solution to violent extremism; and (2) CVE efforts are best pursued at the local level, tailored to local dynamics, where local officials continue to build relationships within their communities through established community policing and community outreach mechanisms" (White House 2011a).

The strategic implementation plan

In December 2011, the White House released the *Strategic Implementation Plan for Empowering Local Partners to Prevent Violent Extremism in the United States*

(SIP), which set forth a series of concrete actions intended to specifically counter violent extremism that were consistent with the Strategy. Through SIP, the federal government hoped to achieve several long-term objectives, including:

- Establishing platforms throughout the country for including communities that may be targeted by violent extremists for recruitment and radicalization into ongoing federal, state, and local engagement efforts;
- Supporting that engagement through a task force of senior officials from across the government;
- Supporting community-led efforts to build resilience to violent extremism;
- Expanding analysis in depth and relevance and sharing the results with those determined to need it, including governor-appointed homeland security advisors, major cities chiefs, mayors' offices, and local partners;
- Training federal, state, tribal, and local government and law enforcement officials on community resilience, CVE, and cultural competence and requiring that training meet rigorous professional standards; and
- Ensuring local partners, including government officials and community leaders, better understand the threat of violent extremism and how they can work together to prevent it (White House 2011b).

SIP outlined a series of activities to counter violent extremism. The goals were to be accomplished through existing funding and by prioritizing certain resources already available to relevant departments and agencies. Some of these activities were specific to CVE, while others addressed broader nonsecurity policy objectives while also having an indirect effect on countering radicalization to violence (White House 2011b). Through the activities described in SIP, the federal government sought to foster a whole-of-government approach that leveraged existing public safety, violence prevention, and resilience programming while placing local United States Attorneys in a leadership role. The intention of SIP was to ensure closer coordination between international and domestic efforts focused on CVE while ensuring that attention was paid to both physical and virtual environments (White House 2011b).

Three-city pilot project

In April 2014, the White House announced the establishment of pilot programs in Boston, Massachusetts; Los Angeles, California; and Minneapolis, Minnesota. Each of these programs was organized under the leadership of the local United States Attorney and was intended to have federal agencies work more closely with local authorities, faith leaders, and others to expand local partnerships needed to prevent ideologically motivated violence.[4]

CVE task force

In January 2016, the Department of Homeland Security (DHS) and the Department of Justice announced the creation of a CVE task force, which would be led by DHS and the Department of Justice, with additional staffing provided by representatives from the FBI, National Counterterrorism Center, and other departments and agencies. The goal of the task force is to enhance the nation's CVE efforts by (1) synchronizing and integrating whole-of-government CVE programs and activities; (2) leveraging new CVE efforts, for example, those of the DHS Office for Community Partnerships; (3) conducting ongoing strategic planning; and (4) assessing and evaluating CVE programs and activities (U.S. Department of Homeland Security 2016).

The CVE task force will organize federal efforts into several areas, including (U.S. Department of Homeland Security 2016):

- **Research and Analysis.** The task force will coordinate federal support for ongoing and future CVE research and establish feedback mechanisms for CVE findings, cultivating CVE programs that incorporate sound research into their designs.
- **Engagements and Technical Assistance.** The task force will synchronize federal government outreach to and engagement with CVE stakeholders and will coordinate technical assistance to CVE practitioners.
- **Communications.** The task force will manage CVE communications, including media inquiries, and leverage digital technologies to engage, empower, and connect CVE stakeholders.
- **Interventions.** The task force will work with CVE stakeholders to develop multidisciplinary interventions such as mental health treatment, faith counseling, and educational support.

Challenges

There are critics of both the strategic direction and implementation of federal CVE efforts. Privacy, civil liberty, and some Muslim organizations have raised concerns over what they interpret as the Strategy's unfair emphasis on targeting Muslims and Arab Americans. Further, the American Civil Liberties Union has raised concerns about the Strategy's emphasis on "counter-narratives" and potential government censorship. Others, including some members of Congress, hold the opposite view, suggesting that the president's Strategy may address violent extremism too broadly and that federal efforts should prioritize the threat posed by Islamic violent extremist (Collins and Lieberman 2011; King 2011). Other concerns have focused on resources allocated to and management of the Strategy, as well as a lack of performance metrics. Some have cited the lack of progress as an indicator that the Strategy is failing. Concern has been raised over how the Strategy draws a distinction between programmatic efforts to prevent ideologically motivated attacks from those efforts intended to prevent non–ideologically motivated mass casualty attacks. Law enforcement and mental health experts have pointed to common behavioral and psychological characteristics present within the group of offenders who commit mass casualty attacks and have suggested that focusing on the threat of targeted violence and mass casualty attacks broadly is programmatically a more effective approach than limiting the focus discretely on CVE (Weine and Cohen 2015).

Understanding and Managing the Threat: Expanding Opportunities for Intervention

Who becomes a violent extremist in the United States?

There is no single economic, religious, ethnic, cultural, or educational profile for a violent extremist.[5] However, a growing body of research and analysis reveals that extremist causes resonate with a subset of our population who are vulnerable to such influences because of their psychological and life experience characteristics (Weine and Cohen 2015). A subset of these individuals will commit violent acts to further these extremist narratives. A review of past cases involving ideologically motivated violence illustrates that many of these individuals come from problematic family environments[6] and feel disconnected from their community. Many have suffered a series of life failures and are searching for some cause or group connection that provides them with a sense of belonging or meaning (Weine and Cohen 2015). These individuals tend to spend a lot of time alone, online, viewing violent postings and playing violent virtual games (Weine and Ahmed 2012). A significant subset of these people present underlying mental health issues, and some have a history of criminal behavior (Weenink 2015). In many cases, while these individuals gravitate toward an extremist cause to justify violent behavior, they rarely achieve more than a superficial understanding of the ideology itself. In short, these are disaffected young people searching for something that provides meaning to their lives—and they are finding a deep and meaningful connection with extremist and terrorist groups such as ISIS or finding meaning in the social connectivity that comes from adopting the cause that others have adopted (Haque et al. 2015). Understanding these dynamics is important because it explains why extremist narratives seem to resonate with a growing number of young Americans and provides insight into potential intervention opportunities but also calls into question strategies that emphasize counter-narrative development.[7]

Managing the threat through assessment and intervention

A growing number of law enforcement officials believe that operational efforts to counter violent extremism will benefit if they become intertwined with broader community-based, multidisciplinary violence prevention efforts directed at preventing targeted acts of violence and mass casualty attacks.[8] These community-based efforts would complement traditional law enforcement strategies (investigation, arrest, and prosecution) with systematic processes to identify, assess, and manage potential threats in the "precriminal space," that is, prior to the violation of law (Meloy and Hoffman 2013). "Threat assessment and management, by its nature, is a multi-disciplinary approach drawing from a variety of fields to enhance understanding of the nature and dynamics of targeted violence. Practitioners also draw upon a range of disciplines in developing and implementing strategies to prevent, disrupt, and mitigate the likelihood and impact of acts of violence" (Deisinger and Randazzo 2016, 3). Threat assessment and management through intervention in the pre-criminal space provide the foundation for efforts to counter violent extremism within that same local environment.[9]

Intervention efforts work best when local law enforcement officials work with community members, mental health professionals, faith leaders, and educators to detect individuals who pose a risk of committing a violent attack and intervene prior to such an occurrence. Emerging models of intervention emphasize early attention to underlying causal issues (mental health, family, social, and so on) before such issues lead to violent behavior. Law enforcement may be involved in this early stage, but it could also include some other type of support, such as mental health support.[10]

A growing number of local communities across the nation have employed this type of approach (Weine and Cohen 2015). Replicating best practices in which individuals deemed "high-risk" are "redirected" away from violence holds promise in not only preventing violent extremism but also preventing other types of mass casualty attacks and even gang-related violence.[11] Future federal efforts should focus on incorporating behavioral risk assessment methodologies as an element of broader investigative strategies and violence prevention efforts. Furthermore, the federal government should expand support for locally based, multidisciplinary violence prevention efforts that seek to leverage, when appropriate, community-based, multidisciplinary intervention efforts. This support should encourage cohesive and structured collaboration achieved through the establishment of multidisciplinary teams that combine community, mental health, and law enforcement components to provide five levels of capability (see Figure 1).

(1) **Community-level pattern detection, reporting, and referral:** Educate community members to identify indicators of and patterns associated with an increased risk for violence. Establish communication pathways to enable community members to inform those authorities responsible for conduct of a formal risk assessment.

(2) **Behavioral risk assessment:** Establish, train, and maintain a cadre of community-based professionals (law enforcement, mental health, and so on) to assess an individual's risk for violent behavior (this assessment should look beyond whether elements of a crime are present).

(3) **Disruption:** If elements of a crime have been met and/or an individual is in the mobilization stage, traditional law enforcement strategies should be employed to prevent a violent attack.

(4) **Intervention and containment (for use in precriminal space):** Establish, teach, and maintain a cadre of community-based professionals to implement strategies that address causal factors directly. The goal is to reduce an individual's social or psychological commitment to violence and includes increased engagement among the individual and local community members and agencies.

FIGURE 1

Targeted Violence: Five Community Intervention Decision Points

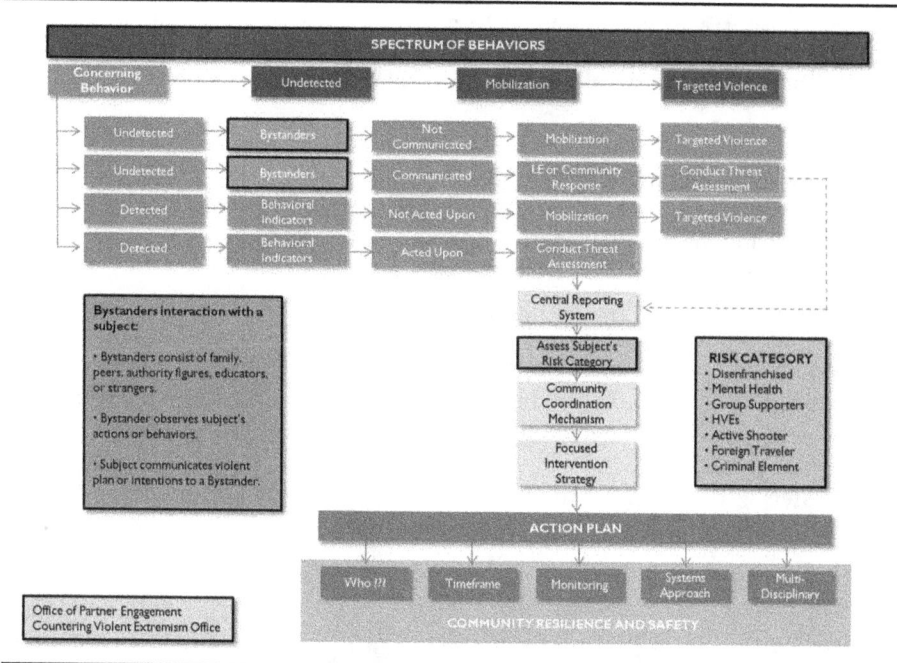

SOURCE: Courtesy of the FBI Office of Partner Engagement.

(5) **Monitoring and assessment:** Establish, teach, and maintain a cadre of community-based professionals to monitor and assess an individual's risk for violent behavior as intervention efforts proceed and measure the impact that the program as a whole is having on priority outcomes (Weine and Cohen 2015).

To be successful, government and nongovernment authorities must have a consistent understanding of the goals and objectives of these efforts. In many cases, efforts to expand opportunities for non–law enforcement intervention will occur in local communities where there exists a high level of distrust between community members and law enforcement. As efforts begin to foster multidisciplinary collaboration, it is critical that these efforts be carried out in a transparent manner. It should be clear that while law enforcement "disruptions" of terrorist plots are important and will continue, that the primary goal of these activities is to prevent violence through the application of non–law enforcement intervention activities. Community members may question whether this "whole-of-community" approach is subterfuge and really intended to enable law enforcement surveillance by encouraging "neighbors spying on neighbors." To counteract these concerns, it is crucial that communication among key stakeholders and all planning efforts are open and transparent to all members of the community. Ultimately, however, community trust will come through the actions of those implementing this whole-of-community approach. Therefore, as a matter of practice and policy, these efforts must demonstrably focus on the following (FBI 2016, 4):

- Enhancing a community's resilience to violence;
- Increasing awareness about the forms and dynamics of violent extremism;
- Enhancing information sharing among those stakeholders who can provide support and services to high-risk individuals;
- Facilitating disengagement programs to turn at-risk individuals away from violent behavior;
- Leveraging school-based programs, enhanced mental health services, counseling, and other non–law enforcement opportunities to deter individuals from embracing violence to further extremist ideologies or other perceived grievances; and
- Fostering the ideals of diversity, inclusion, and tolerance while upholding constitutional freedoms and rights under law.

Conclusion

Aggressive law enforcement efforts remain necessary to counter violent extremism, but they alone are no longer sufficient. The United States is moving to an approach to CVE that recognizes the limitations of "detect and arrest" in the new threat environment; traditional law enforcement tactics must be supplemented by approaches that engage local communities and civil society to identify at-risk individuals and to develop other, earlier forms of intervention.

The federal government simply does not have the resources to conduct surveillance and investigate the expanding number of individuals who derive inspiration from terrorist groups or extremist ideological causes. Furthermore, traditional counterterrorism-related investigative strategies may be insufficient to prevent acts of targeted violence. Accordingly, we must incorporate behavioral risk assessment methodologies into the investigative processes associated with terrorism tips and lead evaluation. We must also empower local efforts to strengthen critical partnerships among law enforcement; the communities they serve; and others such as mental health professionals, educators, and faith leaders. Countering the terrorist narrative is not enough—we should adjust our efforts to counter violent extremism and prevent mass casualty attacks to take into account the behavioral dynamics of this offender population. Finally, we must create holistic and collaborative ways to detect, assess, and intervene in situations where individuals may exhibit the behaviors and indicators of violent extremism in order to prevent a violent attack.

Notes

1. This is not to say that the nation does not face a serious threat from international terrorist organizations that seek to attack the United States at home or its interests abroad. Clearly it does. Foreign terrorist organizations such as al-Qaeda, its affiliates, and the Islamic State continue to plot and plan attacks against the United States and still seek to recruit, train, prepare, and control those who will conduct attacks against airplanes, mass transit systems, airports, and other locations where people congregate. These terrorist groups operate in zones of conflict or ungoverned spaces in the Middle East and parts of Africa and seek to gain control of territory and resources, but they also focus on attacking the West.

2. At the time, the FBI reported that there were open investigations in all fifty states.

3. Attacks by violent extremist are not limited to those inspired by the ideology of groups such as ISIS and al-Qaeda. Nor is the use of mass casualty attacks limited to those who are inspired by extremist ideology. In fact, at the same time that we are experiencing an increase in violent extremist behavior within the United States, there has also been an increase in mass casualty attacks by individuals seeking recourse from some non–ideologically inspired grievance.

4. The Strategy rightfully acknowledges the importance of connecting efforts to prevent ideologically motivated violence with broader local activities focused on violence prevention. However, in practice, the emphasis of federal efforts to date has been on engagement with Muslim organizations through local "round-table" events and developing strategies to counter the narrative of terrorist groups such as the Islamic State. The Strategy's initial emphasis on engagement with Muslim and Arab American organizations overlooks two key factors. First, those at risk of becoming radicalized to violence (even adherents to the ideology of groups such as ISIS) do not all come from the Arab American or Muslim communities, and some adopt violent extremist ideological views that have nothing to do with Islam. Focusing attention primarily within the Muslim or Arab American communities may result in overlooking individuals from outside those communities who may represent a threat. Second, while countering the narrative is a worthy goal, the majority of those who become violent place a stronger value on the social connection and life meaning that come from joining a cause versus the substance of the ideology. Therefore, understanding and addressing underlying issues influencing why these narratives are resonating with a growing number of young people is an important goal versus simply providing a counter-narrative.

5. As it relates to those inspired by the ideology of groups such as ISIS, some come from the Muslim community, but others do not. Some embrace Islam during the radicalization process, but others do not. In an article entitled, "Why Are Young Westerners Drawn to Terrorist Organizations Like ISIS?" the authors write, "The reasons that youths join terrorist organizations such as ISIS have little to do with being poor, brainwashed, a Muslim, or a psychopath, and more to do with vulnerabilities in human nature exacerbated by aspects of Western society. … For those westerners in transition, marginalized, lonely, lost, bored, uncertain, spiritually or existentially dispossessed, burdened by too much freedom, and empathetically selective, ISIS and other shallow but contagious ideologies will remain tempting as quick fixes for the deep predicaments inherent to the human condition" (Haque et al. 2015, 10).

6. Dysfunctional family environment and disconnection from community are some examples. A recent FBI study found that 74 percent of cases of ISIS-inspired radicalization can be attributed in large part to unhealthy family dynamics.

7. ISIS has employed a highly sophisticated and dynamic social media campaign in an effort to inspire people in Western Europe and the United States in particular to conduct violent attacks at home and to do so independent of the organization's command and control structure. Using social media provides ISIS an adaptable method of communication; if a site gets shut down, they simply create a new one. But the success of these efforts has more to do with the content of the postings. These are postings that are specifically designed to appeal to and inspire young westerners. They are short and in English, the speakers use Western slang, and the videos are scored with hip hop and rap music. They romanticize the cause of these extremist organizations and the conditions in which they operate, but, more importantly, they convey a promise to the viewer that they could be a meaningful part of a great cause, and therefore their life can have meaning. And while these postings may offer false hope, they are intended to be attractive to and resonate with people who are searching for some meaning in their life and for something to belong to—for those individuals, these postings are very powerful.

8. While programmatically the approach employed by individual jurisdictions may vary, an operational model for countering violent extremism has emerged that prioritizes greater collaboration among law enforcement personnel, neighborhood organizations, mental health professionals, educators, and faith-based entities who work together to identify and prevent acts of violence by high-risk individuals.

9. CVE is solely focused on preventing acts of violence by those motivated by extremist ideologies. The goal is not to monitor or restrict extreme thoughts or speech.

10. One key challenge that local leaders face is how best to bring together law enforcement, mental health professionals, faith leaders, educators, community advocates, parents, and peers to assess risk and develop intervention strategies specific to the precriminal space. Success requires all stakeholders to move beyond a strict "identify and arrest" approach. Instead, strategies should include an emphasis on intervention in the pre-criminal space that goes beyond criminal justice approaches and focuses also on detecting risks and getting help for those who need it. A growing number of jurisdictions are exploring how to expand multidisciplinary violence prevention efforts to incorporate detection and mitigation of potential mass casualty violence. For example, the Safety Net Collaborative in Cambridge, Massachusetts, aims to "foster positive youth development, promote mental health, support safe school and community environments, and limit youth involvement in the juvenile justice system through coordinated prevention, intervention, and diversion services for Cambridge youth and families"; see www.cambridgema.gov. This program has become one of the foundations of the Boston Strategic Plan to Counter Violent Extremism, which was produced through the White House–led Three Cities Countering Violent Extremism initiative (U.S. Department of Justice 2015).

11. Deerborn, Michigan; Cambridge Massachusetts; and Rutland, Vermont, all have mature programs and are examples of "best practices."

References

Alpert, Bruce. 15 February 2015. FBI director says probes into homegrown violent extremists reach all 50 states. *The Times-Picayune*.

Collins, Susan, and Joe Lieberman. 3 August 2011. Lieberman, Collins react to administration strategy to counter violent extremism. Washington, DC: U.S. Senate Committee on Homeland Security and Governmental Affairs. Available from www.hsgac.senate.gov.

Deisinger, Gene, and Marisa Randazzo. April 2016. Targeted violence in schools: Understanding mental health and managing risks. *Police Chief Magazine*. Available from http://www.policechiefmagazine.org/magazine/index.cfm?fuseaction=display_arch&article_id=3491&issue_id=92014.

Federal Bureau of Investigation (FBI), Office of Partner Engagement. January 2016. *Preventing violent extremism in schools*. Washington, DC: FBI.

Gumbel, Andrew. 25 June 2015. Beyond Dylann Roof: Inside the hunt for domestic extremism in the digital age. *The Guardian*.

Haque, Omar Sultan, Juhye Choi, Tim Phillips, and Harold J. Bursztajh. 10 September 2015. Why are young westerners drawn to terrorist organizations like ISIS? *Psychiatric Times*.

King, Peter. 3 August 2011. King statement on Obama administration violent extremism strategy. Available from www.peteking.house.gov.

Meloy, J. Reid, and Jens Hoffman. 2013. Threat assessment and threat management. In *International handbook of threat assessment*, eds. J. Reid Meloy, Stephen D. Hart, and Jens Hoffmann, 3–17. New York, NY: Oxford University Press.

U.S. Department of Homeland Security. 8 January 2016. Countering Violent Extremism Task Force. Washington DC: Department of Homeland Security. Available from www.dhs.gov.

U.S. Department of Justice. 15 February 2015. *Pilot programs are key to our countering violent extremism efforts*. Washington, DC: U.S. Department of Justice. Available from www.usdoj.gov.

Weenink, Anton W. 2015. Behavioral problems and disorders among radicals in police files. *Perspectives on Terrorism* 9 (2). Available from http://www.terrorismanalysts.com/pt/index.php/pot/article/view/416/html.

Weine, Stevan, and John D. Cohen. 2015. *Moving beyond motive-based categories of targeted violence*. With support from Dave Brannegan. Argonne, IL: Argonne National Laboratory.

Weine, Stevan, and Osman Ahmed. 2012. *Building resilience to violent extremism among Somali-Americans in Minneapolis-St. Paul*. Final Report to Human Factors/Behavioral Sciences Division, Science and Technology Directorate, U.S. Department of Homeland Security. College Park, MD: U.S. Department of Homeland Security.

The White House. August 2011 (2011a). *The national strategy for empowering local partners to prevent extremism in the United States*. Washington, DC: The White House.

The White House. December 2011 (2011b). *Strategic implementation plan for empowering local partners to prevent violent extremism in the United States*. Washington, DC: The White House.

Building Resilience Against Violent Extremism (BRAVE), the World Organization for Resource Development and Education (WORDE)'s community-based approach to countering violent extremism (CVE), has gained international recognition for its approach to CVE and its emphasis on research-driven strategies. This article provides an overview of the BRAVE model and suggests practical steps for how to structure an effective, research-based CVE program, based on the BRAVE experience.

Keywords: BRAVE; WORDE; CVE; violent extremism

Building Resilience against Violent Extremism: A Community-Based Approach

By
HEDIEH MIRAHMADI

Violent Extremism: An Increasing Threat

Preventing violent extremism—both within the United States and abroad—will remain a national security priority for the upcoming administration, given the multifaceted and expanding nature of the threat. There are a wide range of actors and movements that compose the threat matrix—including sovereign citizens; militia groups; issues-based extremists, such as eco-terrorists; ideologically linked gangs/organized criminal networks; and Islamist extremists, such as ISIS, al-Qaeda, and Al-Shabab. Islamist extremists compose a fraction of the overall threat in the United States (Kania and Kramer 2011; see also Shane 2015),[1] but in other regions, these groups claim responsibility

Hedieh Mirahmadi is founder and a board member of the World Organization for Resource Development and Education (WORDE). An expert in countering violent extremism (CVE), she is a consultant to several federal and local government agencies and serves as a senior advisor to the FBI, Countering Violent Extremism Section. She has testified before the U.S. Senate and the House of Representatives on violent extremist threats and has coauthored numerous reports and manuals on violent extremism.

Correspondence: hedieh13@gmail.com

DOI: 10.1177/0002716216671303

for the majority of terrorist attacks, political instability, civil strife, and sectarian discord.

In addition to recruiting individuals to support violent extremist organizations (VEOs) abroad, some organizations such as ISIS (also known as the Islamic State or ISIL) and al-Qaeda encourage radicalized individuals to carry out attacks on U.S. soil. To complicate matters further, most plots, such as the 2009 Fort Hood shooting carried out by Nidal Hassan, are executed by "lone-wolf" terrorists who are not connected operationally to a larger foreign terrorist organization. Such attacks pose significant challenges for law enforcement officials to identify and disrupt (Southern Poverty Law Center 2015).

Underutilized Resources in the Fight against Extremism

Interviews with community leaders in Indonesia, Pakistan, Egypt, the UK, and the United States indicate that parents, teachers, religious leaders, counselors, and social service providers may be best positioned to identify individuals vulnerable to radicalization, and to mobilize resources to intervene should these individuals become radicalized. Community-based approaches can be effective in building resilience against violent extremism (Mirahmadi, Farooq, and Ziad 2010), but they remain an underutilized resource.

The U.S. government first articulated a strategy to leverage community resources to tackle violent extremism with the release of the 2011 White House *Strategic Implementation Plan for Empowering Local Partners to Prevent Violent Extremism in the United States*. While the plan recognizes the role communities can play in collaboration with law enforcement agencies to protect America, it does not specify how public officials should establish those relationships; nor does it include any benchmarks for partnership. The plan also does not provide guidelines for how law enforcement can refer radicalized individuals for interventions or how community groups might conduct interventions with radicalized or at-risk individuals. In short, while the plan articulates a commitment to empowering communities, it does little in terms of providing guidance, funding, or resources to encourage the development of such initiatives. This article is a step toward filling that void: I provide an overview of a community-based countering violent extremism (CVE) program—Building Resilience Against Violent

NOTE: The views presented in this article are those of the author and do not necessarily represent the views of the U.S. government. The author would like to thank the important contributions made to development of the BRAVE model from its public and community partners in Montgomery County including Reverend Mansfield Kaseman and Bruce Adams in the County Executive's Office; Police Chief J. Thomas Manger; Assistant Chiefs McSwain, Reynolds, and Hammill of the Police Department; Ms. Uma Ahluwalia and Jay Kenney of the Department of Health and Human Services; Rabbi Batya Steinlauf; Reverend Carol Flett; Imam Faisul Khan; Ms. Mimi Hasannein; and Imam Jamil Dasti, as well as countless other faith leaders who serve as the cornerstone of the effort to promote social cohesion and public safety. This project would also not have been possible without the tireless efforts of WORDE staff, including Mehreen Farooq, Samia Haque, Nouf Bazaz, and Mona Haggag.

Extremism (BRAVE)—and reflect on what it tells us about building research-based CVE programs.

BRAVE: A Community-Led Model

Recognizing the increasing violent extremist threat, the World Organization for Resource Development and Education (WORDE) established the first community-led CVE program in the country to prevent radicalization. Launched in April 2013, and informally known as the "Montgomery County model," the initiative is now being replicated as the BRAVE model in other counties across America.

The model utilizes an evidence-based collective-impact approach to increase the citizen's role in upholding public safety—including intervening in the lives of vulnerable individuals before they choose a path of violence.

Understanding Radicalization

Though the U.S. government and its allies have spent millions of dollars in research to determine what causes radicalization, there is still no such thing as a terrorist profile, and no single factor can predict who will become a terrorist (Horgan 2009; Horgran 2014, 87).

What we do know from empirical research on convicted terrorists and terrorist incidents are some common indicators that exist in many of those cases, which may make an individual more vulnerable to recruitment and radicalization.

WORDE utilizes a "cluster model" approach,[2] which groups factors into five clusters to provide a systematic way of measuring potential risks for an individual who may be more vulnerable to radicalization and recruitment by extremist groups. These potential risk factors include sociological motivators, psychological conditions, ideology/belief/and values, political grievances, and economic factors. These potential risk factors can apply to any form of violent extremism (see Figure 1).

In the matrix in the figure, each bubble represents a set of *potential* risk factors or drivers of violent extremism. Because there are no studies to date that have demonstrated a causal link between any one risk factor, or combination of factors, and an individual becoming a terrorist, use of the term "risk factor" is not predictive of who will become radicalized. The matrix provides a structural guide to explore variables that have a potential to contribute to one's radicalization.

Within each category, there are multiple "push" and "pull" factors highlighted that may influence an individual's susceptibility to radicalization. Push factors are "the negative social, cultural, and political features of one's societal environment that aid in 'pushing' vulnerable individuals onto the path of violent extremism." Pull factors are "the positive characteristics and benefits of an extremist organization that 'pull' vulnerable individuals to join" (Hassan 2012, 18). It is important to note that these factors can independently have an effect on an individual, or several factors can overlap and have a cumulative impact.

FIGURE 1
WORDE's Potential Risk Factors in a Radicalization Matrix

Five Potential Risk Factors that Might Influence Radicalization

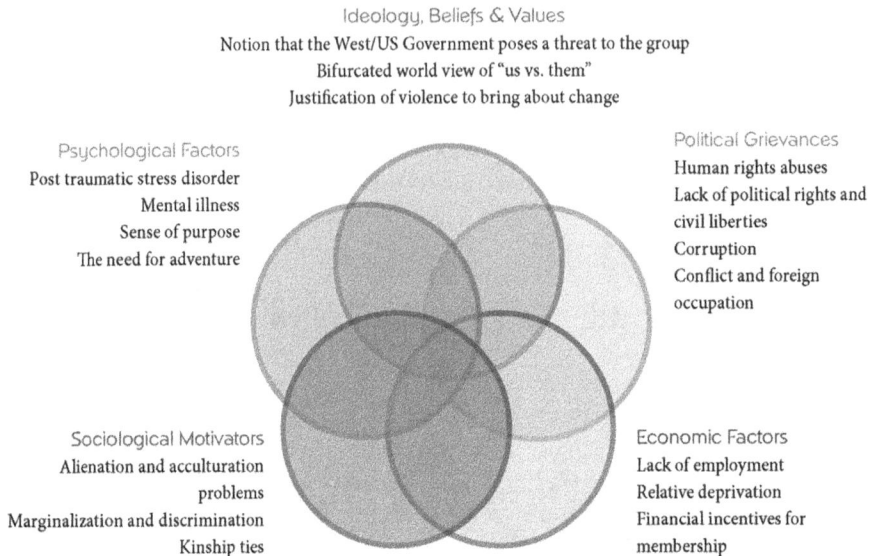

Ideology, Beliefs & Values
Notion that the West/US Government poses a threat to the group
Bifurcated world view of "us vs. them"
Justification of violence to bring about change

Psychological Factors
Post traumatic stress disorder
Mental illness
Sense of purpose
The need for adventure

Political Grievances
Human rights abuses
Lack of political rights and
civil liberties
Corruption
Conflict and foreign
occupation

Sociological Motivators
Alienation and acculturation
problems
Marginalization and discrimination
Kinship ties

Economic Factors
Lack of employment
Relative deprivation
Financial incentives for
membership

© WORDE

A Closer Look at Potential Risk Factors

Sociological motivators

That sociological factors, such as group dynamics and kinship ties, and in particular, familial, tribal, and peer groups, have contributed to radicalization is well documented in previous research (Davis et al. 2009; see also Saltman and Smith 2015).[3] A 2006 study of European extremists, for example, noted that for more than 35 percent of the sample population, social networks that had existed prior to joining militant groups played a critical role in the radicalization process (Bakker 2006). Such networks can exert peer pressure and other means to influence individuals to support extremist activities.

Individuals who are socially alienated are also at greater risk of being recruited by violent extremists, because these groups often offer a social network, or a place where lonely individuals can cultivate a sense of belonging (Kruglanski et al. 2009; Sageman 2011, 122; Saltman and Smith 2015, 9). A recent study conducted in partnership with WORDE and researchers at the University of Maryland found that immigrants who struggle with acculturation and identify with neither their heritage culture nor the culture they are living in are at an increased risk of feeling marginalized and isolated. The study found that experiences of discrimination often make the situation worse and could lead to greater support for radical, fundamental groups (Lyons-Padilla et al. 2015).

Further, a lack of protective resources can lead to greater vulnerability, especially for youth. Protective resources are social and psychosocial factors that can stop, delay, or diminish negative outcomes, such as radicalization (Weine and Ahmed 2012). These resources often stem from strong families, communities, and trusted institutions and can be provided by parents, extended family, teachers, religious leaders, coaches, and elders. A UK study that tracked women who joined ISIS indicates that there is evidence to suggest that women's strong familial bonds can influence some prospective female migrants at least to delay, if not reject, migration entirely (Hoyle, Bradford, and Frenett 2015). Often protective factors provide emotional and practical influence that can prevent vulnerable individuals from radicalizing.

Psychological factors

Psychological factors might also contribute to one's vulnerability and propensity toward violent extremism. One body of research indicates that some people become violent extremists as part of a "quest for significance," or a desire to provide one's life with purpose and meaning (Kruglanski et al. 2009). While developing a sense of personal meaning and significance is a common need for all humans, for some, the inability to derive personal significance might increase their propensity to join a group that offers acceptance and a sense of belonging. Moreover, circumstances that erode one's sense of self-worth, such as personal trauma, shame, humiliation, and discrimination, have also been asserted to play a major role in cultivating support for violent extremism (Lyons-Padilla et al., forthcoming).

Searching for a sense of purpose is often associated with the need for adventure, glory, and other thrill-seeking complexes (Botha and Abdile 2014). Extremist groups capitalize on this and attempt to recruit individuals to join them by utilizing action-oriented videos that feature scenes of militants training, fighting, and celebrating battle victories, or by sharing personal testimonies of fighters who joined their cause to escape their mundane lives. Such narratives might have a particular appeal to young men and women during their formative years (Botha and Abdile 2014).

Mental illnesses, in particular post-traumatic stress disorder (PTSD), are posited as another major push factor toward violent extremism. Individuals exposed to prolonged periods of violence often exhibit psychological symptoms akin to PTSD (Homeland Security Institute 2009), which in turn might lead to a greater propensity and vulnerability to engage in revenge or violent acts (Davis et al. 2009).

Studies have also posited that depression may make some susceptible to radicalization (Bhui, Everitt, and Jones 2014). While there is no evidence to suggest that terrorists have higher levels of severe mental illness than in the general population, symptoms of depression and anxiety seem to be more prevalent in those who sympathize with violence or terrorism (Bhui, Everitt, and Jones 2014). This is particularly relevant for lone offenders, given that 61 percent of lone-wolf terrorists (those who act alone and have no history of belonging to a certain extremist group) had previous contact with mental health services (Bhui, Everitt, and Jones 2014).

Ideologies, beliefs, and values

Violent extremists often utilize radical ideologies, beliefs, and values[4] to foment intolerance and hatred and to justify the use of violence to address grievances. It is important to note that violent extremism is not limited to any single faith community. In fact, previous studies indicate that individuals of all faiths have perpetuated terrorism (Krueger and Laitin 2008). Moreover, religiosity in itself is not an indicator of vulnerability to radicalization.

Over the past 50 years, however, the use of Islamic discourses to justify terrorism has become increasingly prominent. For example, Osama bin Laden's first *fatwa* (religious opinion) against the United States issued in 1996 begins with numerous references to the Qur'an and *hadith* (prophetic traditions), which provide a religious overtone to his justification for the use of violence in response to his grievances with U.S. foreign policy (PBS 1996). Several other *fatwas* issued by extremist clerics such as Anwar al-Awlaki (Al-Awlaki 2010) issue calls to support antistate violence and are heavily interspersed with religious rhetoric. These edicts are based on understandings of religious texts that rely on literalistic interpretations, and deviate from or circumvent more than 1,400 years of scholarly exegesis. Previous studies (Carpenter et al. 2010; Task Force on Confronting the Ideology of Radical Extremism 2009) and public opinion data (Ghitis 2014) indicate that the vast majority of Muslims around the world reject these concepts. However, extremist ideologies resonate among some individuals, particularly those who have a limited understanding of their religion, such as recent converts. In a 2004 study, only 18 percent of violent extremists were determined to have received religious primary or secondary education (Sageman 2004). Some leave extremist groups when militants' deviant interpretations of religious texts are revealed. In a 2010 study of twenty-five former violent extremists, former militants cited al-Qaeda's inaccurate interpretation of Islam as a major factor in their decision to leave (Jacobson 2010).

In addition to espousing deviant ideologies, violent extremists posit several extremist narratives, such as the "West" has launched a war against Islam and Muslims (Silber 2009). Al-Qaeda, ISIS, and other terrorist groups contend that Muslims must unify to defeat this threat and reestablish an Islamic state, or Caliphate.

Violent extremists often propagate a bifurcated worldview in which Muslims are at odds with non-Muslims and in a constant state of conflict. Although ascribing to such a worldview would not necessarily lead one to engage in violence, previous research suggests that it can create a propensity to affiliate or support terrorism in various ways (Borum 2014).

For example, violent extremist worldviews are often framed within simple, binary "us versus them," "right versus wrong," or Manichean "good versus evil" rhetoric, all of which represent value monism. Unlike value pluralism, in which multiple values are considered equally valid and respected, extremist beliefs are underpinned by value monism, the understanding that a particular viewpoint is absolute and often nonnegotiable. According to Liht and Savage (2013), "the inability to make trade-offs between competing values results in low complexity reasoning." This myopic reasoning promotes intolerance and is often used by extremists to justify *takfirism*, or violence against those who do not ascribe to their belief structures.

Perhaps the most prevalent deviant religious concept is the centrality of combative jihad to Islamic practices. It was traditionally interpreted by Islamic scholars to represent many aspects of Islamic practices, ranging from serving God and mankind, to struggling to submit to the will of God. Jihad can include armed combat, such as a defensive war; however, there are several strict rules and conditions that must be considered before militant jihad can be sanctioned. Extremists such as Abdullah Azzam, a key mentor of Osama bin Laden, argued that anyone, at any time, has a personal responsibility to engage in jihad. This reasoning appears in several major *fatwas* encouraging violence against the West issued by Osama bin Laden and al-Qaeda leader Ayman Zawahiri (Davis et al. 2009). Although religious scholars, political leaders, and academics have refuted these radical ideologies, extremists have made combative jihad a central tenet of their ideology.

Political grievances

Political grievances against a state are often a major factor in why individuals become radicalized. These grievances may be due to unpopular foreign policies or economic, social, or cultural practices sanctioned by the state; weak infrastructure; limited rule of law; inefficient judicial structures; unequal resource distribution; limited political rights and civil liberties; and repression of oppositional groups. States' failure to address these grievances can eventually delegitimize a regime, which increases the likelihood that an oppositional group will use violence to resolve those grievances (Sprinzak 1990). Moreover, oppositional political parties are most likely to use terrorism when they have large-scale ambitions of regime change and the establishment of a new social order (Noricks 2009).[5] This is particularly relevant for organizations such as ISIS or al-Qaeda, which intend to subvert established regimes to build a new supposed "Islamic" state.

Foreign interventions such as drone strikes and the presence of foreign military troops or bases are common political grievances. For example, the deployment of 10,000 U.S. forces in Saudi Arabia during the 1991 Gulf War was heavily criticized by Osama bin Laden. Following the twin bombings of the American Embassies in Nairobi and Dar es Salaam, an organization with ties to Osama bin

Laden issued a communiqué warning that additional attacks would occur unless U.S. and Western forces withdrew from Muslim countries (Kifner 1998). Effective recruiters draw on these global themes and then make them relevant at the individual level by appealing to personal senses of injustice, relative deprivation, or collective humiliation.

Previous studies indicate that the perception of foreign occupation also has a correlation with incidents of terrorism. For example, in a study of suicide campaigns from 1980 to 2001, suicide bombers were determined to be particularly likely to target democracies that are perceived to be foreign occupiers (Pape 2003).

State repression is considered particularly powerful in mobilizing opposition groups. The state's use of excessive violence against oppositional figures not only delegitimizes the state but also legitimizes the use of violence by activists. Furthermore, state repression can create and reinforce the notion of martyrdom (Della Porta 1995), a popular theme among extremists.

Limited political rights and civil liberties—including a lack of political representation, perceptions of political discrimination, and feelings of disenfranchisement—facilitate a sense of alienation and hopelessness, which may influence vulnerable individual's participation in radical milieus (Helmus 2009). The lack of civil rights and civil liberties, compounded by distrust of the government, is a particularly powerful narrative among vulnerable individuals.

Government corruption is also a major source for political grievances and contributes significantly to the perceived illegitimacy of a regime. Allegations of corruption can stem from usurping power, embezzling state funds, or from serving the needs of foreign governments.

Economic factors

The relationship between economic factors—such as poverty, unemployment, and relative deprivation—and the propensity to support violent extremism is arguably one of the most contested issues in the field of terrorism studies. Some studies that rely on national survey data suggest that unemployment or low levels of income do not necessarily lead one to become a terrorist (see, for example, Krueger and Maleckova 2003). Other studies indicate that lack of gainful employment and other poverty indicators have been identified in some regions as a driving factor of recruitment and radicalization (see, for example, Mesøy 2013). For example, in Somalia, Mali, Syria, Pakistan, and Afghanistan, violent extremists target their recruitment efforts in poor communities, by providing social welfare assistance, employment, cash handouts, and scholarships to impoverished individuals to gain support (Mirahmadi and Farooq 2010; Mirahmadi, Ziad, and Farooq 2014). Similarly, Turkish foreign fighters in Iraq and Syria cite financial incentives such as stipends of $150 per day for fighting with groups such as ISIS (Yeginsu 2014). In one study of al-Shabaab fighters, more than half of the respondents indicated that economic considerations played a major role in their decision to join (Botha and Abdil 2014). Half reported being unemployed at the time that they joined the group, while the other half reported being largely in low-wage jobs. It is noteworthy that respondents who cited economic reasons for joining al-Shabaab were apt to view the organization as a reliable employer. It is also worth noting that disincentives play a critical role in individual's decisions to provide material support to VEOs.

In addition, feelings of relative deprivation, the discrepancy between what individuals believe they are entitled to and what they obtain or experience as their circumstances permit it, are a prominent push factor of violent extremism because they can fuel frustration and aggression (Taspinar 2009). Feelings of relative deprivation can stem from perceived economic inequalities, discrepancies of national resource allocation, or even political disenfranchisement. VEOs often reinforce relative deprivation, by drawing on victimization narratives, which posit that Muslims are discriminated against by the broader society and, as such, receive fewer resources.

Translating Research into Action: Four Core Components of the BRAVE Model

Extensive research into the theories of radicalization and decades of empirical work on social integration revealed the four core components of what would become the BRAVE model for CVE (WORDE 2016). First, engage a wide range of stakeholders—including faith community leaders, public officials, law enforcement officers, educators, and social service providers—in a way that promotes trust, respect, and positive social interaction. The goal here is that these participants become a cohesive community network, committed to public safety and serve as an early warning network of trusted adults. More than 300 faith-based institutions and community service providers have participated in the Montgomery County, Maryland, pilot initiative.

Second, educate the stakeholders with the information they need to be an informed and aware citizenry dedicated to public safety. It is important to note that the scope of the collaboration cannot be limited to terrorism. Designed to respond to the needs of each locality, the network should also address issues such as disaster preparedness, treating mental illness, and responding to acts of hate or targeted violence.

Historically, terrorism has been treated as the exclusive purview of law enforcement, but the BRAVE model empowers the wider community with knowledge to recognize warning signs of radicalization or recruitment so many more actors can intervene in the precriminal space. To date, WORDE has trained hundreds of first responders, teachers, and faith community members with the latest information about violent extremism and other public safety threats.

Third, once a community becomes an informed and aware public, it has the opportunity to connect vulnerable individuals to a variety of professionals for intervention. Fourth, professionals who are culturally competent and trained in trauma use a multidisciplinary approach to provide counseling and other direct services, such as positive youth development classes or vocational training, for those identified as vulnerable. Although no one can prove a counterfactual—that services prevented someone from becoming a terrorist—one can prove through preclinical and postclinical assessments that clients have had a reduction in potential risk factors and an increase in protective factors.

In Montgomery County, Maryland, we also integrated a licensed clinical social worker (LCSW) into the police department. The LCSW is an independent contractor, employed by the Department of Health and Human Services, but embedded in the Crisis Intervention Team of the police department. Her case files are subject to protected health information rules, so the community can use her as a resource without worrying that it would lead to a police investigation.

Utilizing both innovative and traditional assessment tools, we can measure outcomes and efficacy of the treatment provided. Since the program is a clinical model and follows the protected health information guidelines of professionals, client information is kept entirely outside the purview of law enforcement unless a client's behavior triggers the statutory duty to warn a health care or law enforcement professional.

Lessons Learned

Having now applied these principles for more than 3 years in Montgomery County, Maryland, with more than 3,000 participants, and beginning to apply the program in Prince George, Maryland, and Denver, Colorado, there are some important lessons that stand out:

Whole-of-community approach: The BRAVE model involves diverse faith and ethnic communities, purposively and strategically brought together to reduce stigma of any single faith community. Programs that have singled out the Muslim community have been negatively perceived and only exacerbated the lack of trust or cooperation between the community and law enforcement (Schanzer et al. 2016). Such programs rarely led to more tips on potential threats and provided a lot of negative propaganda for the recruiters who claim that the West is at war with Islam and Muslims.

It is important to note that cross-cultural collaboration is not always a smooth process, and social science research strongly suggests that merely bringing different groups together, who are likely to view the other group as "not like us," stands to increase intergroup alienation (Bodenhausen 1988; Dovidio, Evans, and Tyler 1986; O'Sullivan and Durso 1984; Wyer 1989). To bridge the intergroup divide successfully, in ways that tend to create lasting change, decades of research have demonstrated that several conditions need to be met, including being brought together as equals by trusted interlocutors, working together toward a common goal, and creating opportunities for consistent cross-cultural interaction (Aronson and Bridgeman 1979; Cook 1984; Riordan 1978).

Bottom-up; top-down: The BRAVE program truly places communities at the forefront; it gives them ownership of the agenda and allows them to define the contours of what CVE programing looks like. Nonetheless, while BRAVE is a civil society–led initiative that is bottom-up, it also employs top-down support. The model would not be successful without support from local government and law enforcement, which confer legitimacy to the endeavor and facilitate broader community participation.

Consistent collaboration: Building momentum and expanding the circle of participation relies on fostering trust through consistent engagement and collaboration on a multitude of issues beyond violent extremism. Rather than focusing only on threats from groups such as ISIS or al-Shabaab, it is important to discuss issues such as online safety of youth, how to prevent cyber bullying, or reducing the incidence of hate crimes.

Cultivating these relationships across social divides is more critical now than ever. Domestic terror attacks are creating fault lines in our societies that will only lead to more violence, if they are not repaired. The separation of Muslims from non-Muslims feeds into the bifurcated worldview of the terrorists who say "it is us versus them; the West against Islam." A comprehensive prevention agenda therefore must include programs that prevent that divide, so that there is only an "us" against the terrorists.

Metrics and evaluation: Last but not least, using a solid, research-based framework to guide engagement strategies, threat assessment, and intervention efforts promotes credibility and ensures financial support for the initiative. The Montgomery County model has been the subject of two federally funded evaluations. The first, funded by the National Institute of Justice (Williams, Horgan, and Evans 2016), indicates that the program has fostered positive social integration in its participants. In fact, there were statistically significant outcomes in twelve out of the fourteen indicators measured—factors such as "I feel welcome"; "I learned about cultures different than my own"; and "I feel a sense of belonging." All these factors help to reduce social alienation, which is posited as one of the motivations for radicalization.

The second evaluation, funded by the Department of Justice, carried out by the Police Executive Research Forum, indicates that the vast majority of participants in the model felt empowered to tackle public safety issues. They had a sense of satisfaction with the quality of speakers and topics presented; had gained new insight/knowledge from the trainings; and appreciated the religious and cultural diversity of participants, and working together toward common goals.

In addition, WORDE conducts its own event satisfaction surveys after almost every event. Whether it is at a training on disaster preparedness for houses of worship or at a workshop on mental health first aid, these surveys indicate that at least 80 percent of those surveyed feel a greater connectivity to people of other faiths, have an increased understanding of people who come from other traditions, and are more likely to engage in help-seeking behaviors to protect their community and loved ones.

Recommendations

With proof of concept based on the experiences in Montgomery County, Maryland, the model shows promise for scale-up and replication in other jurisdictions. However, there are several challenges that the next administration must consider.

1. *Improve federal government coordination in CVE*: Though important steps have been taken to coordinate and streamline the federal government coordination of CVE, much of that has not translated into practical differences at the local level. There is also no attempt to scale and replicate an evidence-based program like BRAVE or to develop a national framework for domestic CVE efforts. Every jurisdiction is left on its own to create a program from scratch, often not based on any research, and the result is an ad hoc collection of disjointed efforts. Such an approach also prevents us from creating a "community of practice" that can be fine-tuned and improved across jurisdictions.

2. *Act in ways that show how CVE is about more than terrorism and Muslims*: An oft-repeated CVE mantra is "words matter," but the pushback to CVE is largely because the actions of law enforcement and federal partners do not match their words. In other words, if CVE is to be truly about more than just terrorism and the Muslim community, then the programming and partnerships for CVE must reflect that. It is not enough to say it; the actions should reflect the words.

3. *Increase community engagement efforts*: To reduce the long-term effects of socially alienated or isolated communities, federal, state, and local governments and law enforcement need to invest and participate in creating and sustaining cross-cultural community engagement efforts in accordance with research-based principles like those used in social integration theory[6] or collective impact models (Kania and Kramer 2011). This will require enhancing U.S. public and private agencies' cultural competency and partnering with civil society to implement these programs.

4. *Provide additional resources*: Communities need resources, not just funding. They need institutional capacity development, training on radicalization and terrorism, and program administration before they will be able to create multidisciplinary, community-based prevention programs as well as diversion programs (see below) that can actually treat radicalized individuals in a way that is governed by the laws of informed consent and monitored by federal or local law enforcement agencies. The Department of Homeland Security's Urban Area Security Initiative (UASI), which enhances regional capabilities to prevent, protect, and mitigate terrorist attacks, major disasters, and other emergencies, could be expanded to assist in this area.

5. *Encourage the development of diversion programs*: Diversion programs, as opposed to prevention, are meant to take a subject off the path of criminal or violent behavior before prosecution or to channel offenders into rehabilitative programs in lieu of incarceration. Such programs are often conducted in close partnership with law enforcement, courts, district attorneys, or nongovernmental agencies because the subjects pose a greater risk to society if not properly monitored. To support such initiatives for radicalized

subjects, law enforcement will need to provide training on radicalization indicators and behavior intervention assessment tools for professionals who have the competency to take on such cases.

6. *Establish and refine metrics for evaluating CVE programs*: Federal funding should require applicants to clearly articulate a theory of change that connects program activities with the potential risk factors[7] that the program seeks to address. Using traditional and innovative evaluation tools, we should be able to determine whether a CVE program reduces vulnerabilities in the program participants.

7. *Incentivize multidisciplinary approaches*: Given that CVE requires a multidisciplinary approach, the federal government should support research on adapting good practices from other prevention programs (e.g., gang prevention, drug prevention) and apply them to the CVE context. Funding agencies could also require CVE programs to be carried out in collaboration with multiple partners, or through a consortium.

8. *Improve access to services*: For many vulnerable communities—particularly new immigrants—unfamiliarity with bureaucratic processes and language barriers can lead to misperceptions that they are being discriminated against by the system. This may reinforce "us-versus-them" mentalities and further validate the feeling that they "don't belong here," the latter of which is also articulated by violent extremist organizations to radicalize vulnerable individuals. There should be extensive training and resources for government funded agencies in particular to increase their outreach and engagement with these communities so that those in the community can better access services and transition to life in the United States more effectively.

9. *Provide communities guidelines on the duty to warn*: Communities that will engage in interventions in the precriminal space must understand and be trained on the regulations around the "duty to warn," which varies from state to state. Such laws are designed to balance the privacy rights of those seeking treatment and the rights of protection from harm for the rest of the public.

In summary, the BRAVE experience has established that long-term prevention (reduction of recruitment and lessening radicalization to violent extremism) requires public and private stakeholders to undergo a paradigm shift that emphasizes trust, collaboration, and multidisciplinary strategies through engagement, education, and specialized interventions. It is a departure from traditional government-led or law enforcement–centric approaches and requires an acknowledgement by all parties that each stakeholder makes a unique contribution to this struggle. It also requires the recognition that all citizens have a role to play in upholding public safety; and while the law enforcement community has an important role to play, it should ultimately play a supporting role to healthcare professionals, educators, and other governmental organizations that are better suited to lead prevention activities.

Notes

1. According to the New America Foundation, non-Muslim extremists are responsible for nearly twice as many deaths in the U.S. than supporters of Islamist extremism since September 11, 2001.

2. A similar cluster model approach was utilized by the Department of Homeland Security (see U.S. Department of Homeland Security 2011).

3. See Saltman and Smith (2015, 13), for a discussion of the conceptualization of "sisterhood bonds" that pull individuals toward joining violent extremist organizations.

4. It is important to note that just because an individual holds radical or extremist views, this does not make them a potential violent criminal.

5. Darcy M. E. Noricks identifies research conducted by Leonard Weinberg, Ami Pedahzur, and Arie Perlinger as instrumental works in the field. See Noricks (2009, 21).

6. Also referred to as Intergroup Contract Hypothesis, there is a whole body of social science research that outlines key factors for how this contact should be structured for maximum benefit.

7. Since there are no studies to date that have demonstrated a causal link between any one risk factor or combination of factors, and an individual becoming a terrorist, our use of the term "risk factor" is colloquial and not predictive of who will become radicalized.

References

Al-Awlaki, Anwar. 2010. A call to jihad. Ansar al-Mujahideen English Forum. Available from azelin.files. wordpress.com.

Aronson, Elliot, and Diane Bridgeman. October 1979. Jigsaw groups and the desegregated classroom: In pursuit of common goals. *Personality and Social Psychology Bulletin* 5 (4): 438–46.

Bakker, Edwin. December 2006. *Jihadi terrorists in Europe*. Clingendael: Netherlands Institute of International Relations. Available from www.clingendael.nl.

Bhui, Kamaldeep, Brian Everitt, and Edgar Jones. 24 September 2014. Might depression, psychosocial adversity, and limited social assets explain vulnerability to and resistance against violent radicalization? *PLoS ONE* 9 (9).

Bodenhausen, Galen V. November 1988. Stereotypic biases in social decision making and memory: Testing process models of stereotype use. *Journal of Personality and Social Psychology* 55 (5): 726–37.

Borum, Randy. 2014. Psychological vulnerabilities and propensities for involvement in violent extremism. *Behavioral Science and the Law* 32 (3): 286–305.

Botha, Anneli, and Mahdi Abdile. September 2014. *Radicalisation and Al-Shabaab recruitment in Somalia*. Pretoria: Institute for Security Studies. Available from www.issafrica.org.

Carpenter, Scott J., Matthew Levitt, Steven Simon, and Juan Zarate. July 2010. *Fighting the ideological battle: The missing link in U.S. strategy to counter violent extremism*. Washington, DC: The Washington Institute for Near East Policy. Available from www.washingtoninstitute.org.

Cook, Stuart W. 1984. Cooperative interaction in multiethnic contexts. In *Groups in contact: The psychology of desegregation*, eds. Norman S. Miller and Marilynn B. Brewer, 155–85. New York, NY: Academic Press.

Davis, Paul K., Kim Cragin, Darcy Noricks, Todd C. Helmus, Christopher Paul, Claude Berrebi, Brian A. Jackson, Gaga Gvineria, Michael Egner, and Benjamin Bahney. 2009. *Social science for counterterrorism: Putting the pieces together*, eds. Paul K. Davis and Kim Cragin. Santa Monica, CA: RAND Corporation. Available from www.rand.org.

Della Porta, Donatella. 1995. *Social movements, political violence, & the state*. Cambridge: Cambridge University Press.

Dovidio, John F., Nancy Evans, and Richard B. Tyler. January 1986. Racial stereotypes: The contents of their cognitive representations. *Journal of Experimental Social Psychology* 22 (1): 22–37.

Ghitis, Frida. 10 July 2014. A spark of good news from the Mideast. *CNN*.

Hassan, Muhsin. 23 August 2012. Understanding drivers of violent extremism: The case of al-Shabab and Somali youth. *CTC Sentinel* 5 (8): 18–20.

Helmus, Todd. 2009. Why and how some people become terrorists. In *Social science for counterterrorism: Putting the pieces together*, eds. Paul K. Davis and Kim Cragin. Santa Monica, CA: RAND Corporation. Available from www.rand.org.

Homeland Security Institute. 23 April 2009. *Recruitment and radicalization of school-age youth by international terrorist groups*. Arlington, VA: Homeland Security Institute. Available from www.homeland-security.org.

Horgan, John. 2009. Individual disengagement: A psychological analysis. In *Leaving terrorism behind*, eds. Tore Bjorgo and John Horgan, 17–28. New York, NY: Routledge.

Horgan, John. 2014. *The psychology of terrorism*. New York, NY: Routledge.

Hoyle, Carolyn, Alexandra Bradford, and Ross Frenett. 2015. *Becoming Mulan? Female Western migrants to ISIS*. London: Institute for Strategic Dialogue. Available from http://www.strategicdialogue.org.

Jacobson, Michael. January 2010. *Terrorist dropouts: Learning from those who have left*. Washington, DC: The Washington Institute for Near East Policy. Available from www.washingtoninstitute.org.

Kania, John, and Mark Kramer. 2011. Collective impact. *Stanford Social Innovation Review* 9:36–41.

Kifner, John. 14 August 1998. Bombings in East Africa: The suspect; wealthy force behind murky militant group. *New York Times*.

Krueger, Alan B., and David D. Laitin. 2008. Kto Kogo? A cross-country study of the origins and targets of terrorism. In *Terrorism, economic development, and political openness*, eds. Philip Keefer and Norman Loayza, 148–73. Cambridge: Cambridge University Press.

Krueger, Alan B., and Jitka Maleckova. 2003. Education, poverty, and terrorism: Is there a causal connection? *Journal of Economic Perspectives* 17 (4): 119–44.

Kruglanski, Arie W., Xioyan Chen, Mark Dechesne, Shira Fishman, and Edward Orehek. June 2009. Fully committed: Suicide bombers' motivation and the quest for personal significance. *Political Psychology* 30 (3): 331–57.

Liht, Jose, and Sarah Savage. 2013. Preventing violent extremism through value complexity: Being Muslim being British. *Journal of Strategic Security* 6 (4): 44–66.

Lyons-Padilla, Sarah, Michelle Gelfand, Hedieh Mirahmadi, and Mehreen Farooq. Forthcoming. The struggle to belong: Immigrant marginalization and risk for radicalization. *Behavioral Science and Policy*.

Lyons-Padilla, Sarah, Michelle Gelfand, Hedieh Mirahmadi, Mehreen Farooq, and Mareike van Egmond. 2015. Belonging nowhere: Marginalization & radicalization risk among Muslim immigrants. *Behavioral Science & Policy* 1 (2). Available from http://gelfand.umd.edu/papers/BSP_2_Lyons_2p%20(002).pdf.

Mesøy, Atle. January 2013. *Poverty and radicalisation into violent extremism: A causal link?* Oslo: Norwegian Peacebuilding Resource Centre. Available from http://www.peacebuilding.no.

Mirahmadi, Hedieh, and Mehreen Farooq. December 2010. *A community based approach to countering radicalization*. Montgomery Village, MD: WORDE. Available from www.worde.org.

Mirahmadi, Hedieh, Mehreen Farooq, and Waleed Ziad. May 2010. *Traditional Muslim networks: Pakistan's untapped resource in the fight against terrorism*. Montgomery Village, MD: WORDE. Available from www.worde.org.

Mirahmadi, Hedieh, Waleed Ziad, and Mehreen Farooq. February 2014. *Afghanistan 2014 and beyond: The role of civil society in peacebuilding and countering violent extremism*. Montgomery Village, MD: WORDE. Available from www.worde.org.

Noricks, Darcy M. E. 2009. The root causes of terrorism. In *Social science for counterterrorism: Putting the pieces together*, eds. Paul K. Davis and Kim Cragin, 11–70. Santa Monica, CA: RAND Corporation. Available from www.rand.org.

O'Sullivan, Chris S., and Francis T. Durso. 1984. Effects of schema-incongruent information on memory for stereotypical attributes. *Journal of Personality and Social Psychology* 47 (1): 55–70.

Pape, Robert A. August 2003. The strategic logic of suicide terrorism. *American Political Science Review* 97 (3): 343–61.

PBS. 23 August 1996. Bin Laden's fatwa. *PBS Newshour*.

Riordan, Cornelius A. June 1978. Equal-status interracial contact: A review and revision of a concept. *International Journal of Intercultural Relations* 2 (2): 161–85.

Sageman, Marc. 2004. *Understanding terrorist networks*. Philadelphia, PA: University of Pennsylvania Press.

Sageman, Marc. 2011. *Leaderless jihad*. Philadelphia, PA: University of Pennsylvania Press.

Saltman, Erin Marie, and Melanie Smith. 2015. *Till martyrdom do us part*. London: Institute for Strategic Dialogue. Available from http://www.strategicdialogue.org.

Schanzer, David, Charles Kurzman, Jessica Toliver, and Elizabeth Miller. 2016. *The challenge and promise of using community policing strategies to counter violent extremism*. Durham, NC: Triangle Center on Terrorism and Homeland Security, Sanford School of Public Policy, Duke University.

Shane, Scott. 24 June 2015. Homegrown extremists tied to deadlier toll than jihadists in US since 9/11. *New York Times*.

Silber, Mitchell D. 19 November 2009. Testimony for the Senate Homeland Security and Governmental Affairs Committee.

Southern Poverty Law Center. 12 February 2015. *Age of the wolf: A study of the rise of lone wolf and leaderless resistance terrorism*. Montgomery, AL: Southern Poverty Law Center. Available from www .splcenter.org.

Sprinzak, Ehud. 1990. Extreme left terrorism in a democracy. In *Origins of terrorism: Psychologies, ideologies, theologies, states of mind*, ed. Walter Reich, 65–85. Washington, DC: Woodrow Wilson Center Press.

Task Force on Confronting the Ideology of Radical Extremism. March 2009. *Rewriting the narrative: An integrative strategy for counterradicalization*. Washington, DC: The Washington Institute for Near East Policy. Available from www.washingtoninstitute.org.

Taspinar, Omer. 2009. Fighting radicalism, not terrorism: Root causes of an international actor redefined. *SAIS Review* 29 (2): 75–86.

U.S. Department of Homeland Security. 16 December 2011. *Assessment: A model for understanding the motivations of homegrown violent extremists*. Washington, DC: U.S. Department of Homeland Security. Available from www.dhs.gov.

Weine, Stevan, and Osman Ahmed. 2012. *Building resilience to violent extremism among Somali-Americans in Minneapolis-St. Paul*. College Park, MD: National Consortium for the Study of Terrorism and Responses to Terrorism. Available from www.start.umd.edu.

The White House. December 2011. *Strategic implementation plan for empowering local partners to prevent violent extremism in the United States*. Washington, DC: The White House.

Williams, Michael J., John G. Horgan, William P. Evans. 2016. *Evaluation of a multi-faceted, U.S. community-based, Muslim-led CVE program*. Washington, DC: National Institute of Justice.

WORDE. March 2016. *The Building Resilience Against Violent Extremism (BRAVE) Model: A collective impact initiative that increases public safety and social cohesion*. Montgomery Village, MD: WORDE. Available from www.worde.org.

Wyer, Robert S., Jr. 1989. Social memory and social judgment. In *Memory: Interdisciplinary approaches*, eds. P. R. Solomon, G. R. Goethals, C. M. Kelley, and B. R. Stephens, 243–70. New York, NY: Springer-Verlag.

Yeginsu, Ceylan. 15 September 2014. ISIS draws a steady stream of recruits from Turkey. *New York Times*.

School-Based
CVE Strategies

By
KATIE MOFFETT
and
TONY SGRO

The Peer to Peer (P2P): Challenging Extremism initiative, which counters violent extremism through youth engagement, is a partnership between an interagency government team and EdVenture Partners, a private organization that manages experiential learning initiatives using a peer-to-peer approach. The initiative tasks university students across the globe to counter extremism among their peers and in their communities, by creating and implementing, over the course of a school term, a social or digital initiative, product, or tool designed to empower their peers and counter hate. At the time of writing, more than two thousand students from more than ninety-five universities in more than thirty countries have been involved in the initiative, which is specifically designed to capitalize on public-private partnerships.

Keywords: youth; extremism; challenge; education; partnership; university; engagement

The importance of educating and organizing youth against violent extremism cannot be understated. Most recruits to violent extremist groups are in their twenties, with some even younger (Soufan Group 2015). It is, therefore, important to reach and influence vulnerable youth before they are radicalized. One strategy

Katie Moffett is a content marketing manager for EdVenture Partners (EVP), where she is tasked with developing the firm's overall content strategy and brand. She has more than 10 years of experience in marketing, including her previous work managing collegiate experiential learning programs with EVP. She now promotes EVP's P2P: Challenging Extremism initiative.

Tony Sgro is the founder and CEO of EdVenture Partners (EVP). EVP has built industry-education partnerships at more than eight hundred universities internationally to address societal challenges by connecting students, educators, and industry leaders. Sgro has more than 40 years of experience in marketing, advertising, and promotion. Sgro and his team at EVP created and manage the P2P: Challenging Extremism initiative.

Correspondence: katie@edventurepartners.com

DOI: 10.1177/0002716216672435

ANNALS, AAPSS, 668, November 2016   145 currently under way, from EdVenture Partners (EVP), leverages the college education market to do just this.

EVP is a private organization dedicated to developing innovative industry-education partnership programs using a peer-to-peer approach. EVP organizes, manages, and facilitates collegiate programs that run as part of a class or student organization. EVP first connects the students with a program partner, a public or private organization or trade association, that is looking to reach the college market. For example, a vehicle manufacturer may want to market its latest vehicle to college students. EVP would then have student teams perform research, design a campaign, and implement this campaign to market the latest vehicle to their peers. Student teams are given a budget and can use this money for their campaigns. The participating students decide what tactics, strategies, and creative direction will work best to both accomplish their set objectives and impact their peers. At the end of the term, students prove the effectiveness of their chosen tactics and approaches to EVP and their program partner. The program is learn-by-doing and, therefore, provides real-world experience.

In fall 2014, EVP was hired by the U.S. government to begin an effort to engage college students in the fight against extremism. Because previous countering violent extremism (CVE) campaigns had been designed by government insiders, the EVP approach was novel, directly activating youth to combat hate and extremism among their peers. EVP had previously worked with the U.S. Department of State, the Central Intelligence Agency (CIA), and the Federal Bureau of Investigation (FBI) on similar collaborations. EVP worked with the White House National Security Council, U.S. Department of Homeland Security, U.S. Department of State, and the National Counterterrorism Center to bring the first iteration of Peer to Peer (P2P): Challenging Extremism to life. The program launched in January 2015 at twenty-three universities worldwide. Facebook joined as a technology partner in fall 2015 to provide additional resources and support to participating university teams.

P2P was one of many exchange programs engaged in the fight against extremism. As Evan Ryan, Assistant Secretary of State for the Bureau of Educational and Cultural Affairs at the U.S. Department of State, put it, "We are always looking for innovative ways to engage new audiences, and the hundreds of brilliant university students participating in P2P are helping us achieve that goal" (Ryan 2016). This article describes the design, development, and implementation of the P2P: Challenging Extremism initiative and provides recommendations on how this initiative can inspire and inform additional CVE youth strategies.

Strategy and Design

EVP uses a peer-to-peer approach, because it believes that individuals are in the best position to reach and motivate their fellow peers to bring about social change. EVP has been using this peer-to-peer method for more than 25 years with successful results, including peer-to-peer programs with Honda in which university students promoted Honda vehicles to their peers. As Tom Peyton, the assistant vice president at American Honda Motor Corporation, Inc., put it, "There is no better way to learn how to talk to students than from students. They study your company . . . and tell you this is working for you, or this isn't working and how to change it."[1]

In any EVP program, students, enrolled in a relevant course or as part of an academic organization at a college or university, become the program partner's on-campus marketing agency. Program partners may be any organization looking to reach and impact the college marketplace. Program partners have included, for example, the American Honda Motor Corporation, American Fuel and Petrochemical Manufacturers, the FBI, the CIA, and Chevrolet. Over the course of an academic term, these nascent student-agencies design, develop, execute, and analyze an integrated marketing and communications campaign on behalf of the program partner. EVP provides students and faculty members with resources and an in-depth project brief that provides parameters and guidelines for their work throughout the term. Each team is required to complete the same objectives and meet the same program milestones. Participating teams submit an overview of their campaign and implementation successes at the end of the term, and top teams win scholarship awards and recognition. The number of colleges and universities competing each term varies by program. Typically, only one team participates per college or university, but this varies.

This experiential learning design has been shown to be an effective and impactful teaching method (Kolb 1984). From the students' standpoint, consulting-based programs within an experiential learning environment provide benefits such as developing leadership skills and using data and information more effectively to make strategic decisions (D'Angelo, Macaleer, and Meier 2015). The peer-to-peer approach is designed to offer a mutually beneficial relationship to all stakeholders involved in the program.

Program Process

Each term, P2P: Challenging Extremism participants follow the program process outlined below:

Setup

For the P2P initiative, EVP and the U.S. government interagency team set the objectives and developed the project brief that all teams from each participating university used as their guide throughout the term. The project brief provided background information on extremism and the U.S. government interagency team and stated the program objectives and target audience. It also defined measures of success and outlined program and submission requirements.

The students brought together through this initiative were challenged to consider not only how they might counter current extremist messaging and violent extremists' use of digital technologies, but also how to empower positive alternative narratives, models, and pathways that advocate for cultural and religious freedoms, economic production, opportunity through the power of innovation, and living in a civil society, for example.

The program objectives were to design, pilot, implement, and measure the success of a social or digital initiative, product, or tool that motivates or empowers students to become involved in CVE among uncommitted populations, a silent majority, civic-minded individuals, or at-risk youth. Uncommitted populations have formed no opinion about the violent extremist narrative and therefore have not been involved in preventing or promoting it. The silent majority are those who oppose violent extremism but currently are not active in raising public awareness about it or broader prevention efforts. Civic-minded individuals are interested in the public good but not necessarily focused on preventing radicalization and/or engaging in grassroots CVE efforts. At-risk youth are those who are exposed to the violent extremist narrative and vulnerable to radicalization.

Students created initiatives, products, and tools to counter violent extremism in these populations by building communities of interest or networks focused on living shared values that counter violent extremism through action. Broadly, the program encouraged students to come up with various campaigns tailored to their communities and that would resonate with their peers. The program is intended to foster creativity and includes a wide spectrum of strategies and ideas for countering extremism.

School confirmations

EVP works to secure participating faculty from around the world, as determined by the U.S. Department of State and Facebook. Targeted countries vary each collegiate term (see Figure 10 for all P2P participants). Faculty members are contacted via personal phone calls and emails to explain the program, the requirements, and extend them an invitation to participate. Faculty members are required to sign an agreement to participate and to ensure their team will work toward the required objectives and deliverables and use funds appropriately. At the end of the term, if all deliverables and requirements are met, each university receives a $500 donation for their participation.

Launch

A representative from EVP is assigned to each team to guide the faculty and his or her students throughout the program. At the start of the term, the EVP representative provides the project brief and access to an online password-protected project workspace for each team. This workspace houses project resources and allows for communication among teammates and with their EVP representative.

To launch the program each term, a kick-off call is held with all teams, the U.S. government interagency team, Facebook, and EVP. Teams may ask questions and get clarification on the challenge during this call.

Implementation

Participating students begin by doing primary and secondary research on extremism and their target market to formulate their plans on how to effectively reach and impact their campus and community.

Student teams then design their campaign plan. Students must submit a creative brief, which outlines their strategy, tactics, and rationale to counter extremism, for approval by their EVP representative. EVP reviews each brief and works with the teams to answer any outstanding questions. Once the creative brief is approved, EVP provides each team $2,000 (USD equivalent) and $400 in Facebook ad credits to implement their proposed plans.

Students implement their social and digital initiatives, products, and tools on their campus, in their community, and across their country to get measurable results. Teams measure the effectiveness of their campaigns and initiatives using a variety of data and postcampaign research.

Measures of success include, for example:

- Number of people who access the web portal of the initiative, product, or tool;
- Number of people who "favorite" the web portal or digital platform or otherwise indicate their support for it;
- Number of people who join the initiative, participate in its activities, and/or download/use a product or tool. Teams should also measure the quality of involvement (participation in a single event vs. volunteering for ongoing activities, support for marketing a product or tool vs. simply downloading it once, and so on);
- Number of students on the team's university campus who are aware of the initiative, product, or tool;
- Number of social media references to the initiative, product, or tool;
- Number of students who create their own initiatives to counter violent extremism as a result of their exposure to the team's initiative, product, or tool;
- Number of organizational partners and/or sponsors for the initiative, product, or tool;
- The degree to which the project is self-sustaining. Examples of potential measures include financial base for continued operation; number of individuals or organizations that have agreed to continue the initiative, product, or tool; number of independent "spin-off" initiatives and their reach; and products or tools that members of the target audience have created and plan to continue using (this is not an exhaustive list of potential measures);
- The degree to which the project inspired others to take action to counter violent extremism and moving from simply informing others about violent extremism to inspiring others to "do something," as measured through qualitative research and testimonials.

During the implementation phase, an EVP representative is available to answer questions, provide support, and keep teams on track with deadlines, reminders, and clarifications.

Submissions and judging

Teams prepare a comprehensive submission detailing all of their efforts. The submission must be electronically delivered to EVP by the end of each term. EVP sorts and organizes all submissions to prepare them for judging. EVP asks nonparticipating academic faculty to act as the judges for the competition. Each submission is judged using a scorecard designed to match the task, objectives, and deliverables of the initiative.

After the first round of judging, EVP tallies the votes to determine top contenders. EVP then distributes the top submissions to the U.S. Department of State, interagency team, and Facebook for final decisions.

Awards

Awards are used to recognize top teams for their work and impact throughout the term. This includes recognition of the participating faculty and school, as well as the individual students who make up the team. Awards encourage competition among teams to work toward a goal and produce an impact. Awards also include national and/or international travel opportunities for students.

Three top overall teams are invited by the U.S. Department of State and interagency team to travel to Washington, D.C., to present their campaigns to an audience of public and private sector officials. Facebook also recognizes an additional top three teams as part of the Facebook Global Digital Challenge. These teams are chosen based on their strategic use and successful integration of Facebook into their campaigns and tactics.

EVP announces top teams, organizes travel and logistics for participating students, and attends rehearsals for each team before the presentations. At both the U.S. Department of State and Facebook presentations, the presenting teams are placed into final ranking based on their campaign successes. Scholarship awards are given for first, second, and third place in the amounts of $5,000, $3,000, and $1,000, respectively.

Starting with the second iteration of the program, honorable mention teams were also invited to Washington, D.C., for a youth marketplace of ideas about countering and preventing extremism. At the youth marketplace, the teams showcased their campaigns and successes. The marketplace allowed government officials and private-sector attendees to see a broad spectrum of strategies, campaigns, and creative tactics for countering hate and extremism across the globe.

Top international teams are invited to participate in an international visitor leadership program (IVLP) with the U.S. Department of State after the competition. These top students and faculty members travel to different cities across the United States to continue the discussion about countering extremism and their campaigns.

FIGURE 1
One95 Team Members, Missouri State University

Conclusion

At the end of each term, campaign assets, resources, and results from all participating teams are transferred via EVP to the U.S. Department of State, interagency team, and Facebook as actionable ideas that may be used in the effort to combat global extremism. Teams are also encouraged to continue implementing their campaigns (unfunded or with funds from outside sources) after the conclusion of their participation in P2P.

Execution

Pilot program

The pilot program was implemented over the course of the spring 2015 academic term, from January 2015 through June 2015. The pilot included twenty-three university participants and more than six hundred students from ten countries. Teams used a variety of tactics and approaches to empower their communities and peers to reject extremism. Below is a snapshot of the campaigns from the top three teams.

Missouri State University (Springfield, Missouri, United States). Sixteen students formed the team from Missouri State University (MSU). Their campaign, One95, signifies that countering extremism "starts with just one person, one community, and one hundred ninety-five countries, all with one goal: to end violent extremism" (see Figure 1). Campaign highlights included documentary videos, community initiatives, and a tweet-a-thon. The MSU campaign also reached out to a younger audience (Generation Z: 11- to 20-year-olds), providing downloadable lesson packets to educators with worksheets, posters, trivia games and more to use when educating their students on extremism. The campaign included a virtual international exchange between Allen Village School in Kansas City,

Missouri, and The American Nicaraguan School in Managua, Nicaragua. In all, the campaign garnered more than 174,000 social media impressions and reached seventy-five countries.[2]

Curtin University (Perth, Australia). The team from Curtin University was an honors-level social media class comprising fifteen undergraduates. The focus of this team's campaign was the creation of a mobile application called 52Jumaa, which translates to 52 Fridays (see Figure 2). This interactive application provided personalized experiences and challenges to users, while encouraging positive behavior among Muslim youth. The user would select goals she or he would like to achieve, such as "being more helpful to others." The application then provided challenges that corresponded with the behavior, such as "feed a homeless person." If the user completed the challenge, she or he would get a reward in the application from one to three stars. A puzzle was completed after twelve stars. Users were encouraged to collect stars and complete puzzles. The application is downloadable for free and adaptable to different cultural and religious backgrounds.[3]

Mount Royal University (Calgary, Alberta, Canada). The Mount Royal team consisted of seventy-five students from three different marketing classes. The theme of their campaign was, We Are Not Them, abbreviated as WANT. The WANT movement was based on five pillars—community, connection, peace, understanding, and insight—and it was designed to show that violent extremists are a misrepresentation of the Islamic religion and the Muslim culture. The WANT movement consisted of a week-long promotion on campus with different outreach and educational tactics (see Figure 3). Tactics included a portrait project that sought to create a dialog between Muslim and non-Muslim peers by displaying black-and-white photographs of university students with sound clips that described the students and dispelled myths and misconceptions.

The team reported that their campaign reached more than 246,700 audience members, with $10,450 worth of earned media and an average of 5 minutes of engagement from those who interacted with their campaign.[4]

Second iteration

The second iteration ran over the fall 2015 academic term, from August 2015 through February 2016. This installment saw an increase in participants with forty-five universities and more than nine hundred students from seventeen countries. The total campus population reach of all participating schools was more than 800,000. The second iteration saw even more variety in campaign tactics. Below are snapshots from the top three U.S. Department of State teams as well as the Facebook Global Digital Challenge winners.

Lahore University of Management Sciences (Lahore, Pakistan). A team of six students from the course "Introduction to Western Political Philosophy" at Lahore University of Management Sciences designed the "FATE - From Apathy to Empathy" campaign. This campaign addressed the desensitization and apathy

FIGURE 2
The Mobile Application, 52Jumaa

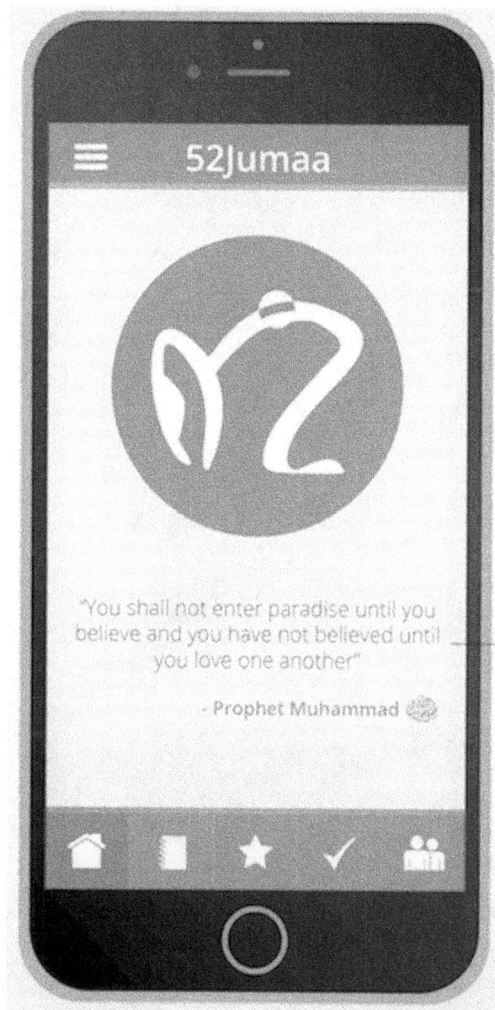

toward extremism that students saw in their society. To address these issues, the team approached them from multiple angles, including awareness, education, tourism, female empowerment, and activism. To increase awareness, the team created the #IChallengeExtremism campaign that asked for students to write personalized messages on cards to protest extremism (see Figure 4). The educational arm of their campaign included distribution of pamphlets at Rehmat Ali Boys High School to inspire the students there to stand up to the apathy of extremism. The tourism angle included partnering with a local tour company to lead a tour through Lahore, going to different religious communities to inspire peaceful coexistence. The idea was to share the religious diversity of Lahore with

FIGURE 3
Creative Piece Designed by the Team at Mount Royal University

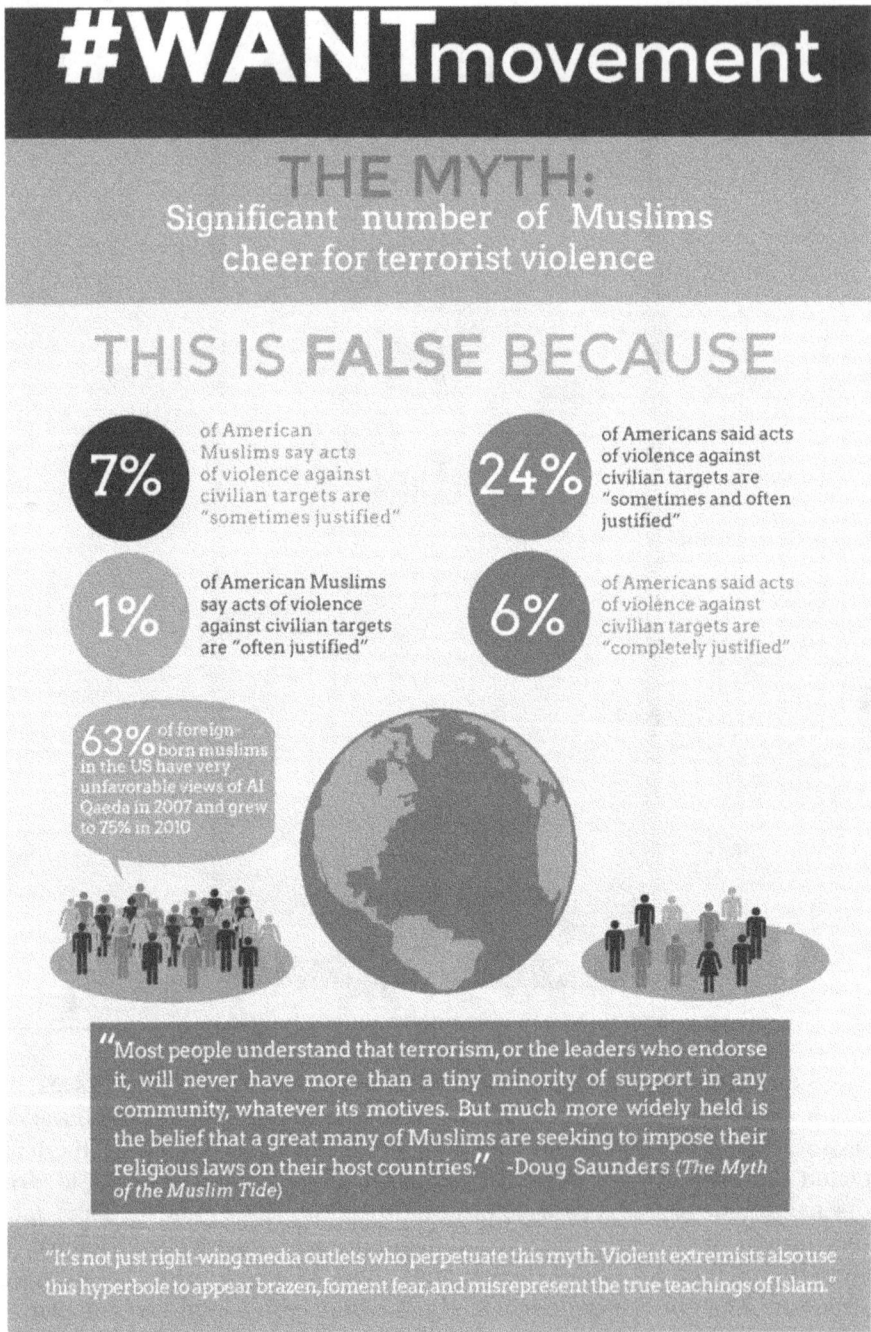

#WANTmovement

THE MYTH:
Significant number of Muslims cheer for terrorist violence

THIS IS FALSE BECAUSE

7% of American Muslims say acts of violence against civilian targets are "sometimes justified"

24% of Americans said acts of violence against civilian targets are "sometimes and often justified"

1% of American Muslims say acts of violence against civilian targets are "often justified"

6% of Americans said acts of violence against civilian targets are "completely justified"

63% of foreign-born muslims in the US have very unfavorable views of Al Qaeda in 2007 and grew to 75% in 2010

"Most people understand that terrorism, or the leaders who endorse it, will never have more than a tiny minority of support in any community, whatever its motives. But much more widely held is the belief that a great many of Muslims are seeking to impose their religious laws on their host countries." -Doug Saunders (*The Myth of the Muslim Tide*)

"It's not just right-wing media outlets who perpetuate this myth. Violent extremists also use this hyperbole to appear brazen, foment fear, and misrepresent the true teachings of Islam."

FIGURE 4
Participant in the #IChallengeExtremism Campaign

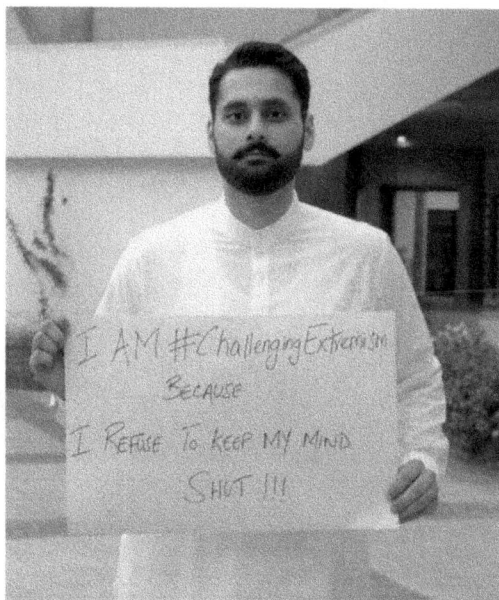

tourists to counter extremism and promote the revival of tourism. The team reported that their campaign received more than 448,000 Facebook impressions, more than one thousand Twitter impressions, 338 website clicks, and 194 Instagram followers.[5]

United States Military Academy (West Point, New York, United States). A team of fifteen in a Combatting Terrorism course at West Point took the approach of building a community to subtly discourage at-risk youth from joining ISIS (see Figure 5). The team wanted to take a different approach than some other campaigns, which outright dissuaded Westerners from joining the Islamic State. The team members believed at-risk youth perceived these campaigns as biased. Instead, the team set out to create a credible online community where at-risk youth could learn, explore, and discuss relevant topics and issues, such as Islamophobia, the meaning of the word *jihad,* and extremism in religious communities. The team used social media to funnel participants to their main campaign platform, their website. The team reported 3,786 page views of their site.[6]

Università della Svizzera italiana (Lugano, Switzerland). The team from Università della Svizzera italiana was made up of twelve students in an E Government course. This team wanted to raise awareness about extremists' historical destruction of monuments and sculptures, such as the destruction of archeological sites at Nimrud, Palmyra, and Hatra, and did so by creating the

FIGURE 5
Team Members Strategizing at the United States Military Academy

FIGURE 6
Faces4Heritage Campaign Logo

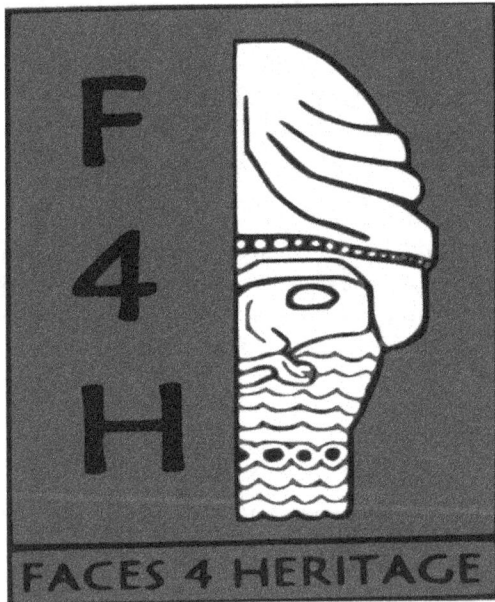

Faces4Heritage campaign (see Figure 6). The campaign included a Facebook tool that allowed users to combine half of their face with an image of one of four historical statues that were destroyed by extremists at the Nimrud Palace,

FIGURE 7
A Creative Piece Designed by the Team at the Turku School of Economics

Nineveh site, or Palmyra site. Their campaign results included 5,846 page views of their website with visitors from more than one hundred countries. Their Facebook page garnered more than twenty-six hundred likes, and the team reported 1,132,355 Facebook impressions at the time of submission.[7]

From the Facebook global digital challenge

Turku School of Economics (Turku, Finland). More than fifty students in a Brand Management course made up the team from Turku School of Economics. This team's approach was to target the increased number of asylum seekers in Finland after learning that these type of refugees are often not provided ample information about their country of refuge. The team's strategy consisted of both online and offline tactics (see Figure 7). Their online strategy included a website and social media; they also created a mobile application, "About Turku," designed to teach users about Finnish society. Their offline events included a football game played among Finns, asylum seekers, and refugees as well as a restaurant day where asylum seekers could share their cultures through food. The team reported 12,700 page views of their website, 650,000 social media impressions, and more than 1,300,000 impressions from print media.[8]

Gulf University for Science and Technology (Kuwait City, Kuwait). A team of twenty-five students from Writing for Public Relations and Advertising courses at Gulf University for Science and Technology created the Raise Your Words campaign (see Figure 8). This campaign was designed to empower the silent majority and encourage open discussions and communications about hate and extremism. The campaign focused on positivity as a narrative. Tactics included seminars on terrorism, a social media contest for sharing quotes about peace and tolerance, a campus event, and social media outreach. The team reported more

FIGURE 8
A Creative Piece from the Raise Your Words Campaign

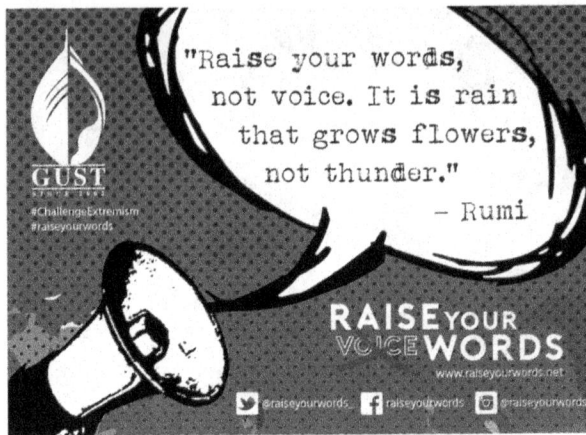

than 530,000 Facebook impressions, more than thirty-four thousand video views, and 276 participants in their social media contest.[9]

University of Arkansas at Little Rock (Little Rock, Arkansas, United States). The University of Arkansas, Little Rock, team consisted of sixteen students in an Integrated Marketing Communications course. The team's campaign, #7Strong, was designed in hopes of uniting the 7 billion people across seven continents. Campaign participants were encouraged to unite against extremism with the #RaiseAFlag campaign, which asked people to flag inappropriate social media content that promoted violent extremism (see Figure 9). The team reported that their campaign reached more than 164,000 on Facebook, had video views of more than seven thousand, and forty-five countries were reached by their campaign.[10]

Third iteration: Spring 2016

The third iteration of P2P: Countering Extremism consisted of fifty-three teams (thirty-three international and twenty domestic) participating, with more than nine hundred students. The final competition and awards for top teams was held at the end of June 2016. The U.S. Department of State awarded first place to Rochester Institute of Technology (United States), second place to Vesalius College (Belgium), and third place to Khazar University (Azerbaijan). Facebook also recognized four top teams: first place was a tie between Laal-u-Anar Foundation (Afghanistan) and Utrecht University (the Netherlands), second place went to College of Europe (Belgium), and third place to Universidad Rey Juan Carlos (Spain).

Continued growth: Fall 2016 and beyond

The fourth iteration of the P2P: Challenging Extremism program is taking place over the fall 2016 college term, from August 2016 through January 2017.

FIGURE 9
Creative material used to promote the #RaiseAFlag campaign

FIGURE 10
Map of P2P: Challenging Extremism Participating Teams, Including Prospective Fall
2016 Teams

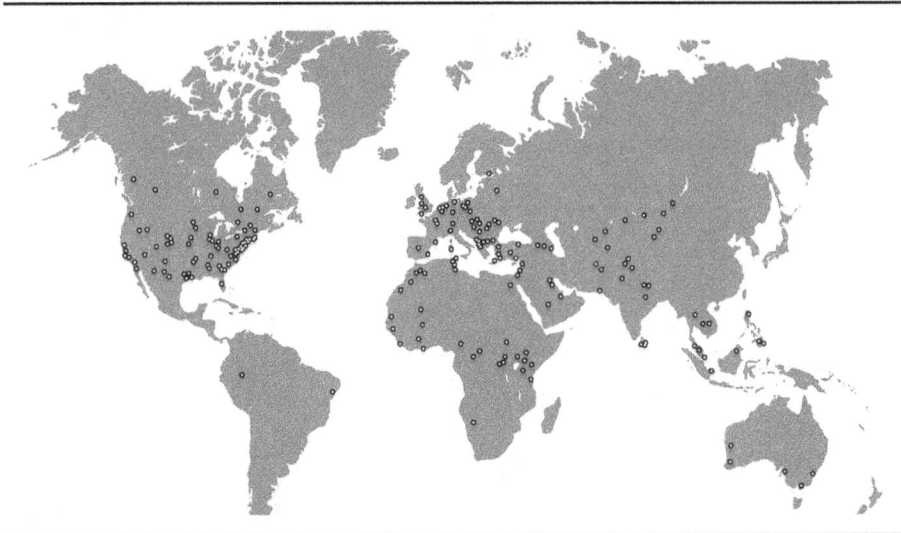

Facebook has decided to greatly increase the global reach of the program to allow
for additional school participants. The goal is to have 50 domestic teams and 125
international teams for the fall 2016 iteration. At the time of writing, there were
50 domestic teams and 119 international teams participating.

Reach and Impact

Key data

The reach of the P2P: Challenging Extremism program can be measured by
the number of participants and the number of universities and colleges involved
in the initiative. The first three iterations of P2P: Challenging Extremism
included more than two thousand student participants at ninety universities in
more than thirty countries worldwide (see Figure 10). The fourth iteration of
P2P: Challenging Extremism is expected to bring the program totals to more
than four thousand students at more than two hundred universities in fifty countries worldwide.

Campaign data

Participating teams are asked to track social media data to measure the online
impact and reach of their campaigns. At the time of writing, data were compiled
from the first two iterations of P2P: Challenging Extremism. In these first two
iterations, the implemented campaigns generated more than 5 million

TABLE 1

Aggregate Social Media Highlights as Reported by Teams Participating From First Two
P2P: Challenging Extremism Programs

Facebook page likes	120,000+
Facebook reach	5,400,000+
Twitter followers	16,000+
Video views (YouTube and Vimeo)	160,000+
Website page views on student-generated sites	84,000+

SOURCE: EVP (2016).

impressions on Facebook, more than 160,000 YouTube views, and gained sixteen
thousand Twitter followers (see Table 1). With the program now entering its
fourth iteration, the numbers continue to grow.

Media hits

P2P's growing popularity has led to numerous media stories about the initiative and the role that college students are playing in CVE efforts alongside the
U.S. government.

Top domestic and international media outlets that have featured the P2P:
Challenging Extremism program include *Wall Street Journal, Time*, PBS
NewsHour, Yahoo News, *Foreign Policy, Daily Pakistan*, National Public Radio,
Yle (Yleisradio), Re / code, and Al-Arabiya.

Students are encouraged to promote their campaigns and the P2P: Challenging
Extremism initiative to their local and national news outlets to produce more
press coverage each program term.

Conference participation

The P2P: Challenging Extremism initiative has been featured at many CVE
conferences and workshops domestically and abroad as well. Both EVP and participating teams have been invited to speak about the program and promote its
efforts in the fight against extremism.

Conferences and workshops featuring P2P include the Sovereign Challenge
(Washington, D.C.), Global Youth Summit Against Violent Extremism (New
York, NY), Security Day in Belgium (Brussels, Belgium), The Radicalisation
Awareness Network (RAN) Education Meeting, 2015 International Counter-
Terrorism Conference (Prague, Czech Republic) and The Commission on
Countering Violent Extremism (CVE) (New York, NY), among others.

Regional events

There are also opportunities within the P2P: Challenging Extremism initiative
for regional events and participation.

Los Angeles. As part of the Whitehouse CVE Summit in February 2015, grant money was provided to Los Angeles to develop community partnership programs. The Los Angeles Police Department used a portion of this grant to expand the P2P: Challenging Extremism program and fund additional university participants in the Los Angeles area. There were five additional Los Angeles–based university participants during the fall 2015 term (six Los Angeles–area schools in total).

The ability to fund the program locally allowed the program to make a larger footprint in the Los Angeles area, and at the same time showed the scalability and viability of the program on a regional level.

Colorado. The Office of Attorney General brought the P2P: Challenging Extremism program to its state. Funding was provided for three university participants in the state of Colorado to participate in the spring 2016 term.

At the end of the spring 2016 term, the U.S. Attorney's Office for Colorado gave an $11,000 grant to Community College of Aurora for placing first among the three Colorado university teams.

National Defense University – Near East South Asia Center. The center is using the Challenging Extremism program to increase participation among universities in the region, as well as to provide additional opportunities for recognition of teams among Near East South Asia (NESA). The center provided funding for five universities in the NESA region over the spring 2016 term.

At the end of the term, all participants in the NESA region, which includes countries in North Africa, the Gulf, Levant, South Asia, and Central Asia, are eligible for the NESA regional awards. These awards recognize the top three teams from the region. This provides additional opportunities for the students to win and for their campaigns to gain recognition. This also allows for regions to focus on the campaigns that are most impactful and meaningful to their area.[11]

Scalability and Program Continuation

"The reason I did this was to maybe change some minds, to start something, some sort of revolution to the way people think. It starts small, it starts with us."

–Student participant, Mount Royal University, Calgary, Alberta, Canada[12]

The P2P: Challenging Extremism program will continue to directly involve youth in countering extremism as it continues to grow and increase its global reach, providing more opportunities to counter hate and extremism via digital and social initiatives, products, and tools. It is important to note that the program also allows the U.S. government to support strategies of intervention and prevention at the domestic community level.

Scalability

Continued domestic and international program growth. The initiative started with 23 university participants, increased to 45 during the second iteration, had 53 in the third installment, and aims to include 150 for the upcoming fourth iteration. By continually increasing the number of universities involved, the program can laterally expand its reach. More universities directly correlates to a larger variety of tactics, more student participants, and more campaigns to counter violent extremism and hate globally.

Regional involvement

Regions can get involved with P2P by providing funding to additional university participants in their region, much like Los Angeles did in the fall of 2015. This not only allows for greater impact of the program in a certain area, but it also localizes the program funding, ownership, and support. With this localized approach, regions are able to establish a partnership with the community to counter and prevent extremism.

Regions can also get involved with the P2P program by hosting regional award competitions. Increasing the competition within a certain area allows for more campaigns to gain recognition outside of the global competition. This approach also works as a motivator, allowing for more students and universities to be honored for their work. Regional competitions have the additional benefit of allowing a region to make a campaign unique to their culture and community.

Campaign continuation

P2P: Challenging Extremism is run on a collegiate term schedule. At the end of the term, student teams are encouraged to continue their work; however, there is not currently funding or assistance in place to aid teams in their efforts. Funding for top teams and teams with highly effective and scalable campaigns should be provided so that teams can continue their campaigns after their participation in P2P. Allowing campaigns to run longer, with economic and logistical support, would lead to more effective campaigns that have a greater reach and impact. Continuing successful campaigns would also allow teams to adjust their campaigns based on social and political events in order to stay relevant.

MSU, from the first term of P2P: Challenging Extremism, has continued its campaign. The MSU team won with its campaign, One95. The team developed a comprehensive campaign to encourage cross-cultural collaboration to fight extremism. The target market for the team's campaign was Generation Z, after its research showed that this younger demographic was being targeted by extremists. Its plan to reach Generation Z included comprehensive education packets including Common Core lesson plans, videos, and trivia games that aimed to educate youth on aspects of extremism and online safety. After the end of the term, the Center Extremism Project (CEP) wanted to continue the One95 brand and education campaign. The team's original brand and website are still in use today, while CEP continues to modify and evolve the brand and materials.

Conclusion

The school-based CVE initiative, P2P: Challenging Extremism, demonstrates a different approach to countering and preventing violent extremism. P2P's peer-to-peer strategy allows for university students, who know their demographic best, to reach their peers and affect change organically. Moreover, with EVP and the backing and support of the interagency team at the U.S. government and Facebook, the initiative gains legitimacy.

Notes

1. As told to EVP after American Honda Motor Company, Inc. participated in an EVP program.

2. Missouri State University team. 27 April 2015. P2P: Challenging extremism: A CVE youth initiative. As submitted to Peer to Peer: Challenging Extremism competition.

3. Curtin University team. 27 April 2015. 52Jumaa: Make the pledge; take the challenge; be the change. As submitted to Peer to Peer: Challenging Extremism competition.

4. Mount Royal University team. 27 April 2015. Want movement: Final submission. As submitted to Peer to Peer: Challenging Extremism competition.

5. Lahore University of Management Sciences team. 11 December 2015. FATE: From apathy to empathy. As submitted to Peer to Peer: Challenging Extremism competition.

6. United States Military Academy team. 11 December 2015. #LetsTalkJihad; learn; talk; join. As submitted to Peer 2 Peer: Challenging Extremism competition.

7. Università della Svizzera italiana team. 11 December 2015. #Faces4Heritage. As submitted to Peer 2 Peer: Challenging Extremism competition.

8. Turku School of Economics team. 11 December 2015. Choose your future. As submitted to Peer 2 Peer: Challenging Extremism competition.

9. Gulf University for Science and Technology team. 11 December 2015. Raise your words. As submitted to Peer to Peer: Challenging Extremism competition.

10. University of Arkansas at Little Rock team. 11 December 2015. P2P: Challenging extremism: Global digital challenge. As submitted to Peer 2 Peer: Challenging Extremism competition.

11. Near East South Asia: Center for strategic studies. n.d. NESA Regions. Available from www.nesa-center.org.

12. As quoted to EVP after the student participated in the P2P competition as part of the Mount Royal University team from January 2015 through June 2015.

References

D'Angelo, Dana C., Andy Macaleer, and Katie Meier. 2015. Consulting-based action learning as an experiential education alternative to traditional co-operative education. *Academy of Business Research Journal* 2015 (June): 52–67.

EdVenture Partners. 2016. P2P: Challenging Extremism aggregate data. Orinda, CA: EdVenture Partners.

Kolb, D. A. 1984. *Experiential learning: Experience as the source of learning and development.* Englewood Cliffs, NJ: Prentice Hall. Available from academic.regis.edu.

Ryan, Evan. 18 February 2016. #ChallengeExtremism together. DIPNOTE: U.S. Department of State official blog. Available at blogs.state.gov.

The Soufan Group. 8 December 2015. *Foreign fighters: An updated assessment of the flow of foreign fighters into Syria and Iraq.* New York, NY: The Soufan Group. Available from www.soufangroup.com.

ISIS and other international terrorist organizations rely on the Internet to disseminate their extremist rhetoric and to recruit people to their cause, particularly through popular online social media applications. Any meaningful counterterrorism strategy must, therefore, account for the ways in which terrorist organizations use the Internet to prey on young, manipulable minds who are drawn to radical ideas and propaganda and to the desire to serve a cause larger than themselves. This article outlines the ways in which extremist organizations use the Internet to ensnare new recruits, analyzes the implications of cyber-recruitment on existing counterterrorism techniques, and suggests ways in which the U.S. government can work with Internet service providers and other major cyber corporations to better address this growing threat.

Keywords: CVE; countering violent extremism; radicalization; Internet recruitment; ISIS

Counter-Radicalization via the Internet

By
KAREN J. GREENBERG

The Threat

Violent extremists and terrorist groups have relied on the Internet as a form of communication since the last decade of the twentieth century. Today's use of the Internet by terrorist organizations is both an extension of prior practice and a new form of outreach. The reliance on the Internet and social media by terrorist organizations as a means of recruitment and messaging has accompanied and abetted the rise of ISIS (also known as ISIL or Islamic State), replacing the more simple

Karen J. Greenberg is the director of the Center on National Security at Fordham Law and the author of Rogue Justice: The Making of the Security State *and* The Least Worst Place: Guantanamo's First 100 Days *(Crown 2016). She writes frequently about national security, civil liberties, and the war on terror.*

NOTE: Andrew Dalack contributed to this article. Thanks also to Matthew Grier and Maxine Jacobson.

Correspondence: greenbergkarenj@gmail.com

DOI: 10.1177/0002716216672635

communication and broadcasts of al-Qaeda and its associates with an onslaught of videos, calls to action, and ideological recruitment messages, all of which sums up to a social media presence that has become essential to ISIS's overall strategy of growth and violence.

ISIS's social media strategy took early form with the Twitter messages that al-Shabaab used for recruitment in Somalia. Seeking fighters for the war in Syria and Iraq, ISIS launched into a highly energized effort of recruitment based on organized propaganda tweets as well as Facebook posts (Berger and Morgan 2015; Berger 2016). Taking this strategy further, ISIS's recruitment efforts turned to the West, expanding exponentially from Twitter and Facebook to include dozens of platforms on the open web, as well as some on the dark web (Cox 2015). ISIS's reliance on the Internet has been central to its identity as well as to its recruitment strategy. Speaking to the cyber savvy of this new generation from which it seeks to recruit, ISIS is self-consciously looking to build a cyber Caliphate, at times referred to as a digital Caliphate in support of its land grab in Syria and Iraq (Atwan 2015).

Internally, they refer to themselves as the Islamic State Electronic Army, a group whose efforts are dedicated to social media messaging on one hand and to hacking and security on the other (Stern and Berger 2015, 173). Toward this end, in January 2014, ISIS announced the creation of the Al-Battar Media Battalion, a Twitter-based team designated to push ISIS propaganda and castigate ISIS opponents (Fernandez 2015, 25). Its use of the Internet has given ISIS an "outsized impact," one that dwarfs the usefulness the Internet had for al-Qaeda (Berger and Morgan 2015, 4). As Federal Bureau of Investigation (FBI) Director Jim Comey explains, "Your grandfather's al-Qaeda, if you wanted to get propaganda, you had to go find it. . . . Now all that's in your pocket. All that propaganda is in your pocket, and the terrorist is in your pocket. It's the constant feed, the constant touching, so it's very, very different and much more effective at radicalizing than your grandfather's al-Qaeda model" (Comey 2015).

Through social media, ISIS speaks directly to the youth it is targeting for recruitment, using the medium that works best for these youth. The average age of foreign fighter recruits worldwide is 27 (Dodwell, Milton, and Rassler 2016). In the United States, recruits to ISIS are slightly younger. Their familiarity with the Internet and social media is a given. Estimates of the impact of the Internet on recruitment to ISIS in the United States are varied, but experts suggest that it outweighs person-to-person recruitment as an initial driver. This online recruitment has involved a multitude of platforms, ranging from email to the partially encrypted platform KIK (Center on National Security 2016).

Within this multiplicity of platforms, Twitter and Facebook have taken the lead in terms of their popularity among violent jihadist wannabes, not surprisingly given that they are the preferred social media platforms among the teenage and adolescent population generally.

To that end, these messages target the young and vulnerable in the United States—isolated individuals tied to their computers in an echo chamber for which reality and other influences are often kept at bay. The new purveyors of Islamic jihad are particularly adept at tapping into the anxieties and angers of broad swaths of young men and women to exploit what might otherwise be the angst of late adolescence, as well as in fomenting action. The content of the recruitment videos and images shows brutal violence against the infidels and intruders, including beheadings. They share videos that show the West harming Muslims; for example, Abu Ghraib imagery has been plentiful in ISIS propaganda and has been used for broadcasting general calls to join and serve the Caliphate.

The success of ISIS's messaging is measurable not just in terms of online follow-ers but in terms of actual recruits. Overall foreign fighter recruits are estimated to be between 27,000 and 31,000, and approximately 250 of them are thought to come from the United States (The Soufan Group 2015). In addition, there are recruits to the cause, if not to the fight in Syria and Iraq, in Western countries. Swearing *bayah*, or allegiance online, has become a regular feature of interactive online communica-tions for those who want to show their commitment to ISIS's jihad.

Though the number of U.S. recruits pales in comparison to those from coun-tries in Europe and elsewhere, there is a strong and successful movement to entice Americans to join the Islamic State in its violent activities not only abroad, as foreign fighters, but at home. As is true globally, much of the recruitment in the United States is done, in part or in total, via the Internet. Since the spring of 2014, nearly one hundred indictments have been made against alleged ISIS recruits, over half are suspected of attempting to travel abroad—or of helping others—to fight in Syria (Center on National Security 2016). With the Internet built into both the identity and strategy of ISIS's evolution, online strategies have been created by the U.S. government as well as by foreign governments to coun-ter the appeal of ISIS as part of their overall counter-radicalization efforts (Stern and Berger 2015, 247). Because the West excels in cyberspace, its expertise and familiarity on the cyber battlefield has led to a strong emphasis on online coun-terterrorism efforts.

The Internet as Countermeasure

Using the Internet as an aid in countering violent extremism (CVE) in general, and ISIS in particular, has taken three main forms: disruption, diversion, and countermessaging.

Disruption

Disruption efforts have relied on a series of technical interventions by Internet companies on behalf of the U.S. government (Waddell 2016). Beginning in 2013, Facebook and YouTube began to aggressively take down propaganda and recruit-ment sites (Berger 2016). In 2014, Twitter reportedly took down tens of thou-sands of these accounts. As of 2016, suspensions authorized by Internet companies have continued. Indeed, in August 2016, Twitter announced that it had shut down more than 235,000 accounts linked to ISIS and other extremist organizations (Prigg 2016). Experts and policy-makers have varied opinions about the effects of these suspensions. Some insist that the suspensions are work-ing to limit ISIS's "ability to grow and spread" (Berger and Morgan 2015). As a

Brookings report on Twitter commissioned by Google points out, "Account suspensions do have concrete effects in limiting the reach and scope of ISIS activities on social media. . . . [T]otal interdiction is not the goal. The qualitative debate is over how suspensions affect the performance of the network and whether a different level of pressure might produce a different result" (Berger and Morgan 2015). Since platforms such as Facebook and Twitter "are global communities, each engaged in a constant process of determining community norms as the use of the platforms evolves," defining what is and what is not "terrorist content" is precarious work that can expose social media platforms to accusations and censorship and undermine their credibility (Greenberg 2015).

Nevertheless, account suspensions are a critical tool for combatting ISIS online. Put succinctly, one report concludes, "The consequences of neglecting to weed a garden are obvious, even though weeds will always return" (Russon 2015). And in fact, the numbers bear out the impact, at least in the short term. Research has shown, for example, that the suspensions have been effective. "The primary ISIS hashtag—the group's name in Arabic—went from routinely registering in 40,000 tweets per day or more in around the time suspensions began in September 2014, to [fewer] than 5,000 on a typical day in February. Many of those tweets consisting of hostile messages sent by parties in the Persian Gulf" (Berger and Morgan 2015, 56).

On one hand, the suspensions tend to enhance a game of cat and mouse, of who can outplay the other in terms of avoiding detection. Industry insiders and technologists tell us that such disruptions are often only temporary. When one Twitter account is taken down, a new hashtag—or several new hashtags—can replace it almost immediately. The user just moves to a new account, a new platform, a new place from which to broadcast its message of violence and hatred. While Twitter, to counter this, has banned the proliferation of sites used for the same purpose, ISIS can load bots—automatic, as opposed to human, transmissions into the system—and flood the digital space, enhancing exponentially the number of screens that have a given message. Still, suspended accounts "rarely fully rebounded to their pre-suspension levels, even when the new accounts were left up. Researchers suspect that this could be the case because the suspension discourages returning users, as well as their followers" (Carman 2016).

In addition, some experts anticipate that these shutdowns drive recruiters and their potential followers to the dark web, where the possibility of a counter strategy stands to be even more elusive. Indeed, ISIS launched at least one propaganda site on the dark web—a portion of the Internet requiring anonymous web browsing, not accessible through regular browsers like Google Chrome, Mozilla, or Internet Explorer—in November 2015, which made its "material more resilient to take-downs" and helped to "protect the identity of the group's supporters" (Cox 2015). Some point out that this result is worth the risk when compared to the damage ISIS can do to the tune of millions of communications a day. Compelling terrorist organizations to operate in secret does make plots more difficult to intercept, experts note; but in the case of ISIS, some argue that it is a trade-off worth making (Burgess 2016).

The goal of those who wish to avoid the dark web option is to focus on human sourcing of messaging; take out the top of the hierarchy; and, in the words of Google Jigsaw's Jared Cohen, "push the remaining rank and file into the digital equivalent of a remote cave" (Cohen 2015). Although ISIS has reportedly set up a dark website as of 2015, it still leaves the vast majority of Internet users sheltered from online exposure to the group's propaganda videos and calls to action (Gilbert 2015). In this way, it becomes a deterrent to recruitment, leaving those who have already claimed membership in ISIS to follow the group to the dark web.

Some point to the usefulness of the open web as a source of information and to the detrimental aspects of pushing ISIS recruits to the dark web. They emphasize the value of collecting data on potential terrorists. Experts agree that there is intelligence value to be gleaned from watching the Internet and keeping these exchanges in the open cyber sphere. As one terrorism expert explains, "In the short term, the most promising way for dealing with the presence of violent extremists and their propaganda on the Internet is to exploit their online communications to gain intelligence and gather evidence in the most comprehensive and systematic fashion possible" (Neumann 2013, 453).

But the value of this may be minimal given the vast amount of activity on the open web and the difficulties of determining the difference between expression and activity. As in terrorism cases generally, identifying the line between extremist expression and terrorist action requires knowledge and judgment. "In this American democracy, we don't want our social media providers to be acting as essentially secret police," said Nate Cardozo, a staff attorney at the Electronic Frontier Foundation. "There is a first amendment right to talk about terrorism. . . . Discussing controversial political, religious, social events of our time is absolutely protected speech. And requiring social media providers to rat out their customers for engaging in their first amendment right to debate important topics is not something that is constitutional" (Ross and Schwartz 2015).

Specific concerns about targeting Muslims have colored the CVE programs initiated by the White House, including those that have engaged civilian groups. One legal counterargument has emerged pointing out that freedom of speech has been regulated in telecommunications for a long time. Telephone harassment is illegal in all fifty states. One comprehensive analysis concludes, "This point needs to be crystal clear: social media companies can and do control speech on their platforms. No user of a mainstream social media service enjoys an environment of complete freedom. Instead, companies apply a wide range of conditions limiting speech, using possibly opaque guidelines that may result in decisions executed on an ad hoc basis. Furthermore, companies typically do not disclose information about who they suspend and why, nor are they required to" (Berger and Morgan 2015, 60).

The choice of whom to monitor, and under what conditions, remains murky and potentially full of legal potholes. Despite the telephone precedents, the regulations for the Internet are less clear. Currently, a variety of new products claim the ability to use algorithms and linguistic analysis and other means to predict who is headed down the road to radicalization. The realistic predictive value of such measures, however, is problematic and largely untested. Moreover, studies suggest that there are too many false positives in this approach. Technologist Bruce Schneier compares the use of algorithms for detecting potential terrorists to the attempts to pinpoint a rare disease, something equally "unique and rare." "When a disease is very rare, if your test tests positive, it's almost always wrong, because your chances of having that disease are one in a million. . . . Out of a million people, 10,000 would test positive—but chances are only one would really have the disease. And you wouldn't know which one. Now imagine the odds are one in 100 million, amid many hundreds of millions of social media postings. Imagine how many posts would be deleted or referred to law enforcement in error" (McLaughlin 2016).

Finally, the thin line between industry monitoring of accounts and law enforcement's involvement is legally troubling inside the industry itself. Tech companies have recently refused to comply with government insistence that the information the companies have access to should be available to the government. Apple refused to design an encryption key for breaking into the phone of one of the San Bernardino terrorists. Microsoft is now protesting the government's gag orders for accounts that are being surveilled and investigated. Facebook and YouTube initially provided for ways to tag terrorist content, but Twitter did not, making exceptions for banning incitements to violence (Stern and Berger 2015; Albergotti and Koh 2014). In October 2014, Twitter sued the government, saying that the government should provide more transparency about what it was doing with this surveillance (Nakashima 2014).

After more than a decade of secretive overreaching by the government—which, when exposed, led to the sunsetting of policies aimed at broad collection of telephone and Internet data—the current appetite for the collection of search engine material and content beyond that openly found on social media platforms could potentially open the fissure between government and cyber businesses even wider. The White House and lawmakers have made an analogy between the detection and reporting of child pornography online to the detection and reporting of terrorists online. In the context of ISIS, the tech companies would be expected to monitor the content put forward by their users and report "terrorist activity" to law enforcement. This not only raises legal and constitutional issues but also issues of expertise: who knows how to identify terrorists or potential terrorists. As some have pointed out, the detection of terrorists could ultimately rely upon a series of vague assumptions, and as terrorists are extremely small in number relative the overall population, this tactic might render the effort nearly impossible (Trujillo 2016).

Diversion and alternative engagement

Diversion and alternative engagement make up the second element of online counterterrorism programs. As early as April 2012, the State Department launched a "viral peace campaign" aimed at individuals in Southeast Asia. The program was designed "to use social media as a way of promoting community involvement and peaceful change" and "to help people craft online strategies that use a whole range of tools—including 'logic, humor, satire, [and] religious arguments'—to match the violent extremists' energy and enthusiasm" (Neumann 2013, 446). Now Google has developed a program of diversion for those who search for certain terms. When a user searches for certain terms or topics, their requests are diverted to nongovernmental organization (NGO) sites where countermessaging occurs. The Google Adwords Grants Program, following the long-term business strategy of Google, gives credits to NGOs to purchase ads for counter-radicalization messaging that will appear at the top of searches identified with the attraction to radicalization (Ward-Bailey 2016). Thus, any nonprofit or NGO can place counter-radicalization ads against search terms of their choosing that carry terrorist or radicalized connotations. For example, the Council on American and Islamic Relations (CAIR) can now create and promulgate ads and narratives countering radical interpretations of Islam that will appear whenever someone enters "violent jihad" into Google. For Google executives, this is about more than rebuttal; it is about hope. "We should get the bad stuff down, but it's also extremely important that people are able to find good information, that when people are feeling isolated, that when they go on-line, they find a community of hope, not a community of harm," a top executive at Google explained (Quinn 2016).

Similarly, nonvirtual counterterrorism strategies suggest alternatives that encourage diversion to those individuals determined to serve a cause larger than themselves—a strong part of ISIS's appeal to American youth (Center on National Security 2016). The United Nation's (UN) Strong Cities program encourages NGOs such as community organizations and youth-oriented organizations to develop their own counterterrorism, counter-radicalization programs independently. In addition, the UN has developed such a strategy in the peace network proposed by the UN's Counterterrorism Implementation Task Force (CTITF). These programs seek to address the underlying reasons for people's interest in ISIS: loneliness, desperation, and naïveté. Some of these programs have also reached out to engage Muslim communities. As a recent synopsis from the Carter Center concludes, "Muslim religious and community leaders have an important role to play in discrediting and preventing violent extremism as they hold unique positions of authority, credibility, and communal ties" (Abadi 2016). Moreover, they often understand the cultural reference points that ISIS propaganda relies on, and can potentially turn youth toward more constructive outlets and activities, as well as helping NGOs to develop models for integration as an antidote to radicalization (Ben-Meir 2015).

Countermessaging

In addition to disruption and diversion, a third and growing element in the government's online counterterrorism strategy has been the dissemination of counternarratives, or countermessages. Following the White House announcement of a counter-radicalization strategy that addressed the role of the Internet in promoting violent extremism, the Center for Strategic Counterterrorism Communications (CSCC) was created in September 2011 in an effort to deter al-Qaeda followers. From 2011 to 2014, CSCC launched aggressive countermessaging against ISIS in both Arabic and English (Fernandez 2015, 4,15).

In February 2015, President Obama held a summit to discuss additional methods of CVE. A year later, in March 2016, the president issued an Executive Order creating the Global Engagement Center (GEC) designed to "lead the coordination, integration, and synchronization of government-wide communications activities directed at foreign audiences abroad in order to counter the messaging and diminish the influence of international terrorism organizations." The GEC is tasked with finding "innovati[ve] and new approaches to counter the messaging and diminish the influence of international terrorist organizations."[1]

These counternarratives fall largely into two categories. The first category includes discussions of Islam that correct misreadings of the Koran and the Muslim religion. These online efforts parallel nationwide programs in which individuals are taught by Imams and others schooled in knowledge of Islam that killing and suicide missions and brutality are anathema to traditional Islam. This strain of counternarrative has been central to counter-radicalization programs world wide, from Saudi Arabia to Indonesia to the UK. They rely to some extent, however, on an individual being connected to a mosque or a larger community. This approach is out of sync with the known details of the lives of many ISIS recruits. In reality, individuals in the United States who are drawn to ISIS are often loners who do not necessarily interact with a mosque or respond to authority of an imam (Callimachi 2015). At least one expert has suggested that Muslim leaders need to rise to this challenge, finding ways to connect with distant youth and "enhance their media capabilities and communication strategies so that they can effectively discredit ISIS propaganda" (Abadi 2015). Here, as elsewhere, the counter narrative is seen as most effective when paired with religious leaders making similar efforts offline, "through the use of local dialects, shorter and interactive sermons, safe space[s] for women, and local initiatives for youth" (Abadi 2015).

A second popular counternarrative refutes the idealization of life inside the Caliphate. Instead of a perfect, protected, peaceful life, viewers see images of rape, death, and general suffering for members of the Caliphate. In mid-April 2016, the GEC's webpage posted a series of videos under the title "Life under Daesh." Individual videos in the series included episodes devoted to discreet topics such as "food, healthcare, and violence" under Daesh. The 90-minute videos expose the hypocrisy of ISIS. The videos pit the recruitment promises of ISIS against the realities of life once the recruit arrives. The most recent video, on "family," posits family as the true antidote to ISIS. "Family is LOVE. ISIS is HATRED. Family is TRUTH. ISIS is LIES. Family is DECENT. ISIS is VULGAR." The list goes on.

Returning foreign fighter testimonials have also lately contributed to the debunking of ISIS. This strategy has proven popular in countries where there is a significant number of returning fighters. Although the United States does not have a significant population of foreign fighters, policy-makers still see the narrative as useful to deterrence in the United States. On April 26, the House passed a bill "To require the Secretary of Homeland Security to use the testimonials of former or estranged violent extremists or their associates in order to counter terrorist recruitment, and for other purposes (e.g., community engagement, etc.)" (U.S. House of Representatives 2016).

Those from other countries, who have traveled abroad and found the Caliphate to be other than what was promised, have gruesome stories to tell, and those stories can deter those who are considering joining ISIS (Draper 2014; Kenworthy 2016; Malik 2015). But the question remains, Who should be responsible for generating this counternarrative? The British program, Prevent, as well as earlier counter-radicalization programs in the United States, have led many to conclude that government-sponsored efforts can be ineffective and counterproductive. The government as messenger diminishes the power of the message: "every time officials try to win trust, they are met with the accusation that they are treating Muslims as a 'suspect community'" (Casciani 2014). In addition, as a House Homeland Security report on "Countering Violent Extremist Programs" pointed out, Prevent failed largely because it did not include Muslims before it implemented its program. In fact, because it focused on Muslims as suspects and excluded them in the creation of the program, Prevent "inadvertently created a relationship of mistrust. This compromised the goal of community engagement and support and potentially helped create an environment ripe for extremist recruitment based on the resentment of the British government" (Southers 2015).

The State Department's counternarrative strategy overall has raised eyebrows alongside Prevent over whether, as one official reportedly explained to *The New York Times*, "the U.S. government should be involved in overt messaging at all" (Miller 2015). Given this caveat, and the persistent doubts about the effectiveness of the program, the U.S. government has recently turned to the private sector for online and interpersonal counternarrative programs, enlisting not only NGOs but college students to create countermessaging. "Over the past year, the Departments of State and Homeland Security have partnered with Facebook and EdVenture Partners to create the Peer to Peer: Challenging Extremism program" (Wagner 2015). As part of this program, students from universities across the globe compete against each other to "develop and execute campaigns and social media strategies against extremism that are credible, authentic, and believable to their peers and resonate within their communities."[2] These student-designed strategies involve rudimentary advertising techniques as well as direct engagement, as in chat rooms. At least one of the college-based programs—at West Point Military Academy—consisted of students posing as ISIS members to lure individuals away from ISIS. Several NGOs have also developed their own counternarrative strategies. Over the last two years, a number of notable efforts have been launched, including video series produced by the Arab Center for Scientific Research and Humane Studies and the Institute for Strategic Dialogue (Cohen 2015, 56).

To date, the absence of Muslims in some of these programs runs the risk of diluting their impact. The counternarrative can preach inclusion, but the reality is that the discourse in the country is often publicly anti-Muslim and unwelcoming to those who practice Islam. Prominent voices in politics and elsewhere in the United States, most notably presidential candidate Donald Trump, have called for the exclusion of Muslim refugees and immigrants and the monitoring of Muslim neighborhoods (Kopal 2015). The impact of these attitudes on the narratives of the individuals who are drawn to ISIS in the United States is revealing. Those individuals often feel that they are unable to practice their religion without persecution. As one teenagers who tried to leave the country to fight with ISIS proclaimed, "The truth is, Mama, I could not bear to live in that land, a land that is haram to live in, the land whose people mock my Allah, my beloved prophet, the commands of Allah, his law. The ones who are using my money to kill my brothers and sisters."[3] Such impressions can hardly lead a young Muslim to reasonably expect to have a successful (religious) future in the United States. The messaging that ignores this reality will likely fall on deaf ears.

Countering ISIS's message should involve not only the Internet but the realities for Muslims on the ground. It is important to be especially attentive to the intersection of the reality on the ground and the message being delivered. For example, collateral damage from drone strikes and the mistreatment and abuse of prisoners (Abu Ghraib pictures figure into ISIS propaganda to this day) appear frequently in ISIS videos (Fernandez 2015). Recent reports on countering ISIS's messaging point to the need to avoid lies and deception as part of the counternarrative. Realism in countermessaging on the web reinforces the close connection between online efforts at counter-radicalization and offline efforts at the community and policy levels.

Conclusion and Recommendations

Online counter-radicalization is a delicate business. The manipulative pitfalls are not the only worries. So too are the many constitutional and legal protections. Where and how law enforcement gets involved is tricky. As Peter Neumann points out, "*Constitutional free speech protections* in the United States are extensive, which means that the vast majority of the content that qualifies as extremist or radicalizing would be protected under the First Amendment" (Neumann 2013, 438).

The private sector is not bound by the same constraints. Still, the tactic of assuming a fake identity as a means of promoting a government sponsored message—referred to as "ventriloquism"—has received criticism when it comes to private entities that receive government funding as a condition of either promoting or refraining to promote specific messages (Greene 2000, 4). Once distrust occurs in the private sector, it will likely prove extremely difficult to enact counternarrative strategies of any sort.

In each iteration of its counter-radicalization strategies, the government has mentioned the need to respect civil liberties and to stay within the bounds of the Constitution. But there are a variety of legal and constitutional issues that could be addressed by defining the contours of any new countermessaging strategies. This is for another article, but, overall, there needs to be upfront recognition of the legal parameters of the policies at the government and private levels. For example, the way in which information from the Internet is reported to legal authorities and by whom needs to be vetted and codified, so that there is transparency about how such information collection is done, by whom, and with what level of criminal liability. Along with the Fourth Amendment issues, First Amendment issues will need to be outlined.

While the counternarrative has evolved over time, there is to date scant confidence in the success of these efforts, particularly for the newer programs. One problem with counter-radicalization programs has been the absence of metrics. But online, there can be tangible results. The decline in certain search words and the lack of Twitter hashtags, for example, are eminently measurable. These metrics should be collected regularly and the strategies evaluated in response to what the metrics tell us.

The Internet, the dominant communication space of our era, can be a vital tool against terrorism. For the Internet to be a security ally, it must employ all three aspects of counter-radicalization identified in this article—disruption, diversion, and countermessaging—but it must do so in a way that recognizes the limitations of government and that puts trust in the citizenry and in private companies to coalesce around the notion that a safe society can result from cautionary measures carried out in informed ways.

Recommendations

Recommendation 1. Online counter-radicalization activities should be understood as part of a larger integrated counter-radicalization effort. They do not and should not exist in a void. As much as reliance on the Internet for counter-radicalization makes sense, the Internet should be seen as one tool among many, rather than as a one-stop panacea. Any attempt at curbing the cyber proliferation of extremist materials, in any form, must be made with the understanding that the Internet is not the only battleground. Online countermeasures must be coordinated with similar antiradicalization activities that take place outside of virtual space. Relying on the Internet exclusively, or even too heavily, can have negative consequences. Coordination with other counterterrorism messages will ensure that the Internet programs do not collide with other programs' goals and methods.

Recommendation 2. Disruption can work. Taking sites down can stem the spread of ISIS recruitment. The statistics bear this out. What is important in the disruption framework is who does the disruption; at the time of this writing, private companies have been entrusted with identifying material that needs to be removed. It would be useful to let individuals online report inappropriate and seemingly dangerous content to the companies. This does not preclude the need for private surveillance of the web, but it shifts some of the burden to the consumer.

Recommendation 3. The messenger matters. Who delivers the countermessage online is important, as it is in person. Muslim voices and guidance need to be involved in messaging strategies. To date, policy-makers have made no explicit or systematic effort to include individuals with a deep knowledge of Islamic law and culture or those who understand teens and late adolescents as message generators. Both should be called upon to help devise these programs from the outset to enhance the effectiveness of the programs by reaching the individuals attracted to ISIS online. The messaging should come at least in part from groups and people possessing an intimate familiarity with Islam, the Muslim world, American Muslim communities, and American youth generally. Accordingly, it only makes sense to coordinate meaningfully with Muslim community stakeholders, who understand best that Muslims have just as much of an interest in halting the spread of extremism as anybody else. Further, because people are less likely to trust or even entertain the messenger unless the individual or organization possesses a certain level of credibility, it is necessary that virtual counterextremism messaging is independent not only from the government but also from government-controlled voices.

Recommendation 4. Interactive messaging should take precedence over broadcast messaging. Interactive communications are essential for an effective online counter-radicalization strategy. The point is to engage, rather than to lecture. It is important to engage child psychologists, university psychiatry programs, those who understand Muslim culture, and youth counselors in finding new ways to draw young people away from virtual reality and back into the real world. Online interactivity can provide therapy, an antidote to isolation and alienation, and a growth experience. Talking on Skype, direct messaging on Twitter are but some examples. As one recruit wrote, after she began receiving constant messages and signs of affection from ISIS recruiters, "I have brothers and sisters now. I am crying." Engagement should be as much about countering alienation and isolation as about countering radicalization.

Recommendation 5. Countermessaging should not be static but should alter as necessary with new information about radicalization. Countermessengers should be attentive to the evolving nature of ISIS's message and to detailed information about who joins ISIS and why. There have been gaps between the design of countermessaging programs and the reality on the ground. For example, the idea of using mosques and imams for de-radicalization may only matter if the potential recruits are in touch with those institutions and religious leaders. Moreover, the refutation of ISIS's message needs to be responsive to the current dominant narratives underlying recruitment, whether they be about the Islamic religion itself, the persecution of Muslims, or the foreign policy of the United States.

Recommendation 6. Driving ISIS to use the dark web can be a worthwhile outcome. Getting ISIS off of popular platforms diminishes their reach and their effectiveness. It is akin to pushing them into a cave, as some have noted. Intervention that makes the point of radicalization more elusive gets at the heart of the matter—recruitment—which takes place on the open web where the not-yet-indoctrinated proliferate. Making ISIS relocate its propaganda to the Internet's darkest depths makes people less likely to actually join or act on its behalf. The dark web forces ISIS into the shadows, making it more difficult for American citizens to start down the extremist rabbit hole.

Recommendation 7. Providing valuable, realistic alternative narratives online is essential. Part of ISIS's allure lies in the adventures, missions, and/or inclusiveness it promises to isolated, often troubled, youth. Accordingly, NGOs and others should be empowered to find compelling causes that youth can join online. Because of the relatively young age of ISIS recruits in the United States, the FBI has turned in some cases to diversion rather than arrest. Internet voices should do likewise. Last year, the UN's Counter-Terrorism Committee Executive Directorate even conceded that alternatives to criminal prosecution were desirable, particularly when an individual has not yet attempted to travel to ISIS territory (UN CTED 2015). This avenue should be enhanced and empowered. What other causes can satisfy those who are isolated, disenfranchised, and looking for a mission and a cause greater than themselves?

Recommendation 8. The truth matters; distortions of fact are counterproductive. Those charged with countering the narrative online should not only point out the lies that ISIS spreads, as the State Department program did, but provide valuable, realistic facts. *Manipulation, and impersonation is counterproductive.* As more and more people successfully flee ISIS's grasp, it is becoming easier to publish counternarratives that devalue ISIS's fantastic misrepresentation of Islam. In addition, there are numerous voices that are willing to combat the vicious messages of ISIS. There is no need to stretch the truth or promote propaganda of a different kind. It is enough to make accurate information about ISIS readily available. The perils of losing credibility are immense.

Recommendation 9. Dissemination of narratives of disillusion can have a profound impact. Returning foreign fighters' voices provide a valuable counternarrative. Disillusionment, portrayals of hardship and brutality—even toward members of ISIS—can be an effective form of deterrence, provided that the message is not manipulated or distorted.

Recommendation 10. Metrics. A series of metrics needs to be developed to assess the strength of these programs. For example, decreasing the number of ISIS Twitter followers and decreasing attention to other social media platforms that ISIS uses are important. An increased number of visitors to alternative sites—such as those that offer a hopeful, constructive vision of life in the United States for those who feel alienated, excluded, and are drawn to violence—would also be a useful metric. Here, as elsewhere, social psychologists could also be consulted for ways to measure changes in behavior and attitudes over time.

Recommendation 11. Legal/civil liberties analysis up front. There needs to be a transparent legal analysis that accompanies each of the strategies for online counter-radicalization. This will enable whatever programs are created to persist into the future on strong foundations. Up-front recognition of specific constitutional principles would be preferable to a blanket nod to civil liberties and constitutional principles. The Apple/FBI debate was a harbinger of a growing determination of private companies to safeguard their domains from government oversight and intrusion. Addressing issues of profiling, of surveillance authorities, and of social media regulations sooner rather than later could lead to more consistency and effectiveness in carrying out online antiradicalization strategies.

Notes

1. Executive Order 13721. 14 March 2016. Available from https://www.federalregister.gov/articles/ 2016/03/17/2016-06250/developing-an-integrated-global-engagement-center-to-support-government-wide-counterterrorism.

2. See http://edventurepartners.com/peer2peer/.

3. *Chicago Tribune.* 3 November 2014. Letter by sister of Mohammed Hamza Khan.

References

Abadi, Houda. 2015. *ISIS media strategies: The role of our community leaders.* Atlanta, GA: Carter Center. Available from https://www.cartercenter.org/resources/pdfs/peace/conflict_resolution/syria-conflict/ isis-media-strategies-role-of-muslim-religious-leaders-2015.pdf.

Albergotti, Reed, and Yoree Koh. 21 August 2014. Twitter faces free-speech dilemma. *Wall Street Journal.*

Atwan, Abdel Bari. 2015. *Islamic State: The digital caliphate.* Berkeley, CA: University of California Press.

Ben-Meir, Alon. 28 April 2015. Integration is the open secret to deradicalization. *Huffington Post.*

Berger, J. M. 2 April 2016. ISIS and the big three. Hate Speech International. Available from https://www .hate-speech.org/isis-and-the-big-three/.

Berger, J. M., and Jonathon Morgan. 5 March 2015. *The ISIS Twitter census: Defining and describing the population of ISIS supporters on Twitter.* Brookings Project on U.S. Relations with Islamic World. Washington, DC: The Brookings Institution. Available from https://www.brookings.edu.

Burgess, Matt. 19 January 2016. Google: ISIS must be "contained to the dark web." *Wired.*

Callimachi, Rukmini. 27 June 2015. ISIS and the lonely, young American. *New York Times.*

Carman, Ashley. 19 February 2016. Twitter suspensions may actually be curbing ISIS propaganda. The Verge. Available from http://www.theverge.com.

Casciani, Dominic. 26 August 2014. Analysis: The Prevent strategy and its problems. BBC News.

Center on National Security. 2016. Case by case: ISIS prosecutions in the United States. New York, NY: Fordham Law. Available from http://static1.squarespace.com/static/55dc76f7e4b013c872183fea/t/577c 5b43197aea832bd486c0/1467767622315/ISIS+Report+-+Case+by+Case+-+July2016.pdf.

Cohen, Jared. 2015. Digital counterinsurgency: How to marginalize the Islamic State online. *Foreign Affairs* 94 (6): 52–58.

Comey, James B. 8 July 2015. Counterterrorism, counterintelligence, and the challenges of "going dark." Testimony before Counterterrorism, Counterintelligence, and the Challenges of Going Dark, Senate Select Committee on Intelligence. Available from https://www.fbi.gov/news/testimony/going-dark-encryption-technology-and-the-balances-between-public-safety-and-privacy.

Cox, Joseph. 16 November 2015. ISIS now has a propaganda site on the dark web. Motherboard. Available from http://motherboard.vice.com.

Dodwell, Brian, Daniel Milton, and Don Rassler. 12 April 2016. *The Caliphate's global workforce: An inside look at the Islamic State's foreign fighter paper trail.* West Point, NY: Combatting Terrorism Center at West Point. Available from https://www.ctc.usma.edu/v2/wp-content/uploads/2016/04/ CTC_Caliphates-Global-Workforce-Report1.pdf.

Draper, Lucy. 2 December 2014. Would-be jihadists' letters home reveal unhappy, mundane life in ISIS. *Newsweek.*

Fernandez, Alberto. 2015. *Here to stay and growing combatting ISIS propaganda networks.* Washington, DC: Brookings Institution. Available from https://www.brookings.edu.

Gilbert, David. 19 November 2015. ISIS moves to the dark web to spread its message and avoid detection. *International Business Times.*

Greenberg, Julia. 21 November 2015. Why Facebook and Twitter can't just wipe out ISIS online. *Wired.*

Greene, Abner S. 2000. Government of the good. *Vanderbilt Law Review* 53 (1): 1–69.

Kenworthy, Josh. 18 March 2016. Getting out of ISIS: American man among the few to escape. *The Christian Science Monitor.*

Kopal, Tal. 16 November 2015. Donald Trump: Syrian refugees a "Trojan Horse." CNN.com.

Malik, Shiv. 21 September 2015. Protect ISIS defectors, western governments urged. *The Guardian*.

McLaughlin, Jenna. 20 January 2016. The White House asked social media companies to look for terrorists. Here's why they'd #fail. *The Intercept*.

Miller, Greg. 2 December 2015. Panel casts doubt on U.S. propaganda efforts against ISIS. *Washington Post*.

Nakashima, Ellen. 7 October 2014. Twitter sues U.S. government over limits on ability to disclose surveillance orders. *Washington Post*.

Neumann, Peter. 2013. Options and strategies for countering radicalization in the United States. *Studies in Conflict and Terrorism* 36 (6): 431–59.

Prigg, Mark. 18 August 2016. Twitter's terror crackdown. DailyMail.com.

Quinn, Ben. 2 February 2016. Google to point extremist searches toward anti-radicalisation websites. *The Guardian*.

Ross, Brian, and Rhonda Schwartz. 1 July 2015. Officials: Facebook, Twitter not reporting ISIS messages. ABC News.

Russon, Mary-Ann. 6 March 2015. ISIS Twitter account "weeds": Up to 90,000 spreading jihadi propaganda in 2014. *International Business Times*.

The Soufan Group. 2015. *Foreign fighters: An updated assessment of the flow of foreign fighters into Syria and Iraq*. New York, NY: The Soufan Group. Available from http://soufangroup.com/wp-content/uploads/2015/12/TSG_ForeignFightersUpdate3.pdf.

Southers, Erroll. 16 July 2015. Rethinking countering violent extremism programs. Security Debrief. Available from http://securitydebrief.com.

Stern, Jessica, and J. M. Berger. 2015. *ISIS: The state of terror*. New York, NY: Ecco.

Trujillo, Mario. 8 January 2016. White House sees child porn efforts as model for fighting terrorism. *The Hill*.

United Nations Counter-Terrorism Committee Executive Directorate (CTED). 2015. *Background note*. Available from http://www.un.org/en/sc/ctc/docs/2015/0721Technical%20session%20Group%20III%20-%20background%20note.pdf.

U.S. House of Representatives. 26 April 2016. Combating Terrorist Recruitment Act of 2016. Available from https://www.congress.gov/congressional-record/2016/04/26/house-section/article/H1961-1.

Waddell, Kaveh. 19 February 2016. Twitter's account suspensions are surprisingly effective against ISIS. *The Atlantic*.

Wagner, Kurt. 15 December 2015. U.S. enlists college students to fight ISIS online. Re/Code. Available from http://recode.net.

Ward-Bailey, Jeff. 3 February 2016. How Google plans to fight extremism through search advertising (+video). *The Christian Science Monitor*.

European CVE Strategies from a Practitioner's Perspective

By
JUDY KORN

Countering violent extremism (CVE) is a widely used and defined term. From a practitioner's perspective, it works on three levels: prevention of radicalization, intervention with individuals in danger of radicalization, and de-radicalization. The European Union pursues a holistic approach, which includes transnational collaboration and eliminating possible root causes of radicalization. The focus is not exclusively on national security concerns but also on prevention, de-radicalization, and rehabilitation. European states have developed a variety of CVE strategies, some of which are perceived as centrally controlled, while others are characterized by participative and cooperative structures. At both the European and national levels, collaborative approaches that encompass incorporation of civil society organizations and governmental programs are seen as the most effective in CVE.

Keywords: radicalization; de-radicalization; countering violent extremism; Islamism; prevention

Countering Violent Extremism (CVE) Strategies: Current Challenges in Europe

The development and sustainable implementation of programs capable of preventing people from joining extremist groups and terrorist associations has become increasingly apparent, especially in Europe. The term "countering violent extremism" (CVE) has been greatly discussed and defined. From the viewpoint of practitioners, whose work it is to implement these programs, a clear definition of CVE is

Judy Korn is the founder and CEO of the Violence Prevention Network, where she works with radicalized individuals. In 2007, she was named an Ashoka Fellow.

Correspondence: judy.korn@violence-prevention-network.de

DOI: 10.1177/0002716216671888

essential. We also must take complex action to meet such a complex social challenge.

Collective and national strategies to combat and stave off extremism should dovetail with many social endeavors. These comprise research into the causes of radicalization, prevention through civic and intercultural education, and efforts to address de-radicalization and reintegration of those who have crossed the line into extremism. A CVE strategy must also comprise security efforts, because the path from disaffected youth to violent fighter can be extremely short.

Take, for example, the case of Omar Abdel Hamid El-Hussein. As a schoolboy, he was regarded as a fervent anti-Semite by his fellow students. The Danish criminal prevention service placed him on a list of those who had radicalized while in prison. When he was incarcerated, he announced that after being released, he wanted to travel to Syria to join the so-called Islamic State (von Altenbockum 2015). Two weeks after his release, on February 14, 2015, El-Hussein murdered one person and injured three who were taking part in an event on freedom of opinion. On February 15, he shot a Jewish security guard and injured two police officers during an attack on a Copenhagen synagogue.

Toulouse in March 2012 (Wiegel 2012), Brussels in May 2014 (Lehnartz 2014) and March 2016 (Faigle, Geisler, and Polke-Majewski 2016), Paris in January and November 2015 (Le Devin and Mouillard 2015), Copenhagen in February 2015 (von Altenbockum 2015), and Saint-Etienne-du-Rouvray in July 2016 (Simons 2016)—for all these killings, we see ourselves confronted with perpetrators who were born or socialized in Europe. All these perpetrators could have had access to prevention, intervention, and de-radicalization programs in schools and prisons. CVE strategies in the three countries in question were in place at the time of the attacks, though possibly not yet adequately implemented. All the perpetrators identified to date were also known to the respective country's security agency (Lobo 2016). The Danish case illustrates how comprehensive CVE strategies need to be checked continually for potential loopholes and adapted to new findings. Intervention and, in particular, de-radicalization are still not common in CVE strategies in Europe despite these horrendous experiences. The focus is most often on prevention.

One of the greatest challenges of this new form of violence exerted by young people who have grown up in Europe is its terrorist quality. Perpetrators are usually not spontaneous and instead are focused on targets with great symbolic effect and exposure, and they act with cold-blooded "effectiveness" and brutality.

Antiviolence or therapeutic initiatives that are unspecific tend to come up short as an intervention measure. Efforts that do not take into account the hyper-moral code of ideologized groups and the victimization that results will not be able to prevent actions such as those listed above (for the meaning of victimization interpretations and their processing by de-radicalization in practice, see Buschbom 2015b). Based on my own experience counseling families in which family members have become radicalized, it is clear that the number of young people becoming radicalized is increasing, and that radicalization puts emotional pressure on family members. Therefore, auxiliary and support services for family members are needed. It has also become clear to me, however, that counseling, and especially intervention, for radicalized individuals themselves is necessary. Family members' influence has its limits.

Work with radicalized individuals returning from a crisis area represents another challenge. Being in the middle of international jihad can have a multiplier effect on radicalization. But not all those who travel to Syria inevitably end up in the arms of Islamist combat units. And not everyone who survives the combat missions of militant jihad returns highly radicalized; some, who are deeply disillusioned, knock again on the doors of family members; others are deeply traumatized; and often both apply. Peter Neumann from King's College in London describes the group of returnees: there are "some who return who are without doubt dangerous—they are in the minority. There are those who are disillusioned and traumatized who need psychological support. But it is not yet clear to most what to do next" (Steffen 2015).

People whose lives had previously been dominated by academic and professional failures, dysfunctional family situations, or a general criminal environment are usually the victims of indoctrination. It is mainly people who are faced with a lack of future prospects in their homelands who seem to be particularly susceptible to Islamist extremism (for the correlation between biographical experience and its interpretation by the individual ideology, see Buschbom 2016; for processing by de-radicalization in practice, see Buschbom 2015a).

Fired up by the so-called refugee crisis in Europe, the rise of right-wing extremist and right-wing populist forces has led to a third challenge that Europe is sure to face for many years to come. It was not only in Germany that the influx of refugees in 2015 led to polarization, radicalization, and violence. "According to the BKA (German Federal Office of Criminal Investigation), it registered 1,005 criminal acts [in 2015] directed at facilities occupied by refugees. This figure was 199 the year before. 901 of these crimes were attributed to the right-wing scene as politically motivated criminality. The number was only 177 in the whole of 2014" (*Zeit online* 2016). These violent attacks against refugees and their accommodations must be dealt with by the penal system, but they must also be factored into the framework of prevention and de-radicalization as laid out in a comprehensive CVE strategy.

The rise of right-wing parties in many countries in Europe, such as the Front National (France), Alternative für Deutschland (Germany), the Schweizerische Volkspartei (Switzerland), the Freiheitliche Partei Österreich (Austria), the Danish Volkspartei (Denmark), the Fidez ("Hungarian Civic Alliance") (Hungary), the PiS ("Justice and Fairness") (Poland), and the Sweden Democrats (Sweden), is an endorsement of the violence toward refugees. This is where classic CVE approaches have had no effect. If things are to change, a pan-European alliance of democratic powers, along with frank debate on the anxieties and demands of the voters who support these parties, is an absolute requirement.

The Three-Level Approach: Prevention, Intervention, De-Radicalization

To counter the radicalization of young people, a three-level approach, comprising prevention, intervention, and de-radicalization/disengagement, is indispensable.

It has allowed different target groups to be approached, enabled a flexible methodology, and allows for cooperation among different professional fields and social organizations. Approaches that are based on these three levels are part of many European CVE strategies. Because of the varying degrees of radicalization, specific prevention, intervention, and de-radicalization measures necessitate differentiation and the "best fit" must be determined on a case-by-case basis.

Preventive measures are used to strengthen "tolerance of ambiguity," to build resilience, and to, therefore, prevent radicalization. Such measures are usually unspecific, with the objective of strengthening positive personality traits and reducing susceptibility (in this case, to radicalization). The target of such preventive measures is people who are only slightly ideological; that is, they are not entrenched in a specific ideology nor do they have violent tendencies. They are often resentful of those who are perceived as "different." In such cases, group-specific initiatives (such as political and/or interreligious education) are required to strengthen tolerance of that which is *different* or *foreign* (tolerance of ambiguity) and to illustrate the appeal of democracy and diversity. Therefore, prevention efforts should target those who might be at risk of religious or political radicalization at an early stage in intercultural and interreligious dialogue and broaden their knowledge of democracy, human rights, and religions, for example.

Arming practitioners with the appropriate skills, such as awareness training (e.g., teachers, specialists in child and youth services, the police, and those working in the penal system), is also key in preventing extremism and radicalization.

Intervention measures are directed at those with a discernible risk of becoming radicalized. If we pay attention to the root causes of radicalization, such as alienation, loss of belonging, and social exclusion, we will find members of social groups that have less power or influence over societal development or those who have fewer possibilities to shape their lives. Intervention can take place within many social entities. Schools and the penal system are the most obvious. Comprehensive awareness training for staff can enable early intervention into the radicalization processes. Confronting ideological positions and radicalized behavior with pedagogic group training and one-on-one coaching fosters self-reflection and change among participants. A dialogue that is free of moral judgments allows clients to question their own reasons for moving toward radicalization, thereby opening up a chance to dissolve these ideologies in the early phase.

De-radicalization and disengagement support come into play when radicalization is advanced and there is a risk that young people will endanger themselves and others, by travelling to a war zone and after returning, for example. Exit programs are directed at those who have already decided to turn their backs on extremism. The objective here, besides (re)integration into society, is to confront the ideological interpretation regime, because the decision to exit is only the start of a long detachment process from previous thought patterns. Other programs provide opportunities for dialogue to people who have yet to make the decision to exit. This approach can trigger distancing from an ideology and radicalized group and allow for an eventual exit from the extremist scene and renunciation of the ideology. The target group for this approach comprises radicalized people, some of whom have strong violent tendencies. If a person joins an extremist group with the will to go so far as to kill for his convictions, the primary objective is to avert any risk to themselves (the radicalized individuals) and others. The de-radicalization process takes a long time.

To be effective in the long term, a comprehensive CVE strategy must include all three levels in the abatement and prevention of extremism. Only then can different groups, from undecided and politically disinterested pupils to highly radicalized potential killers, be targeted effectively.

Joint and National European CVE Strategies

One of the major achievements of the European Union (EU) is that it has made it easy to move freely within European borders. This gain in freedom for many entails the possibility of misuse by a few (such as terrorists). Collective approaches to fighting terrorism and preventing radicalization are therefore an absolute requirement within Europe. In addition to numerous agreements to exchange data and share information relevant to security, and the cooperation of police and the judiciary,[1] the EU adopted the European Union counterterrorism strategy in 2005. This strategic commitment "to combat terrorism globally while respecting human rights, and make Europe safer, allowing its citizens to live in an area of freedom security and justice" (Presidency and CT Coordinator 2005) is split among four levels: prevent, protect, pursue, and respond.

Including *prevention* as a key part of the strategy to combat terrorism indicates a broader evaluation of the phenomenon; it is not simply a national security issue. The European approach implies that countering extremism is not just a remit for the security services, police, and justice system, but also defines (as laid out in the three-level approach mentioned at the start) responsibilities for social entities for preventing and combating radicalization and extremism. Educational institutions, changing labor market policies, and promoting intercultural dialogue and long-term integration are also key actors and steps in preventing individuals from taking part in terrorism and getting at the root causes of radicalization. Therefore, this strategy forms—parallel to the international approach—the foundation for a cross-resourced and interdisciplinary course of action to prevent and combat extremism. The decision to include prevention in its strategy shows that the EU does not differ from the approach of the United Nations: "The UN's global anti-terrorism approach in 2006 also called for a holistic strategy that encompassed the conditions conducive to terrorism" (Nünlist and Frazer 2015).

Notwithstanding the many Member States that are investing huge sums of money in the prevention of extremism, challenges in European prevention and de-radicalization initiatives still abound. Since the beginning of 2013, the number of returning foreign fighters has grown steadily, and thus the issue of reintegration was moved to the top of the political agenda in Europe. The Council of Europe agreed in 2015 to equalize the criminal proceedings—countries are obligated to criminalize various acts of terrorism—and most of the governments agreed to work closely with the national security services to secure risks that the returnees can pose, and identify terrorists at an early stage (Council of Europe,

Directorate of Communications 2015). In addition to the security issues and law enforcement agreements, there is a broad understanding among European governments about the necessity of prevention, de-radicalization, and rehabilitation efforts in response to radicalization and terrorism.[2] Criminalizing, accusing, and arresting will do little to change minds.

It is arguably for this reason that the European Commission also set up the Radicalisation Awareness Network (RAN) in 2011.[3] The primary purpose of this network is to bring together experts, now more than two thousand, from all EU Member States to discuss CVE and exit strategies. Sharing experiences, developing new approaches jointly, and disseminating expertise throughout the whole of Europe is rendered possible by dialogue among practitioners, policy-makers, and academics. The goal of this network is to make exclusive knowledge of CVE approaches accessible to many and to support Member States in the development of national and regional strategies to prevent and combat extremism. This approach relies on a participative and cooperative strategy for developing solutions for one of Europe's most significant social challenges. Political decision-makers are not the only ones involved; the discussions also involve practitioners and theoretical experts who work with individuals who already are, and who are at risk of being, radicalized.

Several times a year, teachers, policemen/women, court and prison employees, social workers, psychologists, disengagement practitioners, and victims of terrorist attacks from all over Europe meet to share experiences with experts and to gain new insights into how the growing problem of radicalization is being combated. The objectives of this European knowledge transfer are to develop local level approaches, which take into account the specific, regional situations, and to formulate recommendations related to specific issues for political decision-makers.

The European Parliament has also passed the resolution, "Prevention of radicalization and recruitment of European citizens by terrorist organizations," which "highlighted the importance of combining de-radicalization programs with measures such as establishing partnerships with community representatives, investment in social and neighborhood projects ... aimed at disrupting economic and geographical marginalization, and mentoring schemes for alienated and excluded young people considered at risk of radicalization."[4] This resolution strengthens the European method of a cross-disciplinary approach.

Despite the intention to cooperate across Europe and develop and implement measures under joint basic assumptions, the EU is nothing more than an alliance of independent nations. Intervening in national law is largely impossible, be it for countering terrorism or preventing extremism. The majority of resolutions are cooperation commitments and coordination strategies. Their basic assumptions are reflected in national law, and sometimes important elements of an effective cooperation are not always implemented. To name one example, as of April 2016, there was still no shared data for all terror suspects and those who pose a public threat that can be updated and viewed by all European countries. This allows, for example, (potential) terrorists to move unhindered between countries because the police and security services have no shared information about them, either on the European or, in part, on the national level. Here data protection has taken priority over the safety of citizens, and bureaucracy prevents speedy implementation of applicable law. Nevertheless, different countries have developed national CVE strategies within Europe. Generally deemed the most comprehensive so far is the Prevent Strategy from the British government.

Britain

In 2003 the British government developed and implemented a project in response to the increasing risk of radicalization and terrorism, which was the precursor to Prevent. A combination of primary preventive measures, such as workshops and debates and targeted intervention, for those at risk of radicalization and those already radicalized, were developed with Prevent. The program was implemented across the country at a massive financial cost. Although the program had positive effects, it also had ill-judged outcomes because it was implemented so quickly. Criticism was leveled, for example, at the fact that the first few years saw the program's financing channeled to organizations that were part of the spectrum of extremism itself rather than part of the sector combating extremism.

Critical voices (such as David Cameron who was then in the opposition) commented in 2008: "Public money that is meant to be used to combat extremism has ended up in the hands of extremists" (Cameron quoted in Vidino and Brandon 2012). These challenges were comparable to the initial difficulties of the "Action Programs against Aggression and Violence," which the then–Minister for Youth and today's Bundeskanzler Angela Merkel initiated in Germany in the early 1990s, and which arguably can be called the first European CVE program. With an annual budget of DM 20m, the program sought to address right-wing extremism between 1992 and 1996, which was on the rise mainly with youths in the five new Federal States. "The pointed criticism levelled at the programme was: 'Skinhead care paid by public purse.' Extreme right-wing youths were able to undergo ideological training paid by the state, and practise their martial arts" (Lüdecke 2013).

In response, the British government introduced mechanisms for checking (potential) contracted organizations. However, the decisions about which organizations should be included in publicly funded programs to combat extremism and radicalization should not be made solely by the individuals who belong to these organizations. In many cases, these individuals can also be representatives of very conservative Muslim communities that cannot themselves be described as radicalized or affiliated with extremism.

The "Channel Programme," an element of Prevent, has been just as criticized. In this program, those who already are defined by the police or security authorities as radicalized, or those who are at risk of being radicalized due to their affiliation with a vulnerable social group are assessed individually by a coordinator with regional responsibility. Depending on the degree of radicalization, the respective intervention steps are initiated and the police and security services get involved (if applicable). That this program is controlled by the British police evoked a sense of being "spied on" within Muslim communities, although many public and nonpublic organizations at the local level are involved (Vidino and Brandon 2012). Following the revision of Prevent in 2011, the decision was made to safeguard long-term financing for the "Channel Programme" in the Counter-Terrorism and Security Act (2015), despite criticism from Muslim communities.[5]

To build on the program for prevention and intervention, and particularly because Great Britain identified around one thousand prisoners in Great Britain as extremists or at risk of extremism, the British Prime Minister announced on February 8, 2016, that "we [Great Britain] will develop a new prison-based pro-gramme for countering the non-violent extremism that can lead to terrorism and violence and this will focus on those at risk of radicalisation, regardless of the crime they originally committed – as well as those convicted of terrorism offences. And to deal with the most serious cases, just as we introduce mandatory de-radicalisation programmes in the wider community, we will also introduce these in our prisons."[6] In August 2016, a review of Islamist extremism in prisons, during probation, and in youth justice centers (Acheson 2016) was published by the Ministry of Justice. Key measures to be implemented include:

- creating a new directorate for security, order and counterterrorism, which will deliver a plan for countering extremism in prisons and probation ser-vices;
- instructing governors to remove extremist literature and putting in place a thorough process to assess materials of concern;
- boosting plans for rapid responses by intervention teams to terrorist-related incidents;
- improving extremism prevention training for all prison officers; and
- strengthening vetting of prison chaplains and a range of positions to make sure the right people are in place in prisons to counter extremist beliefs.[7]

The explicit focus of these measures is security rather than targeted interventions that will encourage Islamist extremists to disengage and de-radicalize.

Spain

Although other European countries have also been victims of terrorist attacks, they have not always implemented CVE programs particularly quickly. Spain for example, despite the wave of attacks by Islamist terrorists in 2004, did not formu-late the "Plan Estratégico Nacional de Lucha Contra la Radicalización Violenta" until 2015.[8] The plan essentially defines the national and regional responsibilities in the fight against violent radicalization. At the heart of Spain's approach is the Coordination Centre for Information on Radicalization. Institutions and citizens can report possible cases of radicalization to the center via a web page, email, or a free hotline. In April 2015, State Secretary for Security Martinez announced: "In its first five months of activity, we have received almost 1,500 notifications, of which 45 percent have been assessed as worthy of police investigation. Forty-seven percent of these notifications have been received via the web page, which substantiates the importance of this method of communication for preventing these threats." According to Martinez, the main focus of all Spanish activities to prevent violent extremism should be juvenile youths, because radicalization can be addressed at an individual level for this group, with the hope of preventing it from continuing. "Quality education and teaching values from a very young age play a key role" in this strategy, including the "teaching of human rights and respect for diversity, fostering critical thought and tolerance." Programs to prevent and combat extremism within the penal system are also part of the strategy.[9] It is not possible at this stage to determine whether this approach has been successful, to what extent experts in civil society or nongovernmental organizations (NGOs) are involved, how the implementation will be carried out in detail, whether central control includes regional requirements, or whether this is a long-term model with sustainable effects.

It is also not possible to gauge the extent to which the lack of prospects for youth, due for instance to a lack of integration into work processes by labor market policies, is being sufficiently addressed. Spain should coordinate this strategy with the Department of Employment, especially since youth unemployment in Spain, at around 45 percent, is double the European average.[10]

The Netherlands

Without having been the victim of an Islamist terror attack, The Netherlands introduced the "Polarisation and Radicalisation Action Plan" in 2007 in the hope that "improving the material integration and sense of belonging of young Dutch Muslims [into Dutch society] … would reduce the breeding ground for radicalization" (Butt and Tuck 2014). Radicalization here was assessed as a consequence of social erosion processes. Efforts to increase integration and social cohesion were put in place to counter negative developments, that is, radicalization.

This preventive plan was not renewed after 2011. However, the action program for combating jihadism (Ministry of Security and Justice, National Coordinator for Security and Counterterrorism, and Ministry of Social Affairs and Employment 2014), published in August 2014, continues to call for a networked and cross-resourced approach to preventing and combating extremism: "Finally, the government is investing in knowledge, expertise and partnerships on local, national, and international levels. Central government and the municipalities concerned will come to agreements on preventing radicalisation and managing social tensions, thus cementing the comprehensive approach and cooperation between municipalities, local partners (welfare, social affairs), educational institutions and the police" (National Coordinator for Security and Counterterrorism 2014).

Denmark

The Danish CVE strategy—A Common and Safe Future—presented in 2009 as a national action plan represents a cross-resourced approach. This plan also includes action in three areas—prevention, intervention, and de-radicalization. Key elements of this plan are based on cooperation structures that were in place before it came into force, such as among schools, social workers, and police.

Anchored in the SSP network, social services and the police focus on prevention of radicalization and exit from extremist groups based on dialogue, awareness raising and direct support. The effort is a supplement to the ongoing crime preventive efforts for people under 18, but now also targets people up to 25. Counter-radicalization is implemented in the crime preventive work based on three levels of engagement: (a) preventative interventions aimed at general socialization and crime prevention; (b) anticipatory interventions aimed at identified vulnerable groups and individuals; and (c) direct prevention and exit aimed at individuals who are already part of the extremist milieu. The strategy is to approach radicalization in the same way as other crime preventive work, which needs both a group related and an individual approach. (Brett et al. 2015)

This linking of different approaches and different departments is implemented along the lines of the well-known "Aarhus" model. This approach of community engagement consists of two areas of intervention. Workshops and dialogues with mosques and cultural societies in the local communities reach the general public. In addition, a task force of first-line practitioners performs risk evaluations of and mentors radicalized individuals.

Belgium

In contrast to the Netherlands, for a long time Belgium did not have a comprehensive national program, despite knowledge of radicalized groups, such as in Molenbeek. The absence of these programs has had massive consequences for the country and the world at large. "He radicalised himself in the prisons of Vorst and Sint-Gillis, where he was an inmate some time ago. Much more than out on the streets," said the sister of Abdelhamid Abaaoud, the supposed backer of the Paris attacks in November 2015. In 2010, Abaaoud was detained following an armed robbery; he met fellow perpetrator-to-be Salah Abdeslam in prison (Biermann et al. 2015). "Afterward, in September 2012, Abaaoud started his wave of terrorism, according to court documents. Over the following two and a half years, he abducted his younger brother Younes, taking him to Syria, and fostered contacts with those around Khalid Zerkani, a notorious protagonist in the Belgian jihadi scene" (Becker and Kuntz 2015).

Belgian politicians finally responded after the attack in Paris in January 2015: "A working group in Brussels will commence to work on de-radicalization. ... Representatives from around the region, as well as of the four districts having the greatest risk potential for radical Islamists—Brussels, Anderlecht, Schaerbeek and Molenbeek—were at the meeting. The meeting was about sharing information, improved monitoring of the phenomenon, and also intervening so that a stop can be put to the level of youth radicalisation" (Kniebs 2015).

Germany

Germany's history gives rise to a particular responsibility to combat extremism, to prevent radicalization, and to de-radicalize. It is hardly surprising, then, that since the Federal Republic of Germany was established, combating extremism has been high on the political agenda, albeit without the term "CVE" finding its way onto a bill or government policy statement.

In 1952, the Federal Agency for Civic Education was set up "to promote the understanding of political issues, to consolidate democratic awareness and to strengthen the willingness for political collaboration."[11] Values such as democracy, pluralism, and tolerance are communicated to the population by publications, trainings, and conferences. Since 2012, the agency has had its own "extremism" department, dedicated mainly to radicalization prevention and de-radicalization.

Because of the federal state structure of Germany, the initiatives for combating and preventing extremism came about in sixteen different states, not just at the national level. Since 2011, and before the series of murders by the Nationalsozialistischer Untergrund (NSU), each of the sixteen federal states has had a democracy center (formerly a state coordination office) that controls the resources and assistance from the state for issues pertaining to right-wing extremism (and Islamism since 2015). These centers are linked into a consultation network that operates nationwide and shares knowledge and experience. These structures, called "a hotchpotch (*Kraut und Rüben*)" (Steffen 2015) by Peter Neumann of King's College London, can be seen as decentralized, participative, and complementary. Over time, this has led to heterogeneity in approaches and expertise, which has allowed for the implementation of long-term and effective approaches. However, maintaining cooperation, knowledge transfer, and experience sharing within this federal entity, which spans professions and disciplines, remains one of its greatest challenges. The unfettered actions of the NSU over many years showed us where lack of information exchange, bickering over responsibility, and lack of cooperation could lead. This might be one reason why the German government released in summer 2016 their cooperative and interdepartmental Strategy to Prevent Extremism and Foster Democracy (Strategie der Bundesregierung zur Extremismusprävention und Demokratieförderung).

A broad landscape of NGOs has developed in Germany to implement government tasks in the social sector. These initiatives focus mainly on the fields of fighting and preventing extremism. Unlike many other countries in Europe, the CVE sector is characterized by civil society engagement and is not controlled solely by governmental players. Even before reunification, the federal government began funding nongovernmental initiatives with extensive special programs (e.g., "Aktionsprogramm gegen Aggression und Gewalt" [1992–1996], "Jugend für Toleranz und Demokratie – gegen Rechtsextremismus, Fremdenfeindlichkeit und Antisemitismus" [2001–2006], "XENOS – Integration und Vielfalt" [2007–2014], "Vielfalt tut gut" [2007–2010], "Toleranz fördern – Kompetenz stärken" [2010–2014], and "Demokratie leben!" [2015–2019]). Given the increased risk of Islamist terrorism and the increase in right-wing extremist attacks on refugees, the German federal government has decided to increase the funding for the current program "Demokratie leben!" from €55m in 2016 to €100m in 2017 (Geisler 2016). In addition, the government is trying to implement a legal basis for promoting democracy and the prevention of extremism to ensure the continuation of such funding streams regardless of election results in the future.

German politicians attach a great deal of importance to these nongovernmental organizations. Extremists perceive the state and its employees as enemies of the respective movement, be it right-wing extremism or Islamism. Any interaction with representatives of the state is appraised from this perspective. Therefore, successful intervention or de-radicalization, which requires a trusting atmosphere and emotional frankness, is difficult, if not impossible. This difficulty is one of the reasons the German government, unlike other European countries, does not intervene alone in CVE and, instead, partners with nongovernmental organizations.

Violence Prevention Network. This strategy is illustrated in the German NGO that the author founded and operates, which focuses on de-radicalization and combating extremism. Founded in 2004, Violence Prevention Network (VPN) has specialized from its outset in the de-radicalization of extremists and those at risk of extremism, unlike many other organizations involved in the fight against extremism. VPN specially designed de-radicalization programs for inmates in the penal system, which met with unusual success in relapse prevention. Since 2001, more than one thousand inmates have participated in the program. At 13.3 percent, the re-imprisonment rate of those who participated in VPNs program stands at close to 70 percent below the national average in Germany.

Since 2004, VPN has worked on this program in the German penal system with assistance from many state and federal ministries. This partnership came about because an external evaluation in the first few years made it clear that the implementation of these kinds of programs by external organizations, which were not part of the German penal system, and thereby did not represent the enemy state, were much more promising than internal prison programs. "The participants were all of the opinion that it is very important to be able to work with trainers who are not employed by the prison" (Lukas 2007). This has been found to be the case in other European countries as well: "initiatives with too much government involvement may be counter-productive. ... Leeway must be given to communities and civil society players to develop initiatives of their own and to determine if and when state involvement is appropriate, and to what extent. This is particularly important in the case of initiatives aiming to mobilize players outside of the mainstream" (Nünlist and Frazer 2015).

Since 2011, VPN has been implementing tailored de-radicalization initiatives in the domain of Islamist-motivated extremism, in conjunction with government interior and judicial authorities. This first (confidential) pilot project in Germany that VPN implemented in coordination with the Department of Public Security at the Federal Ministry of the Interior was the pioneer for today's programs that VPN runs in many of Germany's prisons with inmates convicted of terrorist offences.

In parallel to this program, VPN has developed, in close coordination with security authorities, a program in several federal states that aims to prevent jihadists from increasingly leaving for war zones (such as in Syria and Iraq), by introducing processes to distance themselves from extremist ideologies and enable de-radicalization over the long term.

Using an NGO in a very specialized field of governmental remit, such as combating extremism, clearly illustrates the strategic approach of the government and the NGO community, and VPN is arguably Germany's best practice example. Germany's strategy relies on diverse approaches, innovative concepts of nongovernmental initiatives, and decentralized offerings. The governments at the state and national levels see themselves more as commissioning and coordinating entities than implementing ones.

Germany sees combating and preventing extremism as a continuous political obligation, not as a short-term, ad hoc measure. Only an interdisciplinary and cross-resourced strategy can be a successful countermeasure to extremism. "The dovetailing of different official instruments, the collaboration with other security authorities, the government and civil-socio institutions as part of prevention, and, not in the least, efficient criminal prosecution, represent appropriate resources to stem the threat to internal security in Germany" (Federal Ministry of the Interior 2015).

Conclusions from the European experience

The visible differences among the countries mentioned above are indicative of Europe. The EU directives and resolutions for CVE or counterterrorism generally leave leeway for Member States and must not be interpreted as binding codes of practice. Comprehensive prevention measures are common to all approaches, however. This way, a picture is created within the European community that states' shared values form the foundation for dealing with extremists and those at risk of extremism. What does not result from it, however, is coordinated action, or even a concerted approach. This accumulation of agreed-on but nonobligatory measures and approaches within the EU—all the more so knowing about the international direction and coordination on the part of those behind the Paris and Brussels attacks—is, to the mind of this author, both incomprehensible and negligent.

Some European governments are reacting to the increasing number of terrorist attacks and the growth of extremist organizations with huge budgets for "special programs" or national initiatives to combat extremism. Transferring these budgets to national budgets in the long term, even beyond potential changes of government, is in most cases not guaranteed. This is not sustainable political practice. Such strategies assume that comprehensive measures that counter the causes of radicalization do not need to be implemented in the long term but, rather, hypothesize that these phenomena are temporary and need to be watered down.

Key Factors of Promising CVE
Strategies and Approaches

All CVE and de-radicalization approaches must be appraised in terms of success and transferability within the context in which they take place. National strategies have just as much influence over success and effectiveness as do regional and local conditions. Successful strategies to combat violent extremism and programs for de-radicalization must be implementable in the long term, sustainably effective, and organized flexibly. Ad hoc programs running for a short time deliver little information on which developments are directly linked to which measures. All findings to date on radicalization and extremism indicate that the causes are multifaceted. One-dimensional approaches and concepts for prevention are therefore not effective. The way back for de-radicalized individuals is profoundly individual. There is no one-size-fits-all approach.

Coordinated cross-disciplinary approach

These findings have overarching consequences for the development of programs and strategies. Multifaceted causes can only be rectified or at least ameliorated in a multifaceted way. This requires a coordinated and cross-disciplinary method. Violent extremism is not the sole responsibility of security authorities, the police, or the penal system. Education and labor are only examples of sectors that can become active in combating extremism such as in Paris Banlieues, in Molenbeek, and in other larger European cities. Successful cooperation, be it between different professions or between governmental and nongovernmental institutions, presupposes a high degree of flexibility and trust. Intervention and de-radicalization approaches requiring cooperation with security authorities and NGOs, such as in Denmark, Germany, and Great Britain, presuppose acceptance and appreciation of one for the other. Clear-cut guidelines regarding data protection laws and decision-making powers avert mistrust and promote transparency.

Long-term concepts

Long-term concepts require political actions beyond legislative periods. Short-term pedagogic measures cannot work successfully in prevention or in the implementation of de-radicalization programs. Changing behavior and questioning one's own attitudes, values, positions, and opinions require time. A human being is capable of changing at any time in life; however, a long-term and sustained change requires that we try out what has been newly learned with all its obstacles and unforeseeable challenges. If prevention and de-radicalization are to be truly part of a CVE strategy, the strategy must reflect this in its duration, financing, and scope.

Direct work with extremists

Only a few organizations are turning directly to those moving in extremism networks and circles with the objective of triggering distancing from extremist ideologies. Given the now-visible networks of extremists, such as in Molenbeek, and the terrorist attacks they carried out, it is exactly in this area of CVE that urgent action is needed. Could access have been established to people such as Abdelhamid Abaaoud, Salah Abdeslam, and Ibrahim and Khalid El Bakraoui years ago? This remains an important question.

Continuous evaluation and flexibility

Changing global conditions and politically unstable regions both will have a bearing on the development of extremists at the international, national, and regional levels. A successful CVE strategy must be flexible and react to changing conditions appropriately. The concepts of the strategy, and their implementation, must be continually questioned, evaluated, and, if necessary, modified.

Targeted de-radicalization measures during imprisonment

As indicated at the beginning of this article, being in prison can play a key role in radicalization (Korn 2015). This is where one of the greatest challenges, and at the same time one of the great opportunities, lies. Law enforcement measures, if not combined with de-radicalization and rehabilitation approaches, will be unsuccessful. We have a choice—either lock them up for good or give them a chance to change. Otherwise, highly radicalized individuals will be released from prisons, putting the public at risk, as was the case in Brussels, Paris, and Copenhagen.

Many of the prison sentences for terrorist activities are rather short. Thus, the time frame for "treatment" in the penal system is often too short to trigger long-term changes. A multiagency approach—which involves the process of de-radicalization or exit strategies across diverse professions before, during, and after imprisonment—is more promising than a one-dimensional treatment model inside the penal system. This approach should also be applied to cases where prisoners convicted for nonideological crimes show signs of radicalization. Such approaches require trust and collaboration, as well as a rethinking of certain data protection and data exchange regulations.

Internet: Communication instead of prohibition

Those who are at risk of radicalization or will tend to radicalize can be seen very clearly in the relevant forums of extremist groups on the Internet (Federal Ministry of the Interior 2012) and in social networks. The number of initiatives that create counternarratives, which are believed to be a way of combating such activities and processes on the Internet, is increasing.[12] And the data collected from the Internet by official authorities and civil organizations on the activities of extremists are constantly growing.[13] Nevertheless, there are not as many approaches that enable real contact between individuals at risk of being radicalized or who are radicalized and de-radicalization practitioners. As a result, incipient radicalization processes can take root, and vulnerable individuals can begin to isolate themselves and become embedded in the radicalized scene. Such isolation leads to further distancing from governmental and social entities, thereby impeding the pathways to exit the radicalized scene.

Feeding counternarratives onto the Internet can produce a preventive effect. In contrast, for individuals who view the world around them in an ideologically colored way, such counternarratives will only confirm what they already think they know. Practical experience tells us that de-radicalization efforts that have no contact with those who sow the necessary seeds of doubt only work in rare cases. Online de-radicalization does not and will not work. The key factors for successful de-radicalization efforts are interpersonal relationships and dialogue. Tracking relevant forums on the Internet[14] is hampering the dissemination of extremist ideology. For de-radicalization, however, this approach is not only ineffective but counterproductive. Such approaches only confirm the images of their enemies that radicalized individuals already have. An authoritarian response to extremists only deepens radicalization instead of disbanding it.

Efforts to de-radicalize via the Internet may seem necessary and sensible, but they have been mainly counterproductive. They can be discouraging, and they highlight problems and make them public. Extremists and those at risk of extremism are therefore not reached, and often even become more embedded in the radicalization process. To stop and successfully reverse radicalization, plugging the gap between existing knowledge and necessary, practical actions is an absolute requirement, instead of contradicting the extremists' arguments (which they expect and can easily integrate into the structure of the ideologeme) or simply banning the content. When monitoring social networks online, the objective must be to approach radicalized people and motivate them to participate in debate through direct contact, beyond the virtual world, and to build subsequent relationships that initiate disengagement from radicalization. Unlike in previous approaches, the focus here lies in bringing about change in the target group. Practitioners must build a working relationship through outreach to initiate detachment from extremist groups and encourage the questioning of violent ideology.

Early intervention

The classic "exit programs" begin at a time when the client has already begun to distance himself from the extremists. Other approaches reach people who have not yet questioned their own ideologies and attempt to trigger initial distancing through collaboration between coach and client. This approach can also reach those who would not seek such collaboration on their own. It focuses on distancing processes and detachment from extremist worldviews and thought patterns. Early intervention requires early detection.

Relationship, dialogue, and trust

Effective de-radicalization depends on dialogues between extremists and de-radicalization practitioners. It is about trust, not about arguing against one another. Extremists' communication does not need to be "countered." Change cannot succeed in an antagonistic atmosphere. One of the key factors is the relationship between the practitioner and the extremist. People who feel disenfranchised and regard their life as senseless need someone who is interested in them, not only in their radicalization or offence. They need to feel appreciated. This is the prerequisite for self-confidence, independence, and responsibility.

My overall conclusion, after dealing with many European CVE strategies and approaches, and talking to many CVE practitioners and politicians over the past 10 years, is that CVE is not so much about countering the extremist narrative. It is more about strengthening those who are working for a diverse, democratic, and nonviolent society. It is more about immunizing those who can be recruited by extremist groups in the future. It is more about extending one's hand to those at risk. It is more about sowing doubt in the minds of those who are still convinced. And it is also about counseling those who have doubts and still think about their exit.

Notes

1. See http://eur-lex.europa.eu.
2. See https://www.regjeringen.no/no/aktuelt/youth-against-violent-extremism/id2415272/.
3. See http://ec.europa.eu.
4. See http://www.europarl.europa.eu.
5. See https://www.gov.uk.
6. See https://www.gov.uk.
7. See https://www.gov.uk.
8. See http://www.interior.gob.es.
9. See http://www.lamoncloa.gob.es.
10. See http://de.statista.com.
11. See http://www.bpb.de.
12. See http://www.againstviolentextremism.org.
13. See, for example, http://www.netz-gegen-nazis.de, http://www.no-nazi.net, http://www.hass-im-netz.info.
14. See http://www.jugendschutz.net.

References

Acheson, Ian. August 2016. *Summary of the main findings of the review of Islamist extremism in prisons, probation and youth justice*. London: Ministry of Justice.

Becker, Sven, and Katrin Kuntz. 2 December 2015. Knast, Gehirnwäsche, Krieg. *Spiegel online*.

Biermann, Kai, Philip Faigle, Astrid Geisler, and Karsten Polke-Majewski. 19 November 2015. Der Mann hinter den Mördern. *Zeit online*.

Buschbom, Jan. 2015a. Grundzüge niedrigschwelliger politischer Bildung mit ideologisierten Klientelen. *Interventions* 4:24–32.

Buschbom, Jan. 2015b. Milch der Erniedrigung. *Interventions* 5:24–33.

Buschbom, Jan. 2016. The ideologisation-radicalisation-cycle. *Interventions* 7:19–31.

Brett, Julian, Kristina Bro Eriksen, Anne Kristine Rønn Sorensen, and Tana Copenhagan Aps. 2015. *Evaluation Study - Lessons learned from Danish and other international efforts of countering violent extremism (CVE) in development contexts*. Copenhagen: Danida & Danish Ministry of Foreign Affairs.

Butt, Riazat, and Henry Tuck. 2014. *European counter-radicalisation and de-radicalisation: A comparative evaluation of approaches in the Netherlands, Sweden, Denmark and Germany*. London: Institute for Strategic Dialogue.

Council of Europe Directorate of Communications. 13 May 2015. Press release DC070(2015). Strasbourg Cedex, France: Council of Europe.

Faigle, Philip, Astrid Geisler, and Karsten Polke-Majewski. 23 March 2016. Sie konnten die Mörder nicht stoppen. *Zeit online*.

Federal Ministry of the Interior. 2012. *2012 annual report on the protection of the constitution: Summary*. Berlin: Federal Ministry of the Interior.

Federal Ministry of the Interior. 2015. *Constitution protection report 2014*. Berlin: Federal Ministry of the Interior.

Geisler, Astrid. 19 March 2016. Regierung verdoppelt Ausgaben gegen rechts. *Zeit online*.

Kniebs, Alain. 12 January 2015. Furcht vor Anschlägen – Fokus auf Deradikalisierung. *Belgischer Rundfunk*.

Korn, Judy. 2015. Prison as multiplicator effect. *Penal System Forum* 5:309–11.

Le Devin, Willy, and Sylvain Mouillard. 27 January 2015. Coulibaly, un voyou devenu jihadiste. *Lebération*.

Lehnartz, Sascha. 1 June 2014. Film-Geständnis des Brüsseler Terror-Attentäters. *Die Welt*.

Lobo, Sascha. 30 March 2016. Tiefgreifendes, strukturelles, multiples Staatsversagen. *Spiegel online*.

Lüdecke, Robert. 25 September 2013. Zurück zur Glatzenpflege? *Mut-gegen-rechte-Gewalt*.

Lukas, Helmut. 2007. *Evaluation des Modellprojektes Präventive Arbeit mit rechtsextremistisch orientierten Jugendlichen in den Justizvollzugsanstalten des Landes Brandenburg: 15*. Berlin: Violence Protection Network.

Ministry of Security and Justice, National Coordinator for Security and Counterterrorism, and Ministry of Social Affairs and Employment. 2014. *The Netherlands comprehensive action programme to combat jihadism*. Den Haag: Ministry of Security and Justice, National Coordinator for Security and Counterterrorism, and Ministry of Social Affairs and Employment.

National Coordinator for Security and Counterterrorism. 4 September 2014. Press release: Dutch government strengthens actions to combat jihadism and radicalisation. Den Haag: National Coordinator for Security and Counterterrorism.

Nünlist, Christian, and Owen Frazer. 2015. Countering violent extremism in der Terrorismusbekämpfung. *CSS Analysis in Security Policy* 183:2–3.

Presidency and CT Coordinator. 30 November 2005. *The European Union counter-terrorism strategy*. No. 14469/4/05 REV 4. Brussels: Council of the European Union.

Simons, Stefan. 27 July 2016. Ungenügend. Debatte über Frankreichs Sicherheitskräfte. *Spiegel online*.

Steffen, Wiebke. 2015. Internationaler Terrorismus: Wie können Prävention und Repression Schritt halten? Paper presented at the BKA autumn conference, 18–19 November 2015.

Vidino, Lorenzo, and James Brandon. 2012. *Countering radicalisation in Europe*. London: International Centre for the Study of Radicalisation and Political Violence.

von Altenbockum, Jasper. 16 February 2015. Der Facebook-Dschihadist. *Frankfurter Allgemeine Zeitung*.

Wiegel, Michaela. 22 March 2012. Tod eines Terrorreisenden. *Frankfurter Allgemeine Zeitung*.

Zeit online. 28 January 2016. Fünfmal mehr Straftaten gegen Flüchtlingsunterkünfte.

The first part of the article provides an overview of the efforts, initiatives, and contributions led by the Muslim World to confront the threats of violent extremism. I explore these efforts by highlighting contemporary key initiatives in two major categories: (1) global cooperation and (2) national strategies. The second part of the article provides an analysis of what is required to support the Muslim World in its efforts in countering violent extremism and what is the best approach to integrate these efforts into the wider global commitment to defeat violent extremism. These initiatives need continued support, and I argue that non-Muslim nations must continue to consider the Muslim World a strategic partner in the global efforts to prevent and counter violent extremism.

Keywords: CVE; Muslim World; security; global cooperation; national strategies; GCTF; Hedayah

Countering Violent Extremism Strategies in the Muslim World

By
MAQSOUD KRUSE

In Search of the Muslim World

The effects of terrorism reach across continents, and harm and inflict pain on the whole world. Let us not forget that the Islamic world is both the accused and the victim of terrorism.

—bin Bayyah (2014, 66)

The rise of the so-called Islamic State, also known as "ISIS," "ISIL," or "Daesh," in 2011 generated a serious debate about relationships between Islamic radicalization, Islam, and Muslims (*The Telegraph* 2015; Hamid 2015) and how that

Maqsoud Kruse has served as the executive director of Hedayah, the International Center of Excellence for Countering Violent Extremism, since it was established in December 2012. Based in Abu Dhabi, Hedayah is an independent international think and do tank focused on countering violent extremism (CVE) in all of its forms and manifestations by conducting research and analysis, developing capacity-building programs, and initiating dialogue and communication.

Correspondence: maqsoud.kruse@hedayah.ae

DOI: 10.1177/0002716216671706

dynamic affects the complex reality of global security in confronting Daesh's threat in comparison to other Islamic radical groups such as al-Qaeda (Wood 2015). This ongoing debate led to a broad, yet very direct, question: Where is the Muslim World in all of this?

This question is based on an equivocal perception that the Muslim World is not doing enough to counter Daesh or openly confront Islamic radicalization. There is a perception that Muslims are hesitant to openly and clearly condemn radicalization (Schneier 2015). It is, therefore, absolutely necessary to highlight and explore the significant efforts, major initiatives, and considerable contributions by the Muslim World in the global fight against violent extremism in all of its forms. I unpack these efforts using two major categories.

The first category is "global cooperation," which I use to explore the international partnerships, affiliations, and alliances that have been formed to counter violent extremism. I highlight several key affiliations that showcase the serious commitment that the Muslim World has made to the international community in the fight against violent extremism.

The second category I use is "national strategies," which provides an overview of some of the pioneering efforts within the Muslim World to develop the strategic, legal, community, and law enforcement infrastructures required to facilitate preventative and comprehensive interventions in countering violent extremism (CVE). These strategies are aimed at the grassroots level and seek to build collaborations of community leaders with religious scholars, families, women, teachers, communication experts, and civil society as a whole. Here again, I highlight key contemporary initiatives.

The final section of the article provides an analysis of what is required to support the Muslim World in its CVE efforts and how these efforts can be best integrated into the wider global commitment to defeat violent extremism. The security challenge of violent extremism is constantly changing, and so too is the thinking behind it. There is still much work that can be done, and there are many opportunities to advance global efforts to counter violent extremism.

Global Cooperation

One of the strategies adopted by some Muslim countries for confronting and dealing with violent extremism is joining global multilateral efforts such as the Global Counterterrorism Forum (GCTF), the Global Coalition to Counter Daesh (GCCD), and most recently the Islamic Military Alliance to Fight Terrorism (IMAFT). These partnerships provide a platform for practical engagement with the international community and allow the Muslim countries to be active in the global effort to confront violent extremism.

The Global Counterterrorism Forum (GCTF)

The GCTF is an informal and nonbinding multilateral forum that includes thirty founding members from twenty-nine countries and the European Union

(EU). Its main objective is to promote effective global cooperation in the development of good practices to counter terrorism and to support the implementation of the United Nations (UN) Counterterrorism Strategy (GCTF 2011). The GCTF is based on "cochairing," which aims to foster closer cooperation and diverse collaboration. The United States and Turkey cochaired the GCTF, initially, when it was launched in September 2011. As of this writing, Morocco and the Netherlands serve as cochairs.[1]

Member countries within the GCTF form six working groups, each of which is cochaired by a Muslim country. Four working groups focus on technical themes: Egypt is the cochair, with the United States, of the Criminal Justice and Rule of Law Working Group; the United Arab Emirates (UAE) is the cochair, with the UK, of the Countering Violent Extremism Working Group; Indonesia is the cochair, with Australia, of the Detention and Reintegration Working Group; and Morocco is the cochair, with the Netherlands, of the Foreign Terrorists Fighters Working Group. The remaining two working groups focus on regional themes: Algeria is the cochair, with Canada, of the Sahel Region Capacity Building Working Group; and Turkey is the cochair, with the EU, of the Horn of Africa Region Capacity Building Working Group.[2] In addition to the Muslim countries that cochair the six working groups, the GCTF includes five other Muslim member countries: Jordan, Nigeria, Pakistan, Qatar, and Saudi Arabia.[3]

The Global Coalition to Counter Daesh (GCCD)

The GCCD, launched in September 2014, is a broad coalition that aims to defeat terrorist organization.[4] The GCCD consists of sixty-six members. Members include countries and international organizations; Muslim countries make up twenty of the member countries, in addition to the Arab League.[5] The GCCD is based on four lines of effort to degrade Daesh: (1) financing and economic infrastructure, (2) foreign terrorist fighters (FTFs), (3) stabilization of liberated areas, and (4) counternarrative and countermessaging. For example, the GCCD disrupts and prevents Daesh from raising, moving, and using funds by preventing them from using the international financial system. This is achieved by outing Daesh's senior leaders, facilitators, and financiers; freezing their assets domestically and regionally; and through existing UN Security Council resolutions and the Financial Action Task Force (FATF).[6]

Another way the GCCD is degrading Daesh is by tackling the threat posed by FTFs through the Counter-Daesh Coalition Working Group on Foreign Terrorist Fighters, co-led by the Netherlands, Turkey, and the United States. This group is working with coalition partners to implement the obligations and recommendations of the UN Security Council.[7]

Islamic Military Alliance to Fight Terrorism (IMAFT)

The IMAFT was formed in December 2015 as an Islamic initiative led by Saudi Arabia and includes thirty-four Muslim countries[8] whose goal is to provide an Islamic response to the growing threat of Daesh and to counter all forms of terrorism, violent extremism, and extremism in the Muslim World (Browning and Irish 2015). The IMAFT affirms the principles and objectives of the Organization of Islamic Cooperation (OIC), which calls for member states to cooperate to combat terrorism in all its forms and manifestations and reject all justifications and excuses for terrorism.[9] While the IMAFT was founded on military cooperation, it is not limited to it. The purpose of the Islamic coalition is to provide a comprehensive and holistic approach to defeating terrorism and violent extremism by using multiple methods, including countermessaging; counterideology; and promoting preventative measures that take into consideration conditions conducive to terrorism, violent extremism, and extremism.

National Strategies

Some Muslim countries have developed and implemented national strategies to deal with violent extremism based on their specific challenges, levels of threats, and local considerations. Such countries include Algeria, Bangladesh, Egypt, Indonesia, Jordan, Malaysia, Morocco, Saudi Arabia, Turkey, and the UAE, to name a few. These different strategies provide an insight into the direct steps that governments have taken and allows us to further understand the efforts made by some Muslim countries to advance the fight against violent extremism.

There are two major baskets of "national strategies" that are worth noting here. First is the "multi-axiom strategy," which approaches violent extremism from multiple angles and confronts it at the grassroots level to prevent extremism. The UAE, for example, has used this strategy. The multi-axiom strategy aims at pre-empting the root causes of violent extremism by combining three complementary approaches: security diplomacy, legislative infrastructure, and culture of moderation.

Second is the "de-radicalization strategy," which is based on the development and implementation of rehabilitation and reintegration programs for detained violent extremists. Bangladesh, Egypt, Indonesia, Jordan, Malaysia, Morocco, and Saudi Arabia have all applied this approach. The de-radicalization strategy aims to treat former violent extremists by providing a variety of programs that use reeducation, religious and psychological counselling, and family support for reintegration.

The multi-axiom strategy

Security diplomacy. The UAE took the lead in initiating security diplomacy initiatives as part of its contribution to the global efforts to counter violent extremism. One example of the security diplomacy axiom is the launch of the Contact Group on Countering Extremism at the United Nations Security Council in February 2015.[10] The core objective of this diplomatic initiative is to foster a constructive dialogue at the international level about extremism in order to develop and disseminate concrete solutions for and best practices in preventing violent extremism nationally.

A second example is the two important international centers for CVE that Abu Dhabi hosts: Hedayah, the International Center of Excellence for Countering Violent Extremism; and the Sawab Center. Hedayah is an independent international think and do tank that aims to advance good practices to deal with extremism through research and analysis, capacity building programs, and facilitating dialogue and communication. Hedayah was launched during the third ministerial meeting of the GCTF that took place in Abu Dhabi in December 2012. Hedayah's international steering board consists of twelve members, including Algeria, Australia, Canada, Egypt, the EU, Indonesia, Morocco, the Netherlands, Turkey, the UAE, the UK, and the United States.

The Sawab Center is a digital communications hub that aims to degrade Daesh's propaganda and recruitment efforts through direct online countermessaging. It was established in July 2015 as a joint initiative led by the UAE and the United States as part of their collaboration within the GCCD.

Legislative infrastructure. This axiom provides the legal advancement necessary for CVE. For example, the UAE has enacted Federal Law No. 7 of the year 2014, which was issued in August of the same year; this law provides the legal definitions of "terrorist acts" and expands on the previous Federal Decree No. 1 of the year 2004 on Combating Terror Crimes. In November of the same year, the UAE Cabinet approved a list of designated and affiliated terrorist organizations and groups[11] in an attempt to raise awareness among the public and increase transparency about these affiliations. An "antidiscrimination law"[12] was issued following a decree by UAE President His Highness Sheikh Khalifa bin Zayed Al Nahyan in July 2015; this law criminalizes any acts of discrimination against individuals or groups on the basis of religion, caste, doctrine, race, color, or ethnic origin.

Culture of moderation. The UAE launched several initiatives that aim to promote a culture of moderation across all sectors of society. For example, the UAE established "the Forum for Promoting Peace in Muslim Societies" in March 2014 in Abu Dhabi; this forum gathers scholars and researchers on an annual basis to discuss all challenges and issues related to violent extremism within Muslim societies and to develop effective initiatives to counter violent extremism. It also provides an opportunity for mainstream Muslim scholars and researchers to discuss moderation and combating sectarianism and discrimination as a means to enhance the "Islamic-Islamic dialogue." One of the forum's recommendations was to establish the Muslim Council of Elders (MCE), which will "work together to promote peace, to discourage infighting and to address the sources of conflict, divisiveness and fragmentation in Muslim communities."[13] These initiatives pave the way for the provision of an "alternative narrative" that establishes authentic, positive, and effective messaging that targets Muslim youth and sets the stage for a genuine debate and exchange of thoughts on the true nature of Islam compared to the distorted perception created by violent extremist groups.

One significant outcome of the forum is the Marrakesh Declaration.[14] This declaration was made during a conference hosted by His Majesty King Muhammad VI of Morocco in January 2016. It is based on the historic revival of the objectives and aims of the Charter of Medina, which was declared by Prophet Mohammed (peace be upon him) and provides insights about the rights of religious minorities in Muslim lands, both in theory and practice. The Marrakesh Declaration aims to contribute to the broader intellectual, cultural, and legal discourse surrounding contractual citizenship and the protection of minorities within Muslim societies.

The UAE's efforts exemplify the importance of considering a multitude of factors in preventing and countering violent extremism. A chronological summary of the key initiatives led by the UAE and capturing the multi-axiom approach is provided in Table 1.

The "de-radicalization strategy"

Several Muslim countries have developed rehabilitation and reintegration programs to address the challenge that comes with detained or returned violent extremists. These programs vary in their scope, approach, and effectiveness; "some have a more formally structured rehabilitation program, with dedicated resources, staff, and after-care plans, as in Saudi Arabia. Other programs take the form of looser policy initiatives, as seen in Bangladesh and Morocco, while still others facilitate a de-radicalization process once the decision to pursue that course has already been made by a group or individual, as is the case in Egypt" (Fink and El-Said 2011, 4).

These different programs show the various ways in which reeducation, religious discourse, psychological counseling, and family and financial support are being applied in an effort to de-radicalize populations. It is difficult to establish the effectiveness of these programs or determine their degree of success (El-Said 2012), but they remain important for understanding and appreciating the Muslim World's national strategies in the fight against violent extremism.

Saudi Arabia, for instance, has formed an "advisory committee" within its Ministry of Interior, which is responsible for rehabilitation and reintegration. The advisory committee led to the establishment of the Mohammed bin Nayef Center for Counseling and Advice.[42] The advisory committee comprises four subcommittees: the religious subcommittee, the psychological and social subcommittee, the security subcommittee, and the media subcommittee. Each subcommittee plays an integral role in the de-radicalization and rehabilitation of security prisoners. The religious subcommittee provides counseling through approximately 150 clerics and scholars who engage in dialogue and debate with prisoners. The psychological and social subcommittee comprises approximately fifty mental health specialists and social scientists responsible for assessing and diagnosing prisoners' psychological problems and behavior. The security subcommittee evaluates potential security risks among the prisoners and makes recommendations on their release. It also monitors prisoners after their release. The media subcommittee produces the educational materials used in the counseling

TABLE 1

Chronological Overview of UAE Efforts in Countering Violent Extremism (CVE)

Year	Item
2009	• Cabinet forms UAE Committee on Commodities Subject to Import and Export Control, reporting directly to the Council of the Ministry of Foreign Affairs, in order to tighten export controls on illicit goods (including terrorist financing).[15]
2010	• Immigration and Customs Enforcement (ICE) signed two Memoranda of Cooperation (MOCs) to support training academies of UAE Ministry of Interior and Customs Authority to enhance border capabilities.[16]
	• General Authority of Islamic Affairs and Endowments provides guidelines to mosques for Friday sermons to prevent violent extremist preaching.[17]
	• Dubai authorities discover PETN bomb on commercial flight originating from Yemen and linked to al-Qaeda.[18]
	• UAE hosts Gulf Cooperation Council (GCC) Summit in Abu Dhabi, calls for world counterterrorism center.[19]
2011	• UAE special forces overtake hijacked Dubai-bound ship from pirates in the Arabian Gulf.[20]
	• Dubai hosts first antipiracy conference.[21]
	• Participated in first Global Counterterrorism Forum (GCTF) ministerial meeting in New York; His Highness Sheikh Abdullah Bin Zayed Al Nahyan announced hosting first-ever International Center of Excellence for CVE in Abu Dhabi; UAE is cochair of GCTF CVE Working Group with the UK.[22]
2012	• Implementation of retina-scanning devices at border controls to enhance security measures.[23]
	• UAE hosts second annual Counter-Piracy Conference in Dubai.[24]
	• UAE Ministry of Interior hosts fifth regional field meeting for Project al Qabdah: Counterterrorism for the Middle East and North Africa.
	• Hosted Third GCTF Ministerial Meeting in Abu Dhabi; Launch of Hedayah, International Center of Excellence for Countering Violent Extremism.[25]
2013	• UAE hosts third annual Counter-Piracy Conference in Dubai.[26]
	• Federal Law No. 7 passes, securing Hedayah's place as an independent, international organization.[27]
2014	• Federal National Council (FNC) amends to key money-laundering legislation to better strengthen efforts to combat terrorist financing raised by the International Monetary Fund.[28]
	• UAE and EU sign an agreement to open Chemical, Biological, Radiological and Nuclear (CBRN) Risk Mitigation Center of Excellence in Abu Dhabi.[29]
	• UAE issued Terrorism Law No. 7 of 2014, identifying the legal definitions of terrorist acts.[30]
	• GCTF adopts Abu Dhabi Memorandum on Good Practices for Education and CVE at Fifth Ministerial Meeting in New York City, drafted with support of Hedayah.[31]
	• UAE participates in coalition airstrikes in Syria against Daesh.[32]
	• UAE mission to the UN hosts panel discussion on the role of women in CVE in New York City.[33]
	• Cabinet approved list of designated terrorist organizations and groups in support of Terrorism Law No. 7.[34]
	• Abu Dhabi Police arrest self-radicalized terrorist suspect less than 48 hours after attack on American teacher and attempted bombing of Egyptian-American doctor.[35]
	• Hedayah hosted first Global CVE Expo in Abu Dhabi.[36]
	• UAE Counter-Piracy Week; UAE hosts fourth annual Counter-Piracy Conference in Dubai.[37]
	• Forum for Promoting Peace in Muslim Societies hosts high-level conference in Abu Dhabi on combating violent extremism.[38]

(continued)

TABLE 1 (CONTINUED)

Year	Item
2015	• UAE launches a diplomatic initiative to establish a Contact Group on Countering Extremism at the UN Security Council.[39]
	• Enactment of the Anti-Discriminatory Law, issued following a decree by UAE president, criminalizes any acts that stoke religious hatred and/or which insult religion through any form of expression.[40]
	• The launch of the Sawab Center, a joint UAE/ U.S. online engagement initiative, in support of the Global Coalition Against Daesh.[41]

SOURCE: Based on an internal report produced in 2014 by Lilah El Sayed, Research Associate at Hedayah.

sessions and religious classes for prisoners. It also produces materials that are used in Saudi schools and mosques (El-Said 2012).

The efforts of the Saudi center are being amplified and supported by the "Assakina campaign,"[43] which was formed by a group of Saudi Islamic scholars affiliated with the Mohammed bin Nayef Center for Counseling and Advice and focuses on theological discourse and scholarly debates with violent extremist groups in order to de-legitimize their ideological narrative. The "Assakina" approach is simple and direct: scholars deconstruct the arguments that the violent extremist groups put forward in an attempt to expose their inconsistency and inherent contradictions and to establish a moderate mainstream narrative based on scholarly evidence and supported counterarguments. There is also the "Amman message,"[44] which was originally launched in 2004 by King Abdullah II and was issued by 180 Muslim scholars who advocate for and promote a tolerant interpretation of Islam, as a direct response to violent extremists misconceptions (Fink and El- Saied 2011). This initiative was part of the Royal Aal Al-Bayt Institute for Islamic Thought, which published several reports and led various initiatives on Islamic tolerance and moderation. Morocco has also directly engaged at the theological and philosophical level with the radical narrative of violent extremist groups. For example, Morocco established the Al-Muhammadiyah Foundation,[45] which plays a key role in the rehabilitation and reintegration efforts in prisons through direct religious discourse.

Other Muslim countries, such as Bangladesh, Indonesia, and Malaysia, have also attempted to counter violent extremism by developing rehabilitation programs that are based on bringing together Muslim scholars, with the support of the police, to counter violent extremism teachings in prisons (El-Said 2012). These programs approach each violent extremist on an individual level through counseling, education, and providing financial support to the families of the convicted violent extremists (Fink and El-Said 2011).

Violent Extremism and the Muslim World:
Toward Further Understanding

Knowing is not enough; we must apply. Willing is not enough; we must do.[46]

—Johann Wolfgang von Goethe

The Arab Spring began in Tunisia on December 18, 2010, in the form of a civil revolution against the ruling regime; it was followed by several revolutions, protests, and demonstrations in Egypt, Libya, Yemen, Bahrain, Syria, and many other Arab countries (Dabashi 2012). The Arab Spring also resulted in the overwhelming success of political Islamic movements, which assumed power in three major countries: Tunisia, Egypt, and Libya (Beaumont 2011).

All these movements have roots in, and ideological affiliations to, the Muslim Brotherhood movement in Egypt, which is considered to be the spark that produced all contemporary political Islamic groups (Zahid 2012). The unprecedented rise of Islam as a political and societal force has raised serious questions about its nature and influence compared to traditional secular forces such as the nationalists, socialists, and liberals.

This crucial turning point for the Middle East specifically and the Muslim World broadly triggered political and ideological debates between two major movements within Muslim societies. The advocates of Islamism are part of a fundamentalist Islamic revivalist movement generally characterized by moral conservatism, the literal interpretation of the Quran, and their attempt to implement Islamic values in all aspects of life; advocates of secularism believe that religious considerations should be excluded from civic affairs and public education.

These debates, in the context of current developments—epitomized by the dramatic shift in society that took place during the Arab Spring, followed by the rise of Islamic radicalization—will not only affect the local region but also the rest of the world politically, economically, and ideologically. This article, then, is a contribution to scholarly efforts to conceptualize and anticipate the future of political, cultural, and societal trends and movements in the Muslim World (see, for example, Aljabri 1994; Ibn Sunitan 2004; Moussalli 2004).

It is necessary to understand the complex reality of the political and ideological debates on Islamism and secularism in the Muslim World in order to initiate CVE strategies. It also helps to predict and portray the role that these debates will have and have had in shaping future political ideologies and, hence, the strategies needed to defeat violent extremism. Other countries can learn from the strategic initiatives led by the Muslim World, especially in the arena of religious discourse and the construction of alternative narratives.

The quest for identity among Muslim youth is a central element in why youth are attracted to violent extremism (Friedman 2016). Scholars, religious leaders, and educators can help to steer these young people away from extremism not only by condemning it, but by providing an alternative vision of a promising future that can galvanize the masses and release the collective imagination; in other words, inspire an Islamic Renaissance.

During the first-ever Countering Violent Extremism Communications Exposition (Global CVE Expo), which took place in December 2014 in Abu Dhabi and was organized by Hedayah in partnership with the GCTF, several practical initiatives and communications prototypes emerged from one of its unique activities, the "CVE Hackathon," which aimed to find innovative ways to counter Daesh messaging, specifically online (Hedayah 2014).

The prototypes that received the highest votes from both the attending audience and the online participants from across the globe had one common idea: mainstream, moderate, and progressive Islam is the true antidote to radical Islam. Muslims, more than any other group, have the ability to confront the misconceptions and misleading narratives created by violent extremist groups. However, this is not a challenge for the Muslim World alone; it is a challenge for the international community as well. Therefore, it is imperative that the initiatives led by the Muslim World be supported locally and globally and that these efforts be combined with other CVE efforts across the world.

Notes

1. See https://www.thegctf.org/home.
2. See https://www.thegctf.org/working-groups.
3. See https://www.thegctf.org/members-and-partners.
4. See http://theglobalcoalition.org/about/.
5. These countries include Afghanistan, Albania, Arab League, Bahrain, Bosnia and Herzegovina, Egypt, Iraq, Jordan, Kosovo, Kuwait, Lebanon, Malaysia, Morocco, Nigeria, Oman, Qatar, Saudi Arabia, Somalia, Tunisia, Turkey, and the United Arab Emirates.
6. See http://theglobalcoalition.org/mission/tackling-daeshs-financing-and-funding/.
7. See http://theglobalcoalition.org/mission/impeding-the-flow-of-foreign-fighters/.
8. These countries include Bahrain, Bangladesh, Benin, Chad, Comoros, Côte d'Ivoire, Djibouti, Egypt, Gabon, Guinea, Jordan, Kuwait, Lebanon, Libya, Malaysia, Maldives, Mali, Mauritania, Morocco, Niger, Nigeria, Pakistan, Palestine, Qatar, Saudi Arabia, Senegal, Sierra Leone, Somalia, Sudan, Togo, Tunisia, Turkey, the United Arab Emirates, and Yemen.
9. Joint statement on formation of Islamic military alliance to fight terrorism: see http://www.mofa.gov.sa/sites/mofaen/ServicesAndInformation/news/GovernmentNews/Pages/ArticleID201512159481880.aspx.
10. See https://www.wam.ae/en/news/emirates/1395277105405.html.
11. See https://www.wam.ae/en/news/emirates-international/1395272478814.html.
12. See http://www.thenational.ae/uae/government/anti-discrimination-law-enacted-across-uae.
13. See http://www.muslim-elders.com/en/media-center/establishment-of-the-muslim-council-of-elders-announced/.
14. See http://www.marrakeshdeclaration.org/.
15. See http://www.uae-embassy.org/business-trade/trade-export/export-control-and-combating-terror-financing.
16. See http://www.refworld.org/cgi-bin/texis/vtx/rwmain?page=country&docid=51a86e6416&skip=0&publisher=USDOS&coi=ARE&searchin=title&sort=date.
17. See http://www.awqaf.gov.ae/Affair.aspx?Lang=EN&SectionID=14&RefID=2542.
18. See http://www.washingtonpost.com/wp-dyn/content/article/2010/10/29/AR2010102904395.html.
19. See http://www.emirates247.com/news/emirates/gcc-summit-ends-urges-establishment-of-world-counter-terrorism-centre-2010-12-07-1.326200.
20. See http://www.thenational.ae/news/uae-news/special-forces-rescue-uae-ship-from-pirates.
21. See http://www.aljazeera.com/news/middleeast/2011/04/20114186721819166.html.
22. See https://www.thegctf.org/documents/10162/13878/Co-chairs+Fact+Sheet+-+CVE+COE.pdf.

23. See http://www.refworld.org/cgi-bin/texis/vtx/rwmain?page=country&docid=51a86e6416&skip=0&publisher=USDOS&coi=ARE&searchin=title&sort=date.

24. See http://www.khaleejtimes.com/kt-article-display-1.asp?xfile=data/nationgeneral/2012/May/nationgeneral_May387.xml&section=nationgeneral.

25. See https://www.thegctf.org/documents/10162/30110/Co-Chairs+Fact+Sheet-International+Center+of+Excellence+on+CVE.

26. See http://www.thenational.ae/news/uae-news/uae-to-host-international-counter-piracy-conference.

27. See http://www.alittihad.ae/details.php?id=108191&y=2013.

28. See [in Arabic] http://www.thenational.ae/uae/government/uae-anti-money-laundering-draft-law-amended.

29. See http://www.thenational.ae/uae/government/european-union-sets-up-international-centre-in-abu-dhabi.

30. See https://www.wam.ae/en/news/emirates/1395268768515.html.

31. See https://www.thegctf.org/documents/10162/159880/14Sept19_GCTF+Abu+Dhabi+Memorandum.pdf.

32. See http://www.thenational.ae/world/middle-east/uae-joins-airstrikes-on-isil-bases-in-syria.

33. See http://www.wam.ae/en/news/emirates/1395271537446.html.

34. See https://www.wam.ae/en/news/emirates-international/1395272478814.html.

35. See http://www.thenational.ae/uae/crime/reem-island-murder-suspect-in-abu-dhabi-police-custody.

36. See http://www.hedayah.ae/dialogue-/global-cve-expo-2014-/.

37. See http://www.arabiansupplychain.com/article-10721-report-battling-maritime-piracy/.

38. See http://www.khaleejtimes.com/nation/general/world-s-religious-leaders-call-to-fight-extremism.

39. See https://www.wam.ae/en/news/emirates/1395277105405.html.

40. See http://www.thenational.ae/uae/government/anti-discrimination-law-enacted-across-uae.

41. See https://www.wam.ae/en/news/emirates/1395283046846.html.

42. See http://www.mncc.org.sa.

43. See http://www.assakina.com/.

44. See http://www.ammanmessage.com/.

45. See http://www.arrabita.ma/.

46. See http://www.iep.utm.edu/goethe/.

References

Aljabri, Mohamed A. 1994. *Problems with contemporary Arabic thought* [in Arabic]. 3rd ed. Beirut: Centre for Arab Unity Studies.

Beaumont, Peter. 3 December 2011. Political Islam poised to dominate the new world bequeathed by Arab spring. *The Guardian*.

bin Bayyah, Abdullah. 2014. *The culture of terrorism: Tenets and treatments*. Translated by Hamza Yousuf. Sandala. Available from https://sandala.org/.

Browning, Noah, and John Irish. 15 December 2015. Saudi Arabia announces 34-state Islamic military alliance against terrorism. *Reuters*. Available from http://www.reuters.com.

Dabashi, Hamid. 2012. *The Arab Spring: The end of postcolonialism*. Basingstoke, UK: Palgrave Macmillan.

El-Said, Hamed. 2012. De-radicalising Islamists: Programmes and their impact in Muslim majority states. In *Developments in radicalisation and political violence*, eds. Alexander Meleagrou-Hitchens and Jon Bew. London: ICSR, King's College London.

Fink, Naureen Chowdhury, and Hamed El-Said. 2011. *Transforming terrorists: Examining international efforts to address violent extremism*. New York, NY: International Peace Institute.

Friedman, Thomas L. 17 February 2016. Who are we? *The New York Times*. Available from http://www.nytimes.com.

Global Counterterrorism Forum (GCTF). 23 September 2011. Inaugural meeting of the Coordinating Committee, co-chair's summary. The Hague: GCTF. Available from https://portal.thegctf.org/documents/10162/19433/Inaugural+Coordinating+Committee+Co-Chairs'%20Summary.

Hamid, Shadi. 18 November 2015. Does ISIS really have nothing to do with Islam? Islamic apologetics carry serious risks. *The Washington Post*.

Hedayah, the International Center of Excellence for Countering Violent Extremism. 2014. *CVE global expo summary report*. Abu Dhabi: Hedayah. Available from http://www.hedayah.ae/pdf/global-cve-expo-report-2014.pdf.

Ibn Sunitan, Mohamed. 2004. *The Saudi elites: A study of transformation and failure* [in Arabic]. Doctoral Dissertations Series. Beirut: Centre for Arab Unity Studies.

Moussalli, Ahmad. 2004. *Historical dictionary of Islamic fundamentalist movements in the Arab world, Iran, and Turkey* [in Arabic]. Beirut: Centre for Arab Unity Studies.

Schneier, Marc. 2 January 2015. Why don't more moderate Muslims denounce extremism? *The Washington Post*.

The Telegraph. October 2015. The rise of Islamic State - how the jihadi group conquered territory in Iraq and Syria. Telegraph Video.

Wood, Graeme. 24 February 2015. What ISIS really wants. *The Atlantic*. Available from http://www.theatlantic.com.

Zahid, Mohammed. 2012. *The Muslim Brotherhood and Egypt's succession crisis: The politics of liberalisation and reform in the Middle East*. London: I. B. Tauris.

Conclusion

Keywords: terrorism; countering violent extremism; Middle East; Daesh; ISIS; president; security

Conclusion: Key Themes for the Next President

By
RICHARD A. CLARKE
and
EMILIAN PAPADOPOULOS

When the next president takes office in January 2017, she or he will inherit a broad and difficult set of challenges with regard to countering terrorism and specifically violent Islamist extremism in the Middle East and surrounding region, in Europe and other allied Western nations, and domestically within the United States.

As was the case eight years ago, when *The ANNALS* invited us to edit the volume "Terrorism: What the Next President Will

Richard A. Clarke is chairman of the Middle East Institute and an internationally renowned expert on cybersecurity, homeland security, and national security. Clarke served as a senior White House advisor to three presidents through an unprecedented 11 consecutive years of White House service, including as Special Advisor to the President for Cyber Security, National Coordinator for Security and Counter-terrorism, and Special Assistant to the President for Global Affairs. He also served as Assistant Secretary of State and held other positions in the State Department and the Pentagon. He is author of the New York Times *bestseller* Against All Enemies *(Free Press 2004), among other books. He taught at Harvard Kennedy School, is an on-air consultant for ABC News on terrorism and cybersecurity, and is chairman of Good Harbor Security Risk Management.*

Emilian Papadopoulos is president of Good Harbor Security Risk Management, a boutique consulting firm that advises boards, CEOs, and executives on cyber security risk. He frequently publishes and speaks at industry conferences on emerging cyber security issues. Previously, he advised clients in the Middle East on national security, counterterrorism, and urban security. Before joining Good Harbor, he was a political and economic officer with Foreign Affairs Canada and worked at the Canadian Embassy in Washington, D.C., where he helped to launch the Embassy's Connect2Canada diaspora initiative.

Correspondence: contact@goodharbor.net

DOI: 10.1177/0002716216675825

Face," we are fortunate to have leading practitioners and academic experts contribute to this volume to help the next president understand and address the problem. Key recommendations from each of the authors are summarized in an online appendix to the volume.[1]

Key Themes

Here, we highlight some key themes that extend across the volume. First, *the problem often shorthanded as "terrorism" is actually at least three distinct but related sets of issues*. The first is the near-simultaneous collapse of socioeconomic and political systems in and between a large number of states in which Islam is the predominant religion; the second is the alienation of many Muslims in Western Europe and, to a lesser extent, in North America, combined with a sharp spike in refugees coming into Europe and the subsequent political and social backlash; and the third is a strong but virulent ideological movement battling for control within Sunni Islam, which includes intolerance, violence, and anti-Western activity at its core.

These dynamics interact at the regional, state, organizational, and individual levels. The Middle East is beset by unstable regional and state orders that perpetuate and exacerbate problems within and between states. These dynamics rest in a context of, as Paul Salem describes in his introduction to Part One, "long-simmering dysfunctions of repressive governments; sluggish and unequal economies; growing populations; tightening land and water resources; and unresolved questions of political identity, the role of religion, and social structure." In these conditions, terrorist organizations thrive (and even compete), and individuals are more susceptible to the call of extremism. This, in turn, creates the supply of recruits and resources that the terrorist organizations need to perpetuate instability within and across state lines, further disrupting governance and stability. In addition to being multilayered and complex, the situation is also extremely hard to predict. When we edited *The ANNALS* volume in 2008, few could have predicted the Arab Spring, the Iran nuclear deal, or the conflict in Syria and resulting mass migration into Europe.

The next president needs a strategy that will be adaptive but keep the administration and allies focused in turbulent times. Any strategy that attempts to tackle one problem, for example, a particular terrorist organization or state conflict, without understanding its context and related problems cannot succeed; conversely, with a broader understanding of context, addressing one problem can lead to others being solved. The president needs a cohesive strategy that presses forward simultaneously on regional, state, organizational, individual, and ideological levels.

Second, *none of these related issues is susceptible to a quick fix*, and all will take many years and, in many cases, decades, to alter appreciably. In the extended period ahead, these issues will create ongoing security risks.

After 9/11, then-President Bush called the battle against al-Qaeda "the calling of our generation." Fifteen years later, nearly a generation passed, we are still fighting that battle, and it shows no signs of ending soon. Individual terrorist

leaders may succumb to targeted killings, and terrorist organizations and fran-
chises may rise and fall, but as long as the fundamental geopolitical, demographic, and ideological problems persist, so too will the appeal of violent Islamist
extremism and organizations that harness it to destructive ends.

Today, our counterterrorism efforts are focused on Daesh. U.S.-led efforts are
finally seeing success in disrupting its operations and taking back territory, from
Fallujah to Sirte and possibly even Mosul. These successes are important: Daesh
poses a significant threat, deserves our attention and resources, and must be
defeated militarily and operationally in the near term.

But we must not confuse Daesh losing control of territory with our winning
the battle against violent Islamist extremism. Al-Qaeda will persist, and other
organizations will sprout up to try to take Daesh's place. This is particularly true
since the conflict with Daesh has laid waste to so many cities, destroying homes
and infrastructure and causing mass migration. When Daesh is beaten back, city
by city, the battle risks leaving behind a breeding ground for more extremism, for
a resurgence of Daesh, or for a new terrorist organization. To quell this problem,
the administration and local partners need a plan to fill the vacuum of governance and services, to rebuild and even to resettle the cities that Daesh once called
its own. This same approach applies not only to Daesh but to the United States'
regional and counterterrorism strategy writ large.

Recognizing the persistent, resilient nature of the problem, the next president
must adopt a long-term, even multigenerational view of the problem. The president must develop a strategy for the region and for countering violent extremism
that supports stability, legitimate and good governance, and the reliable provision
of conditions that help local populations to thrive and that eliminates the breeding ground for extremism before it takes root.

Third, *the duration and depth of the current instability might be reduced with the
pursuit of bold, innovative, and well-managed initiatives.* Several authors suggested
large-scale efforts or creative, even controversial, solutions to the problems riling the
Middle East. Paul Salem and Gen. Allen both contemplate major economic investment and trade to spur development and foster interdependence in the region. Marc
Lynch, looking at the state of intractable conflicts and political contests in Syria and
even in Yemen and Libya, observes that "it may be premature in the short-term to
seek the final resolution of the deep political conflicts at the heart of these wars.
Instead, the best chance may be the consolidation of long-term ceasefires and the
de facto, but not de jure, partition of countries into self-governing areas." In Part
Two, authors present a range of effective countering violent extremism (CVE) programs that could have dramatic impact if scaled and resourced properly.

The Obama administration has largely resisted dramatic initiatives in the Middle
East, opting instead for a steady hand that conserves resources; acknowledges the
limitations and risks of action in such an unpredictable, dynamic environment; and
avoids large-scale military deployments that can be counterproductive. In many
ways, particularly with regard to military action, this was wise. Nonetheless, the
next president should consider big ideas, particularly where economic investment
in the region and programs for CVE are concerned.

Fourth, *the study and practice known as CVE is maturing; offers promise in
reducing security risks; and needs continuous, senior-level government*

involvement and support. This may be one of the most significant and promising changes since 2008–2009.

In the immediate post-9/11 environment, our national response leaned heavily on military deployments to the Middle East and on the law enforcement and national security communities to provide public safety in the face of an external threat being introduced surreptitiously into the United States. As time passed, the threat became more complex, with the boundary between international and domestic threats blurring. The Fort Hood shooter, Major Nidal Hasan; the failed Time Square bomber, Faisal Shahzad; and others showed that U.S. citizens could be drawn to violent action in the United States. These incidents showed that individuals could be motivated by the overseas counterterrorism efforts of our security forces or law enforcement efforts domestically; that individuals could act with or without external support; and that they were difficult to detect in advance of acting, notwithstanding the post-9/11 efforts to improve intelligence and federal-local law enforcement coordination.

While law enforcement remains an essential element in detecting threats and preventing violence, a broader, "whole-of-community" effort is being developed. It is premised on an analysis that, with respect to almost every terrorist event that was not detected by law enforcement before it occurred, the pre-event behavior by the eventual perpetrator(s) fit patterns of a predilection toward violence. Further, such behavior was observed by family, friends, and/or authority figures such as religious leaders or teachers but went unreported to law enforcement or any other potential intervention practitioners, typically out of concern about what action law enforcement might take, or because of a lack of understanding, or denial of the implications, of such behavior. That said, law enforcement also realizes that the community model will yield far more potential terrorists than it can responsibly handle. In this model, early identification by informed individuals and by those who observe telltale behavioral patterns becomes critical. While the whole-of-community approach must evolve, it holds great promise to identify pre-event behavior and perpetrators before terrorist incidents occur.

Along with this whole-of-community approach to detection, countless programs are also emerging to counter extremism and the societal and individual conditions that enable it. As President Obama observed, "We cannot use force everywhere that a radical ideology takes root; and in the absence of a strategy that reduces the wellspring of extremism, a perpetual war . . . will prove self-defeating." The president called instead for a strategy that "involves addressing the underlying grievances and conflicts that feed extremism."[2]

In Part Two of this volume, expert authors from around the world review and assess CVE programs that have had great effect and hold even greater promise. Looking across these programs, we observe a few themes about CVE that are important to bear in mind as the field evolves. First, CVE programs need to balance localization with scalability and manage trade-offs between the two. It is important that CVE programs are developed or tailored by local stakeholders and partners for their own environment; there is no one-size-fits-all approach. At the same time, scaling these programs is not only cost-effective but also helps experts and practitioners to learn about the programs—what works and what does not and how to improve them. Second, research about extremism matters and has been useful to date. Governments and civil society should fund more research into extremism, including academic research and CVE field programs with a research component. Finally, measuring the effectiveness of CVE programs matters, but it can be extremely difficult to do so. Governments and civil society that fund CVE programs should require practitioners to explain how their proposed programs address the risks they are designed to mitigate; and to the extent possible, practitioners should identify metrics that can assess the effectiveness of programs over time. Of course, in the near-term, this should not become so bureaucratic that it stifles innovation and experimentation in an emerging field. The next president should use the bully pulpit, federal funds and resources, and influence with allies and stakeholders globally to encourage more programs and research to realize the full potential of CVE.

Finally, *active and creative leadership by the United States is necessary to address the regional challenges and mitigate the security risks discussed in this volume, but U.S. actions alone will be insufficient to achieve significant and lasting results.* While these challenges do directly affect significant U.S. interests and security, both multilateral efforts and effective actions by the nations and societies most directly implicated are required and should be vigorously sought after and supported by the United States.

The current political climate in America runs the risk of swinging the pendulum of foreign policy toward isolationism. That would be a mistake. The United States has an indispensable role to play, as many of the volume's authors agree. As Gen. Allen says in his contribution to this volume,

> No nation on the planet has greater moral and practical convening power, or a broader strategic reach than the United States. . . . Only the United States can form coalitions the magnitude of NATO, or ISAF, or the current global coalition to counter ISIL, and only the United States can lead these endeavors from the front. Where the United States leads purposefully and unambiguously, the strategic direction of the coalition is more certain and compelling.

In the P5+1 negotiations for the Iran deal, too, the United States demonstrated what its leadership can accomplish. The one area in which significant restraint is advisable is when it comes to large-scale military deployments that are not linked to an effective political strategy, as these have shown themselves to be inefficient or, even worse, counterproductive.

The United States is arguably in a better position to have influence in the region than it was eight years ago: the Iran deal reasserted it as a diplomatic leader in the region; the U.S. economy has recovered from the crash of 2007–2009, which necessarily occupied the Obama administration's focus in its first years; and the reduced military presence in Iraq and Afghanistan has provided the military some opportunity to recover from two draining, long wars.

Of course, U.S. leadership does not mean U.S. unilateralism. The United States is at its best in the region when leading a broad coalition and convening all stakeholders, typically including Russia, Iran, the Gulf Cooperation Council (GCC) states, and Turkey. Further, as Lynch argues in his article, "Failed States and Ungoverned Spaces," when agreements can be reached, enforcing them depends on local capacity: "The focus thus far has, appropriately, been on efforts to build competent local forces to play such a role: the training of the Iraqi security forces, the efforts to build the Libyan national army, and the efforts to forge a unified Syrian opposition army." The same is true not only of security forces but of diplomatic and economic endeavors, too.

The president should maintain active involvement in the region, working closely with local partners. The president should resist the temptation to lean on large-scale military deployments that may be ineffective or counterproductive but, instead, use a combination of economic, diplomatic, societal, and purposeful military action in concert.

Concluding Thoughts

Much has changed since our previous volume eight years ago, but elements of the big picture remain remarkably consistent. Eight years ago, we said that "although the outcome of the Cold War was far more crucial to the continued existence of the United States and its values than the current challenges of countering violent Islamist extremism seem to be, there are some often cited parallels between that struggle and the present one. Like the Cold War, this struggle is ideological at its root and will likely take many years to end. As with the Cold War, however, skillful management could eventually cause the threat to go away, not with a bang but a whimper (Clarke and Papadopoulos 2008, 12).

The incoming president faces an important and complex battle against violent Islamist extremism. The interplay between extremism and the unstable regional and state orders in the Middle East, as well as the greater reach afforded extremist groups by the Internet and other new technologies, make the problem even more threatening today than it seemed in 2008–2009. Nonetheless, if the president adopts a long-term, even multigenerational, perspective on the problem and leads a cohesive strategy in the Middle East and surrounding region, the next administration might edge the problem ever closer to going away, not with a bang but with a whimper. We hope that the contributions in this volume help to achieve that goal, and we thank our coeditors and authors for their efforts to that end.

Notes

1. See http://ann.sagepub.com/supplemental.
2. President Barack Obama in a speech to the National Defense University, 2013.

Reference

Clarke, Richard A., and Emilian Papadopoulos. 2008. Terrorism: The first portfolio for the next president. In "Terrorism: What the next president will face," eds. Richard A. Clarke and Emilian Papadopoulos, 6–12. *The ANNALS of the American Academy of Political and Social Science* 618.

CORRIGENDUM

"The Electoral Landscape of 2016," published in *The ANNALS* 667, pp. 50–71, by John Sides, Michael Tesler, and Lynn Vavreck.

Figure 2 is incorrect in the published paper. It presents the overall trend in the Index of Consumer Sentiment rather than the trend broken down by income tercile, as the text describes. The correct Figure 2 is published below.

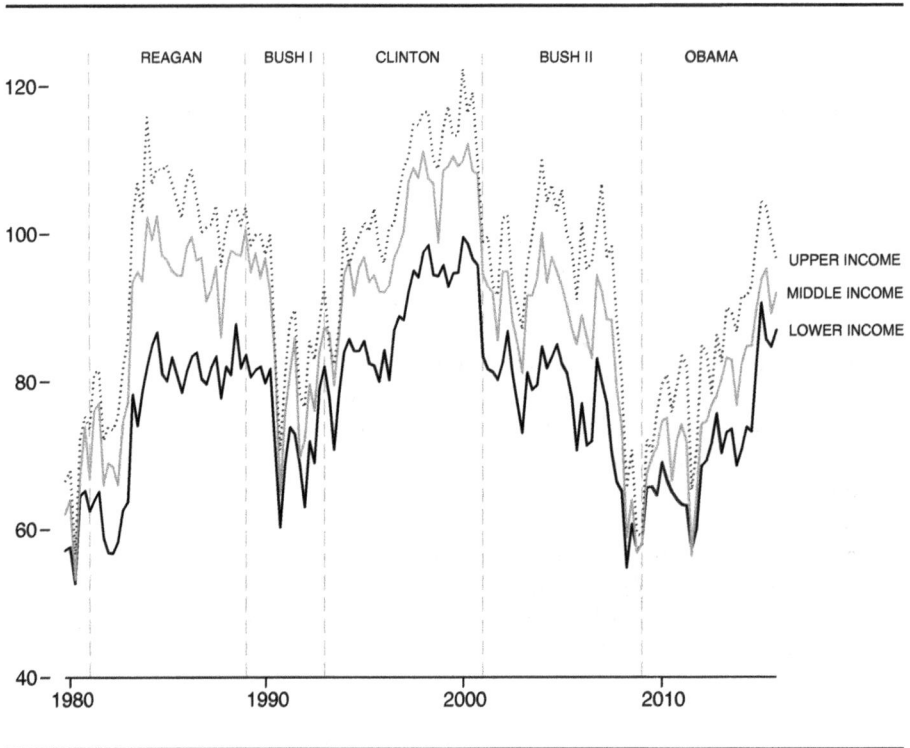

DOI: 10.1177/0002716216670125

0. STATEMENT OF OWNERSHIP, MANAGEMENT, AND CIRCULATION
    P.S. Form 3526 Facsimile

1. TITLE: ANNALS OF THE AMERICAN ACADEMY OF POLITICAL AND SOCIAL SCIENCES
2. USPS PUB. #: 026-060

3. DATE OF FILING: October 1, 2016

4. FREQUENCY OF ISSUE: Bi-monthly
5. NO. OF ISSUES ANNUALLY: 6
6. ANNUAL SUBSCRIPTION PRICE: Institution $994.00
                                                             Individual $118.00

7. PUBLISHER ADDRESS: 2455 Teller Road, Thousand Oaks, CA 91320
    CONTACT PERSON: Graeme Doswell, Head of Global Circulation
    TELEPHONE: (805) 499-0721

8. HEADQUARTERS ADDRESS: 2455 Teller Road, Thousand Oaks, CA 91320

9. PUBLISHER: SAGE Publications Inc., 2455 Teller Road, Thousand Oaks, CA 91320
    EDITOR:
    Thomas A. Kecskemethy, 202 S. 36th Street, Philadelphia, PA 19104

10. OWNER: The American Academy of Political and Social Science
    202 S. 36th Street, Philadelphia, PA 19104-3806

11. KNOWN BONDHOLDERS, ETC.
    None

12. NONPROFIT PURPOSE, FUNCTION, STATUS:
    Has Not Changed During Preceding 12 Months

13. PUBLICATION NAME: ANNALS OF THE AMERICAN ACADEMY OF POLITICAL AND SOCIAL SCIENCES

14. ISSUE DATE FOR CIRCULATION DATA BELOW: July 2016

15. EXTENT & NATURE OF CIRCULATION:

		AVG. NO. COPIES EACH ISSUE DURING PRECEDING 12 MONTHS	ACT. NO. COPIES OF SINGLE ISSUE PUB. NEAREST TO FILING DATE
A.	TOTAL NO. COPIES	539	538
B.	PAID CIRCULATION		
	1. PAID/REQUESTED OUTSIDE-CO, ETC	287	269
	2. PAID IN-COUNTY SUBSCRIPTIONS	0	0
	3. SALES THROUGH DEALERS, ETC.	14	14
	4. OTHER CLASSES MAILED USPS	0	0
C.	TOTAL PAID CIRCULATION	301	283
D.	FREE DISTRIBUTION BY MAIL		
	1. OUTSIDE-COUNTY AS ON 3541	15	15
	2. IN-COUNTY AS STATED ON 3541	0	0
	3. OTHER CLASSES MAILED USPS	0	0
E.	FREE DISTRIBUTION OTHER	0	0
F.	TOTAL FREE DISTRIBUTION	15	15
G.	TOTAL DISTRIBUTION	316	298
H.	COPIES NOT DISTRIBUTED		
	1. OFFICE USE, ETC.	223	240
	2. RETURN FROM NEWS AGENTS	0	0
I.	TOTAL	539	538
	PERCENT PAID CIRCULATION	95%	95%

16. THIS STATEMENT OF OWNERSHIP WILL BE PRINTED IN THE NOVEMBER 2016 ISSUE OF THIS PUBLICATION.

17. I CERTIFY THAT ALL INFORMATION FURNISHED ON THIS FORM IS TRUE AND COMPLETE.
    I UNDERSTAND THAT ANYONE WHO FURNISHES FALSE OR MISLEADING INFORMATION ON
    THIS FORM OR WHO OMITS MATERIAL OR INFORMATION REQUESTED ON THE FORM MAY
    BE SUBJECT TO CRIMINAL SANCTIONS (INCLUDING FINES AND IMPRISONMENT) AND/OR
    CIVIL SANCTIONS (INCLUDING MULTIPLE DAMAGES AND CIVIL PENALTIES).

Graeme Doswell

Graeme Doswell   Date: 08/17/2016
Head of Global Circulation
SAGE Publications, Inc.

In compliance with GPSR, should you have any concerns about the safety of this
product, please advise: International Associates Auditing & Certification
Limited The Black Church, St Mary's Place, Dublin 7, D07 P4AX Ireland
EUAR@ie.ia-net.com

www.ingramcontent.com/pod-product-compliance
Lightning Source LLC
Chambersburg PA
CBHW080248030426
42334CB00023BA/2740

* 9 7 8 1 5 0 6 3 7 8 9 3 0 *